Clinch Mountain Girls

24 Women Grow Veggies, Animals, and a Community

Nancy Withington Bell

Clinch Mountain Girls:
24 Women Grow Veggies, Animals, and a Community
Nancy Withington Bell

Published October 2022
Little Creek Books
Imprint of Jan-Carol Publishing, Inc.
All rights reserved
Copyright © 2022 Nancy Withington Bell
Front Cover Painting: Mildred "Tata" Andres
Author Photograph: Flint Chaney
Graphic Design: Tara Sizemore

This book may not be reproduced in whole or part, in any manner whatsoever without written permission, with the exception of brief quotations within book reviews or articles.

ISBN: 978-1-954978-59-1
Library of Congress Control Number: 2022944768

Jan-Carol Publishing, Inc.
PO Box 701
Johnson City, TN 37605
publisher@jancarolpublishing.com
www.jancarolpublishing.com

To my sister:

Janet Withington Bouchard (1948–2015),

who first showed me the way

In memoriam:

To Linda Anderson Long (1948–2017),

one of the Clinch Mountain Girls

Contents

Letter to the Reader . . . vii

Introduction: Taking the Off Ramp to a Country Road . . . ix

Chapter 1: How Do You Raise a Homesteader? . . . 1

Chapter 2: Back to the Land . . . 15

Chapter 3: Adding a Home to the Homestead . . . 27

Chapter 4: Keeping the Home Fires Burning . . . 49

Chapter 5: The Worth of Water . . . 59

Chapter 6: Growing Our Gardens, Growing Ourselves . . . 73

Chapter 7: Good Food All Year Round . . . 92

Chapter 8: Some Creatures Wild and Small . . . 106

Chapter 9: Sheep and Lambs and Goats and Kids . . . 121

Chapter 10: Some Creatures Wide or Tall . . . 134

Chapter 11: "Just Somethin' to Get Around In" . . . 155

Chapter 12: A Woman's Work: Childbirth . . . 165

Chapter 13: Working at Home and Away . . . 179

Chapter 14: The Creative Life . . . 197

Chapter 15: "Ladies' Meetings" and Other Essential Gatherings . . . 213

Chapter 16: Feeling the Spirit . . . 227

Chapter 17: Family Matters: Holidays, Health, and Accidents . . . 241

Chapter 18: Teach Your Children Well . . . 255

Chapter 19: Meeting the Neighbors . . . 272

Chapter 20: Learning to Get Along . . . 292

Chapter 21: Back to School and Other Changes . . . 308

Chapter 22: Looking Back, Looking Ahead . . . 328

Afterword . . . 347

Biographies of the Clinch Mountain Girls . . . 351

Acknowledgments . . . 357

About the Author . . . 359

Dear Reader,

"Oh, the Clinch Mountain girls—welcome!" we heard as we piled out of vans and station wagons. Okay, they had named us, the several families together who would head for Robin Hood Thrift Store an hour away for much-needed clothes a couple of times a year.

In later years the girls would sit around laughing and telling stories. I volunteered to write some down. I began interviewing the two dozen women, transcribing the tapes, and grouping pieces into a mosaic of our lives. You will find short bios of each of the two dozen women at the back of the book. Look in the Afterword for short descriptions of the Clinch Mountain area and my oral history methods.

Hike with me into a green holler, see a woman chasing a wayward baby goat under the sheets on a clothesline. Now walk into her kitchen to the aroma of bread baking. Please, sit down, open the book, and laugh or sigh at these stories and heartfelt reflections on our lives and struggles, and how we found peace here in the mountain hollers. Enjoy!

Best wishes,

Nancy Bell

Introduction

Taking the Off Ramp to a Country Road

Standing in front of the chilled produce section in a Connecticut supermarket one summer morning in 1970, I felt numb. The colorful, perfect fruits and vegetables encased in plastic, had no fragrance at all. No friendly vendor offered me a sample of a melon or other fruit. I walked out with an empty cart. I had just returned to the States after a two-year stay in rural Iran, serving in the Peace Corps. Adjustment between cultures notoriously takes some time and applies equally to re-entry into your own, which never seems quite the same again.

I was also feeling the vertigo of those times, the frenzy of events and ideas: the Vietnam War, the protests; the fights for civil rights, for women's rights, and for poor people; the assassinations and violence; the metastasizing materialism of the sixties and seventies. But there was also Earth Day; Woodstock; the peace movement; the Pill; and then the passing of bills for civil rights, for voting rights, and for clean air and water. And, the Back-to-the-Land Movement. I was "all shook up" by history-in-the-making.

This book is the oral history of twenty-four women who were part of the back-to-the land movement. What I present in this introduction is not a formal history, but my representative personal history—how it felt to live then, and how I reacted to the events of those times. In brief, it is what led me to Tennessee, to the foothills of the Appalachians.

Through high school and college, the Cold War was an ever-present backdrop to daily activities. With news of revolts in Soviet Bloc countries and the Cuban Missile Crisis, my dad said he thought our granite-walled cellar could serve as a fallout shelter, and he brought home cardboard boxes of canned food to stock it. While in high school, I was devastated by the assassination of President Kennedy in 1963.

As a college junior studying in Japan, I read in *Newsweek Magazine* about the "summer of love" in Haight-Asbury in 1966. Returning to college in Maine, I heard some friends talking about their summer as Freedom Riders in 1967 registering black voters in the South. I decided to write my senior sociology thesis on the black rights movement and the charismatic leadership of Dr. Martin Luther King, Jr. In 1968, three weeks after I submitted my thesis, Dr. King was assassinated. Meanwhile, a former boyfriend started writing to me from Viet Nam. Each night I watched the hair-raising news about the war narrated by Walter Cronkite on CBS.

Immediately after college graduation in 1968, I joined the Peace Corps. During our eight weeks of States-side training, Bobby Kennedy was assassinated. I served in Iran where I not only appreciated the people, but also enjoyed shopping in the bazaar, and learning to cook with local, very fresh ingredients. While in Iran I received news of the killings at Kent State University, and of napalm raining down in Viet Nam. I also learned of the Woodstock Music Festival in 1969, and the first Earth Day in 1970.

In 1971 I moved to Ann Arbor, Michigan. Soon after I arrived, someone bombed the ROTC building in protest over U.S. participation in the Viet Nam War. On the home front, another battle was brewing as women started taking the pill, meeting in "consciousness-raising" groups, applying for jobs in traditionally male-dominated fields, and generally feeling "empowered." (The guys I knew said they were all for women's lib, but they still didn't do the dishes.) We were bombarded with news about Watergate, the hopelessness of politics as usual, and environmental degradation. It appeared that most people's Saturday recreation consisted of going to the mall, and huge cars hogged the roadways. Neither fresh air nor world peace seemed at hand.

Every time I went home to New England, I visited my sister, who was living a '"hippie" life near the coast of Maine. I was so interested in her chickens, her goats, the garden, the compost pile. I felt so free there; it was literally a breath of fresh air. She lived in a community of like-minded people who helped and traded with each other. I even went to a barn dance, where I watched her being swung by her partner to the tunes of a local string band. Despite the hardships of Maine winters, I sensed a lot of joy in the life they were creating. Maybe this way of living could be a response to the meaninglessness I felt in modern urban life.

Those thoughts were a background as I switched my graduate degree course from Middle East Studies to Public Health Nutrition. In two years, in 1976, I finished and applied for a position in Appalachia and was accepted for one in northeastern Tennessee. I figured if I could spend two years immersed in the exotic Persian culture, I could handle two years in a unique culture within the United States. I didn't realize at the time that those two years would become forty (and still counting).

From the beginning I reveled in the beauty of the row upon row of green ridges of East Tennessee. I loved the friendliness and down-to-earth wisdom of the people. Bluegrass and old-time music was a major pastime. The winters were short, and the altitude tempered the heat of summer. I found affordable land, and could start living the life I dreamed of. I felt at peace. Perhaps best of all, I found myself in a unique community. So this is not my story only; it is the story also of twenty-three other women who just happened to move to the same mountain valley in a small area of Tennessee just south of Virginia and Kentucky. They are the "Clinch Mountain girls," and this is our community oral history.

Clinch Mountain, Tennessee

When crossing the long, high ridge called Clinch Mountain to its north side on a winding road with few guard rails up and up, and then down into the equally long Clinch Valley, you are relieved to find the peaceful landscape in shades of green. As you drive along a typical narrow, two-lane road in Clinch Valley, you will see farmland on both sides, with pastures extending fingers up into the coves of Clinch Mountain and over the saddles—topped by steeper, wooded slopes. In early morning, mists rise out of the coves, or hollows, giving the famous smoky look. Small white frame houses are surrounded by barns and weathered sheds. Wildflowers abound in three seasons. You are likely to see deer, rabbits, possums, squirrels, and groundhogs trying to make it across the road, or wild turkeys scratching for grubs in the leaves. Every few miles you will see a small, white church, sometimes with a railing down to a creek for baptisms.

Clinch Mountain, home of country music, is at the western edge of the Southern Appalachians. When the young women arrived in Clinch Valley in the seventies, tobacco was the cash crop, although some men worked as loggers or zinc miners. Small country stores every few miles carried everything from canned food, cornmeal, and candy, to horse tack, overalls, and motor oil. Clinch Valley Road had been paved for only about twenty years. All other local roads were dirt and gravel. But even forty years ago, quite a few of the younger people (mostly men) earned their living working off the farm, traveling over Clinch Mountain to work in a factory perhaps an hour away, in winter braving the often icy north slope of the mountain. Several two- or three-room elementary schools were still in existence into the 1990s in Hancock and Grainger counties, and a one hundred sixty-student K–12 school in Hawkins County.

Newcomers Arrive

Throughout the Seventies and Eighties young people arrived from other states: California, Indiana, Ohio, Florida, New Hampshire, New Jersey, Minnesota, New York, Missouri, Oklahoma, Connecticut, District of Columbia, Georgia, Minnesota, Pennsylvania, Michigan, and Louisiana. The women and men tried homesteading and met with varying degrees of success. Somehow these families eked out a living.

In painted school buses and VW vans newcomers arrived, greeted by new neighbors in overalls and welcoming smiles and even an apple pie. Some of these would-be homesteaders eventually left the Clinch Mountain hollows and valleys, but many stayed. This is the story of the women who stayed, and how on earth they managed it. These were white, mostly privileged, middle-class girls who, with their partners, had to find shelter and water, produce their own food and warmth, deal with waste disposal and trash removal, and in some cases, provide schooling for their children. The electric power often went out and if they had telephones, the service was spotty at best. They lived far from each other down back roads spread out over fifty miles of Hancock, Hawkins, and Grainger Counties. They had unreliable vehicles, and few lived within walking distance of each other. What they did have was the youthful enthusiasm and naiveté to take on a life change more difficult and massive than they could have imagined, and the intelligence, energy, and spirit to succeed. They stuck together and helped each other out. This is the life story of their, and my, community.

Chapter One

How Do You Raise a Homesteader?

Let's go back in time and stroll into the kitchens of about two dozen families, and let's ask each of them to tell us how they raised their daughter to become a homesteader. Of course they would tell us that they did no such thing. It wouldn't have entered their heads that their white, educated, protected, middle class daughters would leave the expectation of a comfortable life with a proper occupation and a home with all the conveniences of modern life. For the most part, at those kitchen tables, we would meet middle class families, in the middle of the century, in the middle of a suburb, with aspirations for college for their daughters, probably for them to become nurses or teachers. Of course the changes no parent can predict result from experiences in college, early jobs, or travel.

Of our group of twenty-four, who were the exceptions to the "rule of the middle"? There were four: an upper class Philadelphia girl educated in private schools; a child of career military parents who moved frequently; a Dutch girl who, with her family, suffered hunger during World War II in Amsterdam; a daughter of a diplomat raised in Ceylon, Kenya, and Washington, D.C.; and a girl raised on a dairy farm in Nebraska in the 1930s. Most of our future homesteaders were baby-boomers.

All these daughters, raised in fifteen different states, were from families of three to six kids, and most came of age as typical white, optimistic, trusting kids of the 1950s. Here are a few snapshots of their young lives and times.

Snapshot: bikes

> We could ride our bikes to the park and go down and play in the creek if we wanted to. *(Carolyn, raised in Cincinnatti, Ohio)*

> I rode my bike everywhere. I wonder how many miles a day we actually rode on our bikes, and how far away we were from home. *(Robyn, raised in Florida)*

Snapshot: communication

> The houses were very close together, and my next-door neighbor, Mary Lou, she was one of my good friends. We'd take tin cans with strings, and she'd put one can in her bedroom, and I'd have one in my bedroom, and that's how we talked. *(Linda, raised in Zenia, Ohio)*

Snapshot: hula hoop marathon

> Mary Lou and I were both hula-hoopers. We both entered a lot of hula hoop marathon contests. We went to a contest in Dayton, Ohio, and they had, like, twelve nights of contests. And I won! [My time] was twelve hours, one minute and twenty seconds. *(Linda)*

Snapshot: playing in the street

> For fun every night in the summer we would play wiffle ball in

the road, and frisbee. *(Karen, raised on Long Island, New York)*

We would be out in the street playin', and if somebody got hurt there was always a mom around to patch somebody up. *(Trudie, raised in Tulsa, Oklahoma)*

Snapshot: on the water

I lived in Detroit, but we had an escape out there on the lake. Every summer grew up fishing and swimming and skiing and sailing and all those water activities. *(Cece, raised in Detroit, Michigan)*

[We were] bogging up the brooks, and catching frogs, and going to the reservoir, and stealing boats—I should say borrowing boats—to play on the island in the reservoir. *(Lee, from Brewster, New York)*

When I was probably only thirteen or fourteen we had a little row boat, and a one-horsepower motor. I'd take my friends, and my dog, and sometimes my goat to town, and we'd get an ice cream cone. *(Alicia, on Long Island, but raised in The Bronx, New York)*

Snapshot: roaming

Right across the street was another row of these little houses, but behind that it was just all pasture land. We just ran all over the place, pretty much, never thinking anything bad could ever happen. *(Trudie)*

In the summer they roamed with their parents, but by car. Five girls visited their grandparents' farms frequently or for a yearly stay. Nine women recalled family trips to parks in other states.

> We would go on family vacations, and we went to almost every state. We camped in campers. We went to 'most all the national monuments, national parks, and state parks. [My dad] just wanted to show us everything. *(Janet, rural Missouri)*

Some experiences made lasting impressions.

> They sent me to summer camp, and [my brother and I] would go for sometimes six weeks at a time. We were in heaven. We were out in the woods like this, and living in screened-in cabins, playing in the creeks, and just learnin' how to be in the woods. I fell in love with the mountains. *(Robyn)*

> I'd see pictures of the mountains, the green, sort of nurturing mountains that are the Appalachians. I just felt, That feels like home, that's where I wanna be. And the first time that I did, finally, when I was seventeen, get to [be there], that sealed the deal. *(Micki, Cincinnatti, Ohio)*

Moving with their families to other states provided cross-cultural experiences for a quarter of the girls. Lauren grew up in Sri Lanka, Kenya, and Washington, D.C. And Tata, an "army brat," moved frequently. When Tata's military family was posted in Germany, they took a multi-country summer vacation.

> We went to Yugoslavia, Italy, Switzerland, Austria, parts of Germany we hadn't been to, and we camped out the entire [three-month] time. It made me completely fearless of camping, of quote-unquote roughing it, things that you'd have to encounter in camping and traveling, and other cultures. I'm real tolerant of

different kinds of people because I grew up always the new kid in the new environment, and you have to be tolerant because you're in someone else's space. So the phrase, "When in Rome do as the Romans do"—I can't tell you how many times I heard that. *(Tata, Louisiana)*

Then there were post-high school experiences. Eighty per cent had some higher education. Seventeen young women studied liberal arts in college or attended art school—half of them away from home in a different state. Two trained as nurses and one as a dental assistant.

Of the remaining four, two dropped out of high school but later achieved GEDs as well as further education. A few mentioned how their education helped them.

> I learned how to find out anything I wanted to know, how to do research, where to go, how to investigate stuff. I learned analytical thinking. My education empowered me to do just about, I felt, just about anything I wanted to do. *(Cece)*

> After I graduated from high school I went straight into a horticultural program at the local state college. *(Micki)*

> I took an organic gardening class to get science credit at Arizona State. That was neat because we would get in a van and drive out to the Arizona State [University] Farm, and everybody in the class had their own garden plot. We did little research projects, but we mainly just had our first trials with organic gardening. *(Beth, northern Ohio)*

Besides higher education the girls "got schooled" in other ways, namely in their jobs. Seven of the twenty-four young women either cooked or served food. Two nurses used their professions on and off while traveling abroad. Two crafted jewelry and macrame to finance travels in the United States. One college grad joined the Peace Corps.

> I worked at a printing press. I was the first woman they'd ever hired to work at a big newspaper press. *(Beth)*

> I wanted to go to Jamaica and live in a tent and paint paintings that I thought would be my new expression of myself based on the knowledge I had gained in college. Besides painting I became the town sign painter! *(Tata)*

> I went to a two-year girls' school called Bennett College in Millbrook, New York, and majored mostly in art, and a friend I met there, she got me a job at the local mental institution. That was my first job. I worked as a nurse aide and then moved to a "mental retardation unit," they called it, to do occupational therapy. So she had one whole building to do arts and crafts and things, and I had another whole building. And, we took the patients camping. *(Karen)*

> I had a chance to go to work at a riding stable where I had ridden as a kid. So I quit this really good job to go and live in this crappy little trailer. I stayed in it for like two days. I kept the job, but I didn't, wouldn't, live in the trailer. [My responsibilities were] training horses, giving lessons, just helping out, like if the vet came or something, stuff like that. It was pretty neat. I liked that a lot. *(Trudie)*

Meanwhile, most of the young women traveled widely. Six went to California, four to Colorado, three to Florida; others to Ohio, Kentucky, Oregon, Wyoming, and Nebraska.

I just stopped places and worked. I was in Montana, right in between two beautiful mountain ranges—Hamilton, Montana, not far from Missoula. I got a job at a bakery. I saw the only woman in town wearing Birkenstocks, and I got a job with her. I would work for about a week, and get some money and go on. *(Robyn)*

Several made it to Woodstock.

Went to Woodstock—in a car that had no gas pedal! My friend put a line from the engine through the vent window of this old station wagon—that later we sold for twenty bucks at Woodstock. And hitch-hiked home in time to see the men land on the moon! I remember trying to get to town [from the festival site]. That was interesting. We didn't try driving our car. You'd get on the backs or the fronts of somebody else's car that was going two inches every little bit. Nobody cared. It was all just part of what was goin' on, and everybody was very accepting. Nobody seemed to mind that there were a bunch of strangers perched on their vehicles. It was a neat time! *(Lauren, raised in Sri Lanka, Kenya, and Washington, D.C.)*

[Lee] has a lot of people there [at her Tennessee home at Thanksgiving]. We were sitting around being ol'-hippies-living-in-the-sticks, and someone said, "Yeah, Woodstock and all that!" Someone else said, "Well how many people here have been to Woodstock?" Half the people in the room—and it was a big room—raised their hands! *(Nancy, rural New Hampshire)*

Nancy Withington Bell

A third of the women traveled abroad, sometimes by themselves. Destinations included England, Spain, France, Greece, Lebanon, Morocco, Iran, India, and Japan.

> I went to Europe for a year. First of all, I cashed in my retirement from [two years of] teaching. That money went a long way in Europe 'cause that was when that book was published, *Europe on $5-a-Day*—and you could definitely do it! And then I could teach on Army bases and Navy bases, do substitute teaching to make money. I was a waitress for a while. I went to Spain for a while, and then went up to Germany and joined friends. *(Carolyn)*

> I went to college at Bates and spent my junior year abroad in Japan. It changes your life to live abroad. *(Nancy)*

> Living in Holland, as soon as you got a chance, you would travel south to where the sun was. France was my favorite country. Also my favorite language in school, and I spoke it well. I traveled in Italy, and in Spain, and then later on, lived in India for about two years. After that, I lived in England for seven years. [In India] I went to the local music college, and I had also a private dance teacher, and went to his house, I think every day. And then, I went to my music teacher also, to his house, to practice there. I learned a lot about how those families lived. *(Yvonne, Amsterdam, the Netherlands)*

> I went in the Peace Corps five days after I graduated [college] and lived in Iran for two years and taught seventh and eighth grade girls. We lived in a Kurdish town, and it was just wonderful in a lot of different ways. Very hospitable people, an

amazing cross-cultural experience. Not many modern amenities, so that was interesting. We had an outhouse and things like that. *(Nancy)*

Other cross-cultural experiences took place in the United States. Pat left Minnesota for a Catholic convent and nursing school in New York City. There she earned a Bachelor of Science in Nursing (BSN).

> I went to High School in Minneapolis, and I guess I was there maybe two [more] years, before I left home for the convent. They were Sisters that did a very inspiring kind of work, and they were a tough bunch. First we went to Ossining, New York, and had some training there, but they had us nursing there right away. They trained us to do everything. We went out every day in the Bronx. It was exciting! Went out by ourselves all over the Bronx on the buses and subways. *(Pat, Minneapolis, Minnesota)*

Meanwhile, Alicia, from New York City, also joined the Dominican sisters at the age of nineteen, earning her BSN, and served with Pat in New York City, Kentucky, and Tennessee until the age of thirty-nine.

> I am the way I am, I think, because of the convent. They were tough old ladies. I mean, they went into homes, any kinda home. Poor people, rats all over, cockroaches. They were tough people, and we learned to be tough, and we learned to make do. I came [to Appalachia] as a nurse, over in Campbell County [Tennessee]. I came for the adventure. It was different. I didn't want to just stay in New York and do the same old whatever. *(Alicia)*

Both Pat and Alicia served there in a four-person convent in Jellico, Tennessee, a coal-mining area, for seven years doing home health nursing, often driving up creeks to reach the remote coal-camp houses in the mountains. Many homes had no running water, no bathroom or outhouse, few or no windows, and sometimes only one room for a whole family.

Sandra moved with her construction-worker husband and small children to several states.

> He got into ironwork, so after that we traveled. We went, like, for a coupla years, in Nebraska. Then we come back to Warner Robbins [Georgia] for a few years. Then we went to Wyoming and then to Colorado. When I was thirty-two years old, I drove one of those big U-Hauls, pullin' a car, from Smyrna [Georgia] to North Platte, Nebraska, all by myself. I guess doing that made me feel like I could do anything! *(Sandra, New York City and rural Georgia)*

California was a particular magnet.

> I found some program called California Rural Apprenticeship Program. They matched up people who wanted to work on farms, organic farms, with farmers. I was just out on my own. I had a truck with a hand-built camper on the back. I ended up visiting a farm outside of Placerville, California. It was called The Famine's End. That's where I really fell in love with the idea of learning to find out what it took to be self-sufficient and live on an organic farm. I was only there a year, but it was a really good experience for me because, well, just the different things we did. We built this beautiful herb garden. They had goats so I learned about goat husbandry, and learning about milking goats every morning and every evening, and making

cheese. They had chickens. I also learned a lot about cooperatives because the owner, Brian, started up this cooperative for everybody that was just kind of settling into the area and building things. What they were starting was a grape nursery, so I helped plant some grape stems in their garden, and that was maybe a half-acre of grapes. *(Beth)*

For three of the eventual homesteaders, the California learning experience included living in an informal commune near Santa Cruz, that they named Harmony Hill.

We hooked up with this man, Forest, and he owned a big piece of land in the Santa Cruz Mountains. We met some people through Forest. It was not all his land. It was land that nobody—the owners never came to it—paid any attention to. So he said, "You'll be fine there." We built little dwellings all over the side of these Santa Cruz Mountains. It was really beautiful in the redwoods. Beautiful. Magical forests. We had one large cabin that was like the central cabin where we had a wood cook stove and a fireplace, and out front we had a big fire pit with chairs all around it. California has nice weather so usually it was fine. Rick and I lived in a teepee for a winter, and then we lived in a shelter that somebody had built, just little, couple of beds. But we used the main cabin. There were a couple of old cabins that people could live in, and they did. But what brought us together was the store and our children. We would take care of each other's children and mind the store. And that was really the binding force. People would come and go, but I'd say it was family, it really was family. It wasn't a drug-based community at all. We ran a natural foods store. That's how we made money and that's how we fed ourselves. And we had a bakery and that brought in some income. We didn't pay rent or anything. We didn't have a lot of money exchanged. *(Carolyn)*

There were maybe, right in that area of Harmony Hill, maybe twenty or thirty people. We'd all gather at the brown cabin, especially for the [outdoor] fireplace there and everything. We would gather there in the evenings. That was the social place of the community, other than like the bakery that was down in Ben Lomond, and the co-op that was in Felton. We kinda gathered there. We were all, to some degree, involved with either the bakery or the co-op or both. *(Cece)*

Up the mountain there was a real house. It wasn't part of our community, but was friendly, and there was a hot shower that we could pay twenty-five cents and have a shower and pay for the electricity. Other than that it was cold showers. There were several teepees, and for a while I lived in one—a small teepee, a sixteen-foot. Which isn't real smart in the redwoods, because of the drip from the trees; in the winter it rains a lot there. *(Judy, rural northern Ohio)*

At Harmony Hill the learning experience included working.

I worked in The People's Natural Food Bakery and The People's Natural Food Coop. It was a good job experience. I worked there as a worker, and then I became the produce manager. I ordered all the produce that we needed for the store. *(Judy)*

> [My husband] Bert and I, we'd get up twice a week and go down to the bakery and make carrot juice. We would squeeze carrots and then we'd box it all up in canning jars and take it down to the co-op. Then they would sell the juice. Bert was into trucking produce. He took me to where people were growing grapes, a cooperative. They sold their grapes to the [food] co-op [in Felton]. *(Cece)*

Harmony Hill residents tried to grow food there, but ran into difficulties.

> Bert and I were doing French intensive gardening. We would go to the co-op and we would get their old oil tins and old green buckets. We'd go down to the McDonalds and get pickle buckets, and drill holes in the bottom of all these, fill them with dirt, and plant squash or tomatoes or something in them. And then the chipmunks would come along, and, ah, have a feast! There wasn't any place to grow anything, and in the redwoods there's no sunshine. *(Cece)*

Carolyn and Cece sum up their feelings about Harmony Hill.

> It was a wonderful time. It's a wonderful way to raise children, in a community. *(Carolyn)*

> I'm still friends with a lot of the people I made connections with there then. That was kind of the founding group for my social activity for the rest of my life, from then till now. *(Cece)*

Harmony Hill was an experience in inventing a life totally different than their suburban up-bringing, an adventure that promoted resourcefulness and community and taught them food-processing skills, although not much about farming and gardening. Only four of the girls had actual working experience on a farm when they were growing up.

> When I was fourteen, my mom and dad divorced, and we went back to Georgia. She's from Georgia. I've picked cotton, I've hoed peas, I've helped with peanuts. They all were big farmers back there [in Georgia]. My uncle was a hog farmer. He raised lots of hogs. I remember many a morning jumping out of bed to help my cousins get 'em back into the fence. Granddaddy, he had chickens, and I remember a cow. I honestly think it was his love of animals that helped me grow up with a true love of animals. *(Sandra)*

> I grew up in Nebraska, on a farm about ten miles out of the town of Red Cloud, Nebraska. It was a several hundred acres farm and [my father] made it a small dairy farm, keeping, I don't know, a couple dozen cattle and maybe a dozen milk cows. [She continues later] My [first] husband decided to have a truck farm [outside Minneapolis], a big farm and raised—at one time we had ten thousand tomatoes staked. *(Alma)*

If only a few of these women had rustic experience with crops and animals and isolated rural lifestyles, what were they thinking when they moved to rural Tennessee? And could the families who raised these girls have imagined their late twentieth century daughters as homesteaders?

Chapter Two

Back to the Land

The social and political turbulence of the Sixties and Seventies resulted in introspection and internal storms for the young women in our story.

When I came back from Europe, it was probably the day before the huge march in Washington to protest the war. That was life-changing for sure, to be there with all these protesters. *(Carolyn)*

The whole idea of ecology, that was one of the reasons why I wanted to come here, too, because of the environment. People that just buy, buy, buy—we're such a consumer-y society. And we're destroying ourselves, in doing this. Well, that was the reason. Self-sufficiency. *(Alicia)*

We had already met these different people in Jellico, these young volunteers that were from college; young men and the war—getting into that. They were so worried about having to be drafted, and sent to Vietnam! Bellarmine [University] students, and then there were Vistas [Vista Volunteers] too, and we got to know them, too. *(Pat)*

There were adventures. For white women, in an era of more relative prosperity and freedom (they had their own cars!), the curiosity of the young could be met with travel, even long trips. A trip could be cross-country or in your head, or both.

My friend and I took a cross-country trip in a Volkswagen van. We went up through New York, and back across Canada. When I got back to California—I had life-changing experiences coming across the country, where we got stoned—I went to the nuns and I said, "I'm just gonna take a break, 'cause I can't come back and work [as a teacher]." And they were wonderful, they were really great. I had also read the book, *Siddhartha*. That was really popular at the time and changed people's consciousness, and so, then, I quit [teaching]. *(Carolyn)*

From getting out of college I got married, and then lived in a commune for a while. It was during the Sixties, and that movement was very much of the hippies and all that. Went to Woodstock, and just sort of liked that lifestyle. I had two little boys. I just felt that I wanted to have the experience of self-sufficiency, and organic living, I guess you'd say. I wanted to raise my kids in a place I thought was free and fun. *(Lee)*

Karen says that she was influenced by visiting Lee in the country, but the romantic idea of life in the country was widespread, and in some cases, an idea held since childhood.

I would live in this cabin. I would have a husband, I would have children. And I would take one of these checkered tablecloths, and a picnic basket, and we would pack our lunch in that, and we would go out of the house onto the hill that was all just beautiful with mountains surrounding. I would spread out the picnic tablecloth, and take everything out of the picnic basket, and then we would all sit down and eat our lunch. That's where we'd have our meals, that's how we would be living. That's my sort of vision when I was thirteen or fourteen. *(Micki)*

I thought, Back-to-the-land! I'll grow my own food and build my own house! And gosh, I had about as much information as the Three Little Pigs when it came to survival! *(Joanne)*

Sometimes a woman went along with a partner's life-long dream.

He wanted to get away from the cold of Minnesota where he'd lived all of his life. He was of the age to retire, and he decided when he retired we would move where it was all four seasons but not so extreme temperatures as Minnesota. So that's how we found [the] little burg of Eidson, and we bought acreage there. We had our own huge garden and had cattle and a couple of milk cows and a couple of goats and so forth. That's how I got down here because he wanted some land, and I knew all about that. I grew up with it. He wanted the experience of having a farm. *(Alma)*

People who lived in San Francisco, especially in the Haight-Ashbury District during the late Sixties, were influenced by the popular "guru," Stephen Gaskin. An instructor at San Francisco State University, he taught a Monday evening class on philosophy near the university until its popularity forced a move.

> [My sister] Tina, Rick, and I would go down to the Family Dog, which was an old nightclub kind of place on the coast, right at the beach in San Francisco, and hear Stephen Gaskin's talk there. He would talk every Monday night. There is a book called Monday Night Class, that I recommend. *(Carolyn)*

Gaskin's lectures incorporated Zen Buddhism, with references to D. T. Suzuki. He wrote a few books, which several of the back-to-the-landers read.

> He had a following of people that he gathered together and said we should go across country and find [land]—and practice what we preach. We should find land, and we should start farming, and raising our children alternatively—out of the system. So he and all his followers bought all these school buses and painted them all these psychedelic colors. They went across country, and they found[ed] The Farm, which is in Summertown, Tennessee, and my sister Tina went with them on the caravan. *(Carolyn)*

> You couldn't live in California any more because we couldn't do what we wanted to do. So that whole caravan of school buses Stephen organized and made this caravan to the east looking for basically what we were doing, [looking for] someplace livable, affordable, where they could run their own show, and have their own land, and do their own thing. *(Cece)*

Stephen Gaskin made a link between Zen practice, mindful living, and the back-to-the-land idea. His ethos included vegetarianism. Articles published about Gaskin's colorful caravan, his books, and word-of-mouth popularized his philosophy with many of the disaffected young people. With his wife, Ina May, he established The Farm, a commune that still exists today although Stephen Gaskin died in 2014. Carolyn, Cece, and Judy followed Gaskin's advice to "go back to the land." In Ohio, Vicki learned about him and his teachings.

> I had been looking through the most recent Whole Earth Catalogue, and I noticed books by Stephen Gaskin, and I think I bought *Monday Night Class* and *Caravan*. I read Stephen's teachings, and his philosophy, and shared 'em with [my boyfriend] Jerome. We decided we wanted to move to Tennessee to be close to The Farm, in Middle Tennessee. It was spiritually based, and pretty much self-sufficient. So, because I loved those philosophies, I wanted to be close to them. So I applied for positions as a teacher in Tennessee, but got one in East Tennessee instead of Middle Tennessee. *(Vicki)*

Vicki and Micki, both from Cincinnati, married brothers, Jerome and Joe Haverland. All four shared a similar philosophy and goals, including a vegetarian diet. Vicki and Jerome moved to Tennessee first.

> I had chosen that we would backpack in the Smokies for our honeymoon. We decided that we would stop and visit Jerome on our way back home after we came down from hiking, Jerome being my ex-husband Joe's brother. He and his then wife Vicki were living here in this area, actually down in Washburn [Tennessee]. That's when we hatched the plan of how Joe and I could be moving here in the very near future. *(Micki)*

Others arrived in Tennessee from different directions, but with similar hopes and beliefs. Pat and Alicia, two members of a four-person Dominican Convent "weren't crazy about" their second posting, in Kentucky. The hierarchy in New York City wanted to talk to them. The nuns rebelled.

> We didn't wanna go, because we had the animals—the chickens and the goats and everything. So we didn't go to all those meetings in New York, and they were getting more and more hostile about it, because they felt like we really didn't belong there [at that posting]. I guess that's what they were thinking. Somewhere along the line they said, "Well, that's it. You have to come back to New York. And behave like a regular nun." And so we said, "No, we're not coming back!" We had an idea then what we wanted to do for sure. We wanted to find an old farm, and garden and raise animals, and live off the land. And get to know people. So, that's what we did! *(Pat)*

All these women, most with families, looking for land, eventually found it in eastern Tennessee, where the terrain was picturesque and property was affordable.

> The land here was extremely cheap. Mountain land was like fifty dollars an acre. Good land was a hundred dollars an acre. So, we knew there was a possibility we could actually own our own place, not have to rent from somebody. That was a big, big, big deal. *(Janet)*

> The reason we came in this direction was, land in California at six or seven thousand dollars an acre, versus land here which at

the time was two hundred or two fifty an acre. No comparison. (Beth)

So how did they find that land? One magazine and a single realtor, Kay Realty, owned by Robert and Nancy Poole Kay, proved surprisingly influential. At least a quarter of this group of women mentioned the Kays' ads in *Mother Earth News* particularly, but also in *Organic Gardening Magazine*, and the *The Smoky Mountain Trader*. *Mother Earth News* was a popular source for ideas on homesteading as well as for advertisements for land. There were other methods of finding a place, such as picking up hitch-hikers!

> We were gonna move back [from San Francisco] to Independence, Missouri, so we came back there to look for a place to rent, and we picked up some hitch-hikers, and they said that they were livin' in Tennessee, and that we could come live there. And we said, okay. So, we loaded up and came to Tennessee. We were questioning whether we should do this or not, and then we got one look at that night-time sky with all those stars, and we said, "This is it." (Janet)

Linda, who had just finished her history teaching degree in Ohio and had had no luck finding a job, visited her recently widowed aunt in Tennessee. Against Linda's wishes, her aunt got her hired at a small local school with just a telephone call. (Aunt Sarah: "She'll take it!")

Though educated as a high school teacher, Linda reluctantly began teaching elementary school, while experiencing loneliness and culture shock.

> Back then, you know, as long as you had a college degree, they didn't care what it was in. So, I taught second grade, which was a real challenge, because I did not know how to teach someone

how to read. So I did a lot of reading of teacher's editions at night, and I thought, Well, I can do this for a year. I had no intentions of staying past one year. None. I really did not like Tennessee. The bugs were big. And I just did not know anyone, and I felt like—I'm sorry, I hate to take this attitude—but I felt like it was so backwards. It's just culture shock, even though I've been comin' down here all my life. I kinda looked at it from a different perspective. I did stay for that year, and then when I went home in summer to Ohio, I would get these letters from these little kids that I had in class. And they would send me their little Mickey Mouse plastic rings, and little doo-dads, and tell me how much they loved me. And I came back! And taught third grade, so I had the same group of little kids. Then [five years later] they put me in eighth grade, so then I had those kids again. By that time I was really starting to look around and think, Look around, look where you are! How beautiful! It's like this property we live on now, if it were in Ohio, it'd be a state park! *(Linda)*

Sometimes a young person can make a life-changing decision in a way that an older person might see as alarmingly casual.

Steven got tired of the fact that other than aspen, there were no deciduous trees in Colorado, I kid you not! He said, "Let's move." I said "Where?" We had this kind of back-to-the-land thing, and I don't know why. We got this really neat book. It just about totally covered everything you could ever want to learn about this, that, and the other [about homesteading]. So eventually we both quit our jobs and sold everything, loaded stuff up into a truck and a trailer, and headed back this way.

Dropped off furniture at my mom and dad's in Kansas City, then went up to Connecticut and dropped off a dog and cat. Then we just started kinda just drivin' around lookin' at land. We came down through Virginia, and it was just raining and raining and raining. Then we crossed the border into Tennessee. And then the sun came out! We pulled into a little real estate office at Brown's Corner [in Rogersville], and they had a picture of this little house in [the village of] Alum Well. I think it was like twelve thousand dollars, a house and five acres. Twelve thousand dollars! Well, we didn't have twelve thousand dollars, but we ended up buyin' it. *(Trudie)*

In semi-rural Ohio a catastrophe propelled Dianna and Bill to move to the Clinch Valley in eastern Tennessee.

[I was] becoming disillusioned with sorta the city coming in on me. My husband and I moved to a farmhouse, and we were pretty much doing kinda back-to-the-land things, heating with wood, cooking with wood, raising our food, and we really did not relate well with the other people in our area and the school that our oldest son was attending. So we had always talked about a place where we could get back to the land and be homesteaders. We really didn't know where that would be. It ended up that our house in Ohio burned down. It burned to the ground. But we had met some friends at a wedding in Ohio, and they lived in Tennessee. She just told me one time, "You need to come and visit us in northeast Tennessee. You might like it." *(Dianna, raised in West Virginia with teen years in an Akron suburb)*

> We stayed with them, Gene and Sally Childs. They took us to parties every weekend and we thought that was just amazing that there were so many like-minded people like us here and having all this natural fun, playing volleyball, and making their own bread, and nursing their children in public, and all the things that I did that were looked down upon when I lived in Ohio. So we felt at home right away. *(Dianna)*

The newcomers came in their loaded-down vehicles, with many hopes, eager to get started, some bringing their small children and even a few animals.

> We went back up [to Cincinnati from the Tennessee visit], and next thing you know, October 1 of that same year, seventy-seven, we were on our way down in our Volkswagen bug, followed by a friend with a van full of everything we had, which wasn't much. We had a bed, an end table, and a lot of house plants. And a guitar. *(Micki)*

> I had a goat, two dogs, two cats, six chickens in my car [a VW], when I got here. We took out the seat, and [the goat] sat in the back. *(Alicia)*

Some of the back-to-the-landers first met at The Farm on the way here.

> The Farm had already been established [incorporating The Farm Midwifery Center]. Ina May Gaskin [Stephen's wife] was there and was already training midwives, had several midwives, and I kept telling Bert, "Well, if I'm pregnant we need to make plans about this. I've gotta have somewhere to have this baby, I

need to be checked out." We went there [The Farm] and stayed for several weeks. I was checked out by the midwives, and Bert worked on the firewood crew along with Vicki Haverland's husband, Jerome, and Bobby Merrithew. So the three guys became buddies, and therefore the wives sorta got to know each other, too. And Jerome and Vicki motivated Bobby and Bert and I to come and look at this area of Tennessee. "It's beautiful, it's mountainous, it has farmable land. It has spring water on a lotta places, and it's livable and it's affordable." *(Cece)*

The abstract became real.

I didn't know much—about the country living. I mean, I lived in Amsterdam, I lived in London, I lived in the cities. You see, I came to the country not as a "believer," but as a tourist! [My husband] Bill was a "believer." Bill was a believer in having a garden, and in doing all this. I came and thought it was great. But, it has never been my "passion," like some of the people here. Like Bill's passion, and Bill's life—the gardening, and all that. *(Yvonne)*

But we are still at the beginning of the story, and just arriving at the homesteading place. It seems idyllic and a great adventure.

I got married, and then lived in a commune for a while, and then decided we really wanted something in the country, and got in a school bus, and loaded everybody up, including the dogs, and the everything, and just started traveling south, and found in Rogersville a little log cabin with fifteen acres. It was thirty-five hundred dollars, and we bought it, right there on the spot! James Richardson had had it listed. We were traveling and just sleeping with a bedroll when we came down. And so, he was showing us things, and he said, "Where are you spending the night?"

We said, "Just alongside the road."

And he said, "Well, that's not going to work."

He took us to an adorable little log cabin that was his cabin—not where he lived—but just a sort of a party cabin, and plopped us down there. It just kind of blew our minds, that, Here's a man that we just met! So, there we were. We were there for about two hours, and he shows up again with his wife and a homemade hot apple pie for us!

So where do you think I might wanna raise children, and where do you think I might wanna live? *(Lee)*

Where indeed?

By fate, fortune, or happy fact, all those families—those California commune dwellers, the tough nuns, the mid-western city dwellers, the education grad on a visit, the idealistic retired couple, the artists, and the just plain wet-behind-the-ears young 'uns—arrived in the same mountain valley in their vans and VW bugs, loaded up with kids, a few animals, guitars, and sparse furnishings.

Chapter Three

Adding a Home to the Homestead

Some homesteaders arrived knowing no one in Tennessee. Others followed relatives or close friends. All were following an idea. It was making that idea a reality that proved to be the formidable challenge. However, they were young, and as Linda put it, "We thought we were havin' fun!"

So, how did they begin? Where did they live while they were looking for a place, or building or renovating a house? For some, renting was an option. One couple got a tip from the rural mail carrier about an unoccupied house.

> [The owner] was willing to rent us this house. Well, "house" is probably an elaborate word for this shack, but it did prove to be our home for five years. He rented it to us for twenty-five dollars a month. It had no plumbing, nor insulation. It was just sort of this box that was divided up into four rooms without doors. *(Micki)*

Another couple found a rent-free situation. Under the invitation from the hitchhikers they had picked up in Missouri, Janet and her husband,

Jesse, lived at the Sunflower Farm commune in a teepee on the side of a hill during their first winter.

> It had a tiny wood stove in it, and it was all real cozy, [with a] little bed. So, every night after dinner, we'd trudge up there with our little sack of wood, and start a fire, and it'd get super hot in there. It was right by a huge creek, and actually, at that time, you could drink the water out of the creek, it was so pure. It was beautiful! *(Janet)*

Dissension between newer members of the commune and the original residents caused the owner to kick everyone out. Janet and her husband went to Florida, and worked building condominiums for a year. Upon returning to Tennessee they moved in with a friend who had decided to grow tomatoes, and helped him build a greenhouse and raise tomatoes that summer.

Then, Janet and Jesse were off to a resort—well, sort of.

> We found out about a place called Mooresburg Springs, which was an old resort that was built around a mineral spring. That was another place that you could go and live for free. We lived there for about a year or two. Part of the time without electricity, part of the time we had it. 'Course, no runnin' water. We just carried it from that spring. The water was orange. You had to clean [the containers] out every single day, or there would be like a layer of this orange—from the minerals. There was an old dance hall there. And there was like eight or ten cabins. *(Janet)*

Meanwhile, Vicki was gradually making her way to the same abandoned resort. On the way from Ohio to her first teaching job in Tennessee, Vicki and her fiancé, Jerome, stayed at The Farm and got married there in August, 1975. Their first rental in the Clinch Valley was a chilly double-wide trailer. They didn't stay in it long.

> The next place we moved to was called Mooresburg Springs, which was an abandoned resort that was active, I don't know, in the twenties, thirties. We went up to visit, and a coupla interesting people [Janet and Jesse] stepped out and greeted us! And those people became our first friends when we moved to Tennessee. We became fast friends, and they told us that we could move into Mooresburg Springs, into one of those cabins. So, sounded like an interesting adventure! We actually did get permission, and the electricity was on. We picked out a cabin, and moved in there probably the early fall. Straight from the city, I had no idea what it would be like living in a not-well-taken-care-of cabin, in an old, old resort. We had to haul our water from the actual mineral springs, which were supposed to be very healthy for everybody, and I think I heard that Teddy Roosevelt had even visited Mooresburg Springs. So we had to haul our water up from the mineral spring, which was quite an incline to the cabin. Jerome didn't have a job. He cut our wood with a bow saw part of the time in the winter. We froze our butts off some of the time though there was a big barrel stove. *(Vicki)*

After about a year, and with Vicki pregnant with her first child, they rented a two-bed-room house in Washburn. She soon became pregnant again, so while living there Vicki traveled to the midwifery center at The Farm in Middle Tennessee for the births of her first two children.

Then they moved again, living with four other adults and six children in one house.

A big, old, old house in Indian Creek, very big and old—and, across the creek. Sometimes we would get flooded in. One couple moved in with us at Washburn, and the woman, Margaret [DeVos], is still a friend. Another couple that we had met on The Farm moved in a while later. That was also a very interesting experience, because I was a pie-in-the-sky optimistic hippie, and I think everything is gonna go really well and happy with everybody, but we sure had a lot to work out with the people we were livin' with. Some of 'em. *(Vicki)*

Meanwhile, way up Clinch Valley in eastern Hancock County on East Pumpkin Valley Road, another group was experiencing communal living in a rental, the "McMillan House."

Newcomers stayed there while exploring the area, looking for a place to rent, or starting to build on their own land. Cece enthusiastically urged back-to-the-landers to come to East Tennessee.

People that came followed us here from California. When we found our place, we sent word back to Carolyn [Novkov], John and Lynn [Gamble], all those folks in California, Judy and Wes [Moore]. "Hey, we found some place that's livable and affordable. If you wanna come out, come on out!" Vivien, Regina, and Wayne and Eileen Rudiger came. A lotta people came and checked it out. Some people stayed; some people left. That McMillan house kinda became a starting, landing place. Carolyn and Rick came. They stayed there a little bit, then they found a place to rent. As somebody found a place to rent, they would move out of there. Somebody else'd come along, and so it all worked out. Kinda "musical houses." *(Cece)*

The McMillan house is gone now, but here's a description.

> It had a kitchen; didn't have a bathroom; had running water, I believe; three rooms and a kitchen. There was Rick and myself, and [our children] Sarah, Rachel, and Joseph; and Cece and Bert [Lakin] and [their daughter] Melissa; and Heather and Margaret [De Vos] and Margaret's baby, Mary Beth. Margaret was then married to Eric [De Vos], whom she had met on The Farm. There was a lot of people in that house—six adults, and six children, twelve people in that house! In the summer we were outside most of the time. Our friend, Vivien, was there also, from Santa Cruz. So we had a lot of people living there. We were the talk of the valley! *(Carolyn)*

Like all the residents of the McMillan "group home," Carolyn and Rick eventually moved to their own place.

> Rick and I found a little house, up on the hill at the end of the valley, a little log house. So we rented this cabin for twenty dollars a month, and in the spring we started working on it. It needed to be chinked, 'cause it had big spaces [between the logs]. So we chinked all the walls, and we moved up there in the fall. [My sister] Tina and [husband] Gary helped us a lot. They would come and visit, and help us do that work. It was a freezing cold house—all we had was a fireplace. It was very cold! It was one degree one morning in the bedroom. One! *(Carolyn)*

This wasn't the last log cabin that Carolyn lived in, nor was she the only newcomer to live in one. Of the places she rented over the following years, at least three were log houses. One had two stories with siding over the logs. After living in that first house for a couple of years, Carolyn and Rick moved to a house near the Clinch River, on Avery Holt's farm.

> We didn't pay any rent. He worked for Avery and that was part of the deal. And then I think he made ninety cents an hour. That was in 1979. There was a hose [from the spring] into the sink so you could have running water. It ran all the time! We had an outhouse. We did have chickens when we lived there. I think we had a duck that was loose in the yard and the kids would play with the duck. Can't remember why we moved out of there. It was nice, it was a great house, it really was. *(Carolyn)*

Next for Carolyn's family of five was another log house, large and recently built.

> We worked out rent and care-taking with the owner. [Living there] was really fun; it was huge. While we were living there Judy and Wes [and their three children] moved in with us for a while till they could find their own place. *(Carolyn)*

Judy, like Carolyn, a former resident of Harmony Hill in California, takes up the story.

> [When] we first came here, we moved in with Carolyn and Rick. [Their house] was a big log-house kit with a small log-house kit attached. They weren't using the whole house. It was too big. The upstairs was empty, so we moved into the upstairs for eight to ten months. *(Judy)*

After a short stay in another house, Judy and Wes moved to—guess what—a log cabin. "We went to a little cabin that our friend Joanne built herself with some help from friends, and we lived there for a few years," Judy said.

Altogether, ten of the women lived in log houses. One advantage was the lower price for an older log house. For some, the cabins reinforced, if only at first, a romantic vision of the simple, bucolic life they had imagined.

When I was dating Gary, he said, "Would you like to see the upstairs?"

Well, the upstairs was a loft. I went upstairs in the loft, and the bed was the proverbial pallet on the floor. It was a mattress. He said, "Look out that window."

The window, you could push open [to one side], and you could look out and see Clinch Mountain, and it was beautiful. I went, "Oh, this is just like *Heidi*!" I was hooked. I think I married him for *him*, and not the house, but sometimes I'm not so sure! *(Nancy)*

The real estate agent took us from one place to another, and every place my eyes started getting bigger. People really lived this far back? And no electricity? It kind of excited me. [It was] a very old, old house. Actually it was two log cabins built side-by-side [of] chestnut logs, and they were both lined with chestnut. Two fireplaces, one at either end. We didn't have much money, so we couldn't do too much. Two big cabins, just no rooms. We used the one for cooking and living, and the other one was the bedroom. *(Sherri)*

Many of the group found land fairly quickly. While they renovated an old house or built a new one, they camped out in various ways.

> We started off living in a school bus, and there were six of us. And then we put in a small, single-wide trailer, like a large travel trailer. So we lived in those two units from October through December. And we had a big [cook] tent. Then we moved into the downstairs of the house we were building on Christmas Eve. (Judy)

Living conditions could provide motivation to make progress quickly, as when living in, say, a truck-bed camper.

> We moved here in a camper, the kind of a camper that goes on the back of a truck, so basically we really, really roughed it when we first moved. [The house] was falling down. Wayne had to rip the porch off and redo it, except for the roof. And he tore walls out. He was just doing the front of the house, temporary till—it was either do that, or a trailer. I didn't want to get a trailer because I was too afraid that then I would never get that house. So, he built this [house]. When he got done I said, "I love this." (Sandra)

Or in a tent.

> This piece of land we ended up with was fourteen and a half acres. It was a great, great price, so it was great. We lived in a tent and had my show tent for craft shows, set up as a kitchen, until a really big storm came. We decided that was really an expensive thing to lose, those show canopies, so we started to

go to town a lot and eat. But we lived in a tent, and built the house, the two of us. We did cook a lot over a fire. *(Robyn)*

Or a trailer.

We lived in a trailer that we got from some other little "hippies" that looked like a silver bullet. Inside had pretty beechwood paneling, and beechwood cabinets. But very tiny—eight feet by forty-eight feet and very interesting. The people that had lived in there before us had made it interesting, too. For instance, they put a free-standing fireplace in the living room, and in order to do that, they had to cut a hole in the ceiling. I don't think they were schooled in this. It was a very here-and-there hole in the ceiling. I imagine that they hoped that the stovepipe and the little cap that went over it, was going to help the rain not go in that hole, but it didn't. Anyway, later, we took that out and we put a skylight there, and we breathed in the kerosene fumes from a kerosene heater. *(Lauren)*

Or a smokehouse (for curing meat).

When we started out, actually we didn't even live in the big house. We lived in the [former] smokehouse. [With Vivien's help] we finished off the nine by thirteen smokehouse first, because the other one was too big of a project. We lived in the smokehouse with a box stove. That was our heat. We lived there while we were fixing up the house. *(Cece)*

Or a barn in the winter, with two small children!

We had heard about this piece of land that was for sale over here on this side of the mountain, and came over here and looked at it, and just really, really loved it, and borrowed some money and bought this piece of property. It was seventy-five dollars an acre. It had no house, but nevertheless, we lived in the barn for a while. That was pretty far out. We didn't have any electricity but we set up refrigeration by digging a hole in the ground, and keeping things cool there. I just had an open fire pit for doing the cooking. I learned how to bake just [over] an open fire in kettles—breads and things. It was alright. But got a little cold, a little cold in the winter! So that's when we started building this cabin here. *(Lee)*

How do you choose your homesteading place? There are ideals of beauty, and there are practicalities.

It wasn't so much about the house. It would have been nice if it was magnificent, but we were buying a piece of land. It had three springs that had never run dry. It had grasslands and forest. It had as much wood as you'd ever need for warming yourself, or building. The house was a little wooden board-and-batten house, no big deal. It wasn't the house we fell in love with. It was the land and the privacy. *(Tata)*

By necessity, the fixer-upper was the choice for many would-be homeowners. And, despite their efforts, they sometimes ended up moving again.

It was way back deep in this holler. You had to go down their driveway, through a gate, then down through their pasture. Then you came to this area that was just a road without any good grading on it that just sort of tilted sideways, so that you were looking down deeper into this holler, into this pasture. You could have easily slid off. Then you got down to the bottom, and there was our place, and the sun didn't shine there very often. There was still ice in May on the steps, but we thought it was grand. There was a little four-room house on the property, and a nice spring, and we built an outhouse, a really nice rock outhouse. I was pregnant, and Claudia, the wife of the other couple [who were co-owners], she was pregnant, so it wasn't long before they bought us out and we moved to another place. *(Joanne)*

That place was not down in a holler, but had a dirt floor and other quaint features.

It was at the corner of Black Sheep Holler [Hollow] and Byrd Creek [Road]. It was just a two-room house [with] a breezeway; there was a kitchen off of the breezeway. It had a lot of outbuildings. We had a hog lot, and a barn for a cow, and fenced pastures. It was pretty nice. It was really cold, though. When winter came, the diaper pail froze inside the house. *(Joanne)*

Meanwhile, Micki's rental situation changed. She moved from the twenty-five-dollar-a-month shack where she had lived for five years.

We weren't making improvements because a) we didn't have money to do that; and b) we weren't planning on living there indefinitely. And when I say there was a bit of a non-improvement, that's because there was a fire in the house at one point while we were living there...

Fire?! We leave that story for later.

We kept hoping that we would find something better. Something maybe that had water, or something. *(Micki)*

Water? We save that for later also. But there was good news at last, as Micki relates.

> A place came up for rent, and this is like two miles down the road. The owners were moving away, and they were looking for somebody to lease this three hundred acre farm with this very together house that had running water; not just one bathroom, but two; had an intact ceiling and roof; had insulation in the walls. Just a dream home as far as I was concerned. We were so looking forward to it, that when we saw the owners of the house head out the valley with their moving truck we jumped into our truck, and drove down to this house [with] the two boys in the truck. It was like a dream come true! It was like the Beverly Hillbillies moved to Beverly Hills.
>
> We came in, and it was carpeted with this Seventies' green carpet all over the floors—avocado, yes, indeed. And we laid down, on that carpet, like we were laying on, like on the beach or on this incredible featherbed in a royal palace. That's what it felt like. And we just lay there, and we looked up at the ceiling that like, was painted white, was like this together ceiling, didn't have any holes in it. I'm telling you, I'll never forget the feeling! It was amazing! Oh my God. I was just pinch, pinch, pinch, pinch myself. And then we had so much fun! We'd go into the bathroom, and, oh, flush the toilet. And there was a bathtub, and we were so excited, we ran the water for the kids to get in

the bathtub right away. It was like, "Wanna get in the water an' play?" It was just, oh God, so wonderful! We were just so overjoyed, overjoyed!

The house had a heat pump and air conditioning, but we never used it. There's a Buck Stove chimney insert, which had a plug-in for a fan to circulate [the warm air], and it did a terrific job heating the house. So we were able to continue using wood, which was really important 'cause the last thing we needed was a power bill. *(Micki)*

Most loved their first homes even when the places needed work.

Our friend, Mary, saw this ad for a farmhouse in Hancock County. It sounded beautiful. It had three porches, and five springs. Oh! It just sounded beautiful, so we drove out here, and we found the place, with their directions.

We couldn't see the house from the road, it was so overgrown with trees. The grass was up to here. College students had bought it from a local person. They had tried to fix it up, so there were little signs of them having done stuff. But you couldn't get up on the front porch. There was a big hole in the middle of the front porch. Anyway, we decided to [try to] make it, and we got the water going. *(Pat)*

It was at the end of the road. It was the only house there. There were creeks that came down either side. It had a barn. It had pasture land, a little bit on each side a three or a four-room house with a small porch. Eventually we added on. But, yeah, it was a neat little house. We painted it yellow, and it had big willow trees out front. *(Trudie)*

Some of the homesteaders lacked basic skills.

> I never used a hammer, I never used a axe, I never used a shovel, a rake, a hoe. My neighbors [taught me] mostly. Or, I watched people repairing the place. *(Alicia)*

And if the house you bought had no windows?

> We had no windows—we had no glass. In the wintertime we would put plastic, heavy plastic up across it, and we would put it on the inside and outside, so they'd have an air pocket in the middle. Then in the summer we would just put screens in there. We just lived hard. We didn't have money. *(Sandra)*

Another use of plastic wrap, when you have to move in quickly—

> [The first house at] Alum Well sold out from under us. We couldn't believe somebody bought it! So we had to get out. This [new house] was framed up, so we got some friends over. I think Bill Young and people from work, and got the roof put on, and then we just wrapped the bottom floor in plastic. We didn't have windows or doors or anything, and really, plumbing, or anything. It was very interesting! It was fun, it was fun! *(Trudie)*

Perhaps a complete renovation was necessary.

> We found this place up in East Pumpkin Valley, forty acres for $13,500. It had a creek bordering it, and it had a spring. It had an old farmhouse that had electricity, but the wiring was very dubious. We put new wiring in the whole thing. And just

mouse-eaten. The outer walls were board and bat [batten]. The inner walls were layers and layers of newspapers that had been stapled up there, some of 'em from back in the forties. When we peeled it, it was nasty. We had to wear masks. You peel the paper off and dead spiders and even mouse skeletons would come down out of the paper. It just disintegrated. It was really a dirty job cleaning that place up, but then we framed it in and insulated it. There was originally three twelve-by-sixteen-foot rooms kinda shaped in an ell, and we divided the middle room into two bedrooms. [One room] was just wide enough that we could get a double bed in. We'd have to crawl up into it. Then the other bedroom became the kids' bedroom. It took about a year. Then [we] put up "wood" paneling [the stores] had at the time. *(Cece)*

A house might have a cool shape, but lack other features.

There was this octagon-shaped room with a chimney in the middle. Where you see the windows, those were openings closed off with plastic. Everything was rough because the person who had made this house had used a chainsaw to cut this wood. It wasn't like really finished. There was this octagon and only one other segment attached to it, which was a sort of a kitchen. There was no running water. I think there was one other little room off the octagon, where the kids slept, and Bill and I slept in a sort of loft situation. We had to climb up a ladder to sleep here. While we were living here we mostly lived in sawdust for a year, trying to get things built on, get real windows, and all that. Actually, Bill worked in the World's Fair [in Knoxville] then, for our first [summer] and I was here alone with the kids for quite a while, for about two weeks in a row. Every night I was dead scared, because there were no door [locks]. Well, there were doors, but no windows. Then the doors you could just open, and I was really scared on my own, until I sort of broke through that, and decided, I've got to sleep! I was afraid of intruders, at night. Like who? I don't know, I had no clue, I had never been here, I had never slept here on my own. Now I don't have that fear anymore. But I know other people, when they come here, some people, they want to make sure that the doors are locked and all. Well, that's what you get with city people, right? *(Yvonne)*

Yvonne described the carpentry they did as "trial-and-error carpentry," an apparently common practice among the homesteaders, including the use of green wood and inappropriate application of chainsaws. And there are so many things to do all at once! But there are priorities.

I remember that the first thing we put on the property was a telephone. After we got some poles put up, we built a little wooden box, and had our red telephone stuck in this box, 'cause we didn't have a house to put it in. We just had a telephone, that's all we had. *(Beth)*

Following are three stories of women who built their houses—with or without spouses—from scratch. All three depended on the skill of horses.

The significant thing I guess about the house was—and a lot of people were doing this—all the lumber that we used in our house we cut off our property with just chainsaws and pulling the logs down off the hills. We did use the first mustang [horse] that we had for pulling the logs off the hills. That was kind of a dangerous situation. All I had at the time for a truck was a Datsun pickup truck, and we bought a long, flat-bed trailer somewhere for three hundred dollars. It seemed like a really expensive purchase at the time, extravagant, like, Why do we need that? We loaded up this trailer with logs, hopefully not too many at a time, pulled it behind the Datsun pickup truck, to P.G. Sizemore's lumber mill, which is up on top of Copper Ridge. That was totally crazy, because that truck was not rated to tow anything, let alone a flat-bed trailer loaded with half a dozen or more logs on it. But we did that.

It was a crazy house—it was built out of four-by-fours—a one-of-a-kind building plan. Didn't put a foundation in. I hated that. We, instead, cut down locust trees and sank [the posts], I think, three feet in the ground. They were probably good size, maybe eight to ten inches in diameter. Like maybe every eight feet we had a locust post in the ground. That's where we built the first floor, was right on top of locust posts, with Ray saying, "This is only temporary." Those were his favorite words, "This is only temporary." He said, "We will come back and fill in a foundation later on." We heard that locust would probably last fifty-plus years in the ground, and that sounded like a forever to us. Fifty years, we won't be around!

It was all green wood, everything. You bring it back from the mill, you start hammering it up. We wanted to have a greenhouse of sorts, so the first incarnation of the house was a three-story—I think it was like twenty by thirty, or twenty-five by forty—basic rectangle, but [with a] shed roof, and it was divided into three floors. So from the second floor up to the top of the third floor [ridgepole] we had diagonal beams coming down [where] we put house windows—they had window panes. Back at the time there were a lot of people that had estate sales or barn sales and you could buy a whole truckload of these windows. Most of them were the same size so they kinda fit together. So there was this slant of windows going from the bottom of the second floor up to the top of the third floor. It was an odd-looking structure, very odd-looking structure. *(Beth)*

After the first cold winter Lee was glad to get out of the barn and start on a house. Like Beth and her husband, Lee also logged with a horse. Her friends and neighbors helped, too.

I found a book that—the how-to books, oh, they're just great!—showed you how to cut, make a wedge, and cut a tree down. Then I had a local person show me how—because I was into it; my [first] husband was not into it, but that's okay. It was my trip anyway. So, [the neighbor] showed me how to use horses. So, you cut down this tree, and then you hook a horse up to this tree, and you drag the tree out of the mountain, and you plop one tree on top of another tree, and somehow it came about. And stones, lots of stones. A lot of people came down from the North that were my friends, and so it was a real community building of this little cabin that actually we're still living in. *(Lee)*

Joanne and her husband Bill, had sold their last place and bought another one, on Sweet Creek. They moved into the tiny shack on the property with their two little girls.

It was one big room and it had a small chimney, so you could put a wood stove there. We had a little loft for sleeping in. It was really dark and dingy and unpleasant, but we lived there a couple of years, and then I started building a log cabin with everybody's help. *(Joanne)*

Bill had left after two years, but Joanne was determined to build a house in spite of working full time. The amazing Tonto George pulled the logs down out of the woods for her.

Geri Kitchen came and helped pull the logs out off the hillside with her trusty horse, Tonto George, who knew more than either one of us did about having a path. He was just wonderful. I had thought I had cleaned up the logs enough to pull them out of the woods. Of course Geri found a lot of fault with that, and she cleaned them up some more. Then I made a trail for Tonto George to bring the logs out, and he didn't like my trail. I mean, talk about humbling, when the horse knows more than you do!

So he took this other trail, and he would bring the logs down to a certain point, and then he would take a right turn, and he would go down another grade off the hillside. He would get to a place where there was sort of an arroyo and he'd turn that corner and he'd brace himself. You could just see him brace himself against what would happen next—the log would roll with his turning and hit these trees and stop. Then he'd take it on down. Then there was a place where I wanted the logs to be piled up, and he would bring them down—this is without anybody at his lead, either—this is just Tonto George working. He'd bring 'em down, and he'd roll them into place so that they were all piling up in a pile! *(Joanne)*

Taking the logs across the bridge to the sawmill was a challenge.

> Then John Hoellman came, and he put the logs on his old logging truck, and he would take 'em to P.G. Sizemore's to be squared up. Bill, before he left, had built this rickety bridge over Sweet Creek. The bridge was made of old telephone poles. There was three of them in a grouping and three more. Then [instead of] flooring the entire area, he only floored each set of the three poles. So, three poles had a decking on them [for one set of wheels], and then there was a space where you could look down into the creek, and then there was another three poles with decking [for the other wheels]. [The bridge] was at sort of an angle to the road so it was difficult to align your tires just right. If one tire went off, you were stuck. So, that was the bridge we were working with—which in and of itself, if you had some driving skills, pretty much you'd be alright. Then one of those poles cracked. And still John drove over them with trucks full of logs! I mean, he just did it! I can never do enough to thank him for what he did. Took the logs over; he then brought 'em back. *(Joanne)*

Every home needs a good foundation—family, friends, community, and cement and sweat.

> Then I did the foundation. I poured the cement and laid the block. I [dug the foundation] by myself, and the chimney foundation. My brother had come, and I was having trouble just laying it out and squaring up the corners, and so he worked with that with me. Then I dug that foundation, and then I dug the chimney foundation. Then he and his wife came back, and

we poured the foundation for the chimney. I had an old bedspring, and that was what we used to reinforce [the concrete]—just put that into the foundation. Oh, we were so muddy and so sweaty and so covered in cement, and we all took a great swim in the pond! *(Joanne)*

As a single parent, Joanne had to "keep her day job." She was a nurse at the tiny local hospital.

So this was weekends and after hours and then, once every two weeks, John and Lee would come up, and sometimes Herb Ferrell would come over, and sometimes other people would come. [Former] patients from the hospital would come and they would work with me, cutting the logs, and putting them in place, and chinking, doing some rock work. Karen Berg and I did a lot of the rock work on the inside chimney. Bobby Merrithew showed me how to lay rock, so that I did the rock work on the outside of the chimney.

Everyone, everyone helped! It was just wonderful. It took two years from the time I started digging the foundation until we moved in. There was still lots of work to do, but it was at a point where we were in! *(Joanne)*

Many of the families cut lumber off their own properties to build their houses and out-buildings, and the pride in self-sufficiency was palpable among the group. Building a small house or reviving an old one was part of living a simple life! No one had the finances to build a professionally designed modern home. Moreover, they were full of energy and adventure and reveled in doing a major project by themselves.

So, yeah, we built our house, and it was not something I'm terribly proud of, other than the fact that it was something we did ourselves! *(Beth)*

Chapter Four

Keeping the Home Fires Burning

Winter is cold in East Tennessee, they say. But, really, how cold was it? "Cold enough to freeze the diaper pail solid," Joanne has stated. Carolyn said that the thermometer read one degree Fahrenheit inside the house one morning. In the mountains temperatures often fall below freezing at night, and it snows. The colder Seventies and Eighties were difficult for the new arrivals.

> I would say the mean temperature in the house in the winter was more like fifty-five, because we didn't have much insulation. So we huddled. We usually closed off rooms and huddled around the stove. If it was a real cold winter or windy day, it came in a lot through the windows, doors, up through the floors, so it was hard to keep it warm. *(Dianna)*

> [Our house] had asphalt shingle siding. But it was only haphazardly on there, so in the winter time, if it snowed, the snow would come blowing through the cracks. It was cold. I typically slept in the winter, when it was really cold, fully clothed, with

hat, and gloves and coat, and when it was *really* cold I wore my boots, as well. *(Micki)*

All we had was a fireplace. It was very cold. Joseph spent most of his first year there in a jumpy swing in front of the fireplace so he could stay warm. 'Cause he couldn't crawl around too much. I would let him out, but you had to be on top of it so he wouldn't crawl in the fireplace. It was cold on the floor, too. *(Carolyn)*

Some tried hot-burning coal, but most rejected it.

Coal had disadvantages. We tried coal one year. That was very warm. It kept our house the warmest it had ever been, but it was very messy, very stinky, and we didn't like it. *(Dianna)*

Heating with wood was challenging. Linda had two children, was teaching school, and her husband sometimes worked in another state.

I'd make a fire in the morning. Sometimes there would be ashes and embers left that you could put some more wood in, and get it going fairly easily. I don't think I was ever gone long enough that it got terribly cold. There were some nights, though, that we had activities, that you may not get home till eight or nine o'clock, and then, building a fire! We had frozen pipes on many occasions. I got a hair dryer, and tried to [thaw] it that way. Sometimes I was not successful, and I just had to carry water till Ron got home and could fix it. 'Cause I could not get under that floor. It's just—that crawl space is—oh, my gosh! *(Linda)*

It's tough with no back-up person when you're heating with wood—even life threatening.

> One winter Dale had gone with Jerome Haverland to Georgia to plant pine trees and make some money for us. He'd taken the vehicle and I didn't have a way to town. It got real cold; it was wintertime. The firewood was up on the middle level there [of the slopes above the house]. I hadn't brought enough firewood down, and I'd gotten real sick with the flu or something. I couldn't get out of bed, and I'd run out of firewood at the door. I'd had the bed right next to the wood stove. The stove didn't have any heat!
>
> If it hadn't been for the dogs I don't think I would have made it through the night, I was so sick. They climbed up on top of the bed, all three of those big dogs. They kept me warm. The next morning I was able to get up and get myself together enough to get a fire going. But I don't think I woulda made it through the night if it hadn't been for those three dogs, I was so very sick. We had water in jugs, and it all froze, which was right next to the bed. I was lucky that I had those dogs with me! It was a "three dog night!" *(Sherri)*

All these homesteading families were cash-poor and resource-rich, including timber. Most of the Clinch Mountain farms typically have tillable bottomland, some sloping pasture, and some woods, often stretching up to the top of a ridge or Clinch Mountain itself. But timing is everything.

> I never got enough wood up, so I would always find that about January I had run out of wood. Then I would go out with my chainsaw, and I would try to cut up some wood, but you know,

the wood would be frozen, so it wasn't very useful. But I never got it all together—not [with] working full time and trying to do everything. *(Joanne)*

I have a [gasoline-powered] wood-splitter that I use. I got one of those years ago, because I didn't have wood when I lived with my "ex." We had "wood for the day." So I got crazy, and I had to learn to use a chainsaw and cut my own wood. It's like havin' food or toilet paper—[like] money, to me! Then a couple of times back then we had two feet of snow. When you have two feet of snow, you can't even find the wood—so I really learned my lesson the hard way. But, you know, you gotta take care of yourself! *(Robyn)*

Right from the start we heated with wood, and it was usually green wood, because we didn't have enough. We couldn't get enough for two years, so we'd have one set for the next year [while burning one set]. So we bought it from this man down the road. He'd just fill up his truck with wood, and it'd be all kinds of different wood. Some of it would be old wood that had been layin' around in a heap. I think we paid him like fifty bucks for a load, or somethin'. He would deliver it. We didn't split it very good. I couldn't split it at all. It had to go into the stove the size it was, and I think we didn't keep that stove all that hot. I was always worried about a fire—creosote in the chimneys and stuff. *(Pat)*

Micki's and Vicki's husbands, the brothers Joe and Jerome Haverland, worked at a sawmill and would bring home leftover slab wood.

> When the log is taken to the sawmill, one of the first things they'll do is square the log, and in squaring the log, that's debarking it at the same time. The slabs had bark on one side and the other side had some of the hardwood. We burned a lot of that slab wood and then supplemented it with what Joe and Jerome would cut with the chainsaw. We also used those slabs to heat our greenhouses, 'cause they were heated with wood stoves as well. *(Micki)*

Lauren traded kerosene heat for wood heat when she moved from the trailer into the house they had built. She organized her six children into a firewood relay that ended inside their house.

> As my boys came along, they were all very proficient with [splitting wood], and they could split wood and stack it in no time at all. In fact, we didn't have a wood shed, and so my favorite thing to do was, we would form a line out of kids, and—kind of a relay thing, pass the bucket thing—we would make two stacks of wood that were, like, two feet wide, and it went clear to the ceiling. That helped that wood to dry out, being inside. It would get so high that somebody had to get on a chair. Someone came right to that chair-person, and handed up the wood, and we'd stack it up there. But, I was not a fan of wet wood, not a bit—it's got its own smell. *(Lauren)*

Ron and Linda were a team.

> Ron's very particular about his trees. It had to be something that was already down; he wouldn't cut it down. Which is good. There was plenty of available stuff. It wasn't always the easiest

in the world to get to, but I helped him some. We'd just go up the hill, and he would cut it [in short sections] and kick it down, and I'd pick it up. Sometimes, along the road he would kick it down, and it'd splash in the ditch-line and sometimes get on the road. I'd have to move it real quick in case a car was coming or something, but we used to think that was fun, too. So, those were the days! *(Linda)*

Wood provides dry, radiant heat.

> Have always heated with wood. The only things that have changed over the years are the stoves. It's a good heat! *(Lee)*

And is good for drying clothes.

> I had clotheslines in the living room that went up over the wood stove. I had a washing machine, and I would wash the diapers and then hang 'em up to dry, and that would be like our humidity in the winter. *(Ceci)*

> Stick 'em up at night, in the morning they're dry. *(Lauren)*

And for canning.

> Canned on a wood cook stove, and to me that was the easiest way I've ever canned. *(Dianna)*

And for "blazing showers."

> [My husband] John came up with this idea of [using] thermal convection, of putting copper coil inside the heat exhaust of this wood stove. [The heat] pushed the water up to a tank that would be up over top of [the stove] and then, just by gravity flow, it went into a little bathing area that we developed. It really did work. The thing that was so amazing was that in the wintertime we often would keep [the water] running because it would blow the safety valve, 'cause it would make such huge amounts of hot water, and so hot that the valve would blow. *(Lee)*

And for baking bread.

> You talk about making bread now! This cookstove was iron. As long as your wood was dry, and the right kind of wood—'cause you have to find out what works for what. Once a week I made six loaves of bread, and it was a tradition always, when it came out, there was a line-up of the kids and John waiting. We would eat one whole loaf of bread when it would come out of the oven. And of course we were milking cows, we had this fresh butter, and so, as we were standing there, we would say, "Poor us, poor us! We got it bad here!" *(Lee)*

There was a certain skill set in each part of harvesting and utilizing wood, from tree selection to building a fire and maintaining an even, adequate amount of heat. Wood cookstoves were notoriously smoky at times, not to mention down-drafts near the mountain.

> We did have a wood cook stove that somehow we had gotten from Joanne, but in order to get it started you had to open all the doors and windows in the house because it would smoke

so badly. But then once it got going you were okay—got the draft going, so I could keep a [fire] going. We had an electric stove, also, but the wood cook stove was nice 'cause it kept us warm, too. And I could keep a big pot of water on it for hot water. *(Carolyn)*

The many styles of cook stoves included ones with beautiful, colored enamel panels. For heating, Warm Morning stoves were quite popular and also Fisher stoves, and the ironically named Suburbans, and even barrel stoves, cut from metal drums.

> The very first stove we had was one of those fifty-five-gallon drums, that they always had directions [for] in *Mother Earth News* on how to build a wood-stove. So, we had one of those drums that was on its side. With some kind of metal-cutting tool, in the round end you cut the door, and I think ours was just propped up on bricks or blocks. *(Beth)*

For that first stove, some needed their first chimneys. Joanne built one with Karen's help. Other women did masonry, too.

> I built a chimney in that house. And remember my saying it's a three-story house? That was a brick chimney, and of course I'd never built anything out of brick before so it took a long time! But I did it! My first chimney! *(Beth)*

Sometimes the house could get smoky, but it could be more serious, like in Micki's first house.

> There was a fire in the house at one point while we were living there. We weren't actually there at the time; Joe and I went up

to Cincinnati. I was pregnant and my dad was having open-heart surgery. By then we were greenhousing our tomato plants, and gettin' going on our farming. So, to keep the greenhouses going while we were gone, Jerome and Vicki came and stayed in our house and then would walk down into the holler to stoke the greenhouse stove. It was just not a "together" chimney scene, and the stove wasn't very together. It was the one that "came with" [the house], the old Warm Morning stove.

In the middle of the night, Vicki reports that she and Jerome woke up and the house was full of smoke. There was a chimney fire! This is one of the drawbacks of not having any water. There was snow all over the ground. There was a heavy snowfall, which turned out to be kind of lucky. But, what ended up happening was, when they saw the fire, Vicki picked up the only thing that she could find that was liquid, which happened to be—you know back then we had the outhouses, and so during the night we used a pee bucket. So she grabbed the pee bucket and she threw it on the flames! And it really didn't amount to much, so it didn't do a lotta good. But in the meantime—and we didn't have a phone, either—so Jerome hoofed up to the nearest neighbor's house to use their phone and they called the Thorn Hill Volunteer Fire Department. They eventually made it out, although there was snow on the roads and it was really, really cold. They made it with their pumper trunk, the old-timey pumper truck—and when they got there it was so cold that when they went to get the pumper started, something had frozen up, and so they could not pump the water out of it!

So what they did, was, they took their axes and chopped a hole through the tin roof and started scooping the snow off the roof down into that hole to put the fire out. And that's what saved the house. So if it had not been snowy, then the whole house would have gone. But what we ended up with then, after that, was not only holes in the walls where the snow would come through, but then we had a hole in our roof! *(Micki)*

In life there are many balancing acts. No one likes to breathe smoke, but a wood fire can smell awfully good, especially that first fire you light in the fall. In wielding an ax or cooking on a wood stove, there is both danger and grace.

Chapter Five

The Worth of Water

No water at the twist of a handle? Most Americans can't imagine it, but rural American households often must obtain their own water. There are no water mains and no water bills—but, there is the expense of digging a well or developing a spring. Pipes must be buried to avoid freezing or damaging. Unless gravity sends water to the house, a pump and pressure tank are necessary. Moreover, scarce resources must be prioritized in acquiring and installing modern conveniences like a toilet, a bathtub, sinks, and a washing machine. The women coped with a lack of facilities in various ways. But everything started at the source.

> I was so enthralled by having such incredibly clean and sweet water that came out of that spring! It was amazing to me. (*Micki*)

If you needed to haul water, you might have to drive five miles or so to a spring where a thick hose had been stuck through rocks into the water source and angled down to the roadside, so anyone could come and get spring water for free. No matter where you carried it from, a good bucket was needed.

> Pickle buckets were these wonderful five-gallon buckets with lids and handles. There was some sort of fast-food burger joint and we could buy these buckets from them for fifty cents, which at the time was a lot of money, but these buckets lasted forever. They had wonderful lids that had the rubber gasket that would seal, so we could haul water in them without spilling. *(Micki)*

So how many five-gallon buckets would be needed?

> I'd fill up nine Dunkin' Donut [batter] buckets every other day. *(Lauren)*

One-gallon jugs came in handy. Some even used barrels.

> [My husband] Gary had a 1946 Dodge Power Wagon, and it had barrels in the back of it, fifty-five-gallon drums. We would go to a spring that is on the Hancock County line. Gary would just pull the truck in really close to that hose, and we would just run that water into about three or four barrels. We had a little side driveway that went up above the house. He would drive the truck up there, and then run hoses. It was far enough above the house that we had gravity feed to the house. *(Nancy)*

One house even had a "cistern."

> There was a cistern under the porch that was made of these fifty-five-gallon drums that were like welded together, but it leaked really badly. It just collected the rain water. Sometimes if we had had a good rain, there was a [hand]pump on the porch, [and] we would pump it up out of the cistern—if we could catch it before

it all leaked out of the holes—and store it in five-gallon pickle buckets. *(Micki)*

Some women were fortunate to have a spring on the property where they were living. But the task of getting water when you needed it could still be onerous. Janet and Vicki each lived for a while at Mooresburg Springs, an old defunct resort, and lugged iron-rich, orange-tinged mineral water up a steep hill. Sherri had clear water, but—

> We had to carry our water two hundred fifty foot uphill from the spring, so Mom [visiting from Indiana] got me a sump pump and then a bunch of garden hoses, so I could turn on the sump pump and get cold water up to the house, and that really changed my life! *(Sherri)*

Then there was attitude! Stamina, imagination, and a sense of humor—all came into play.

> Five-gallon buckets. Put them in the car; take 'em back home. This is running water; you run for it. *(Lauren)*

> I know how many gallons of water it takes to do almost every household chore. *(Sherri)*

> You really learned how to utilize every gallon. It was amazing what you can do with perseverance, and creativity, too. But it was fun, it was fun! *(Lee)*

> We would pass a glass of water around, 'cause that was another thing—we were real conservative using [water] for dishes. So we

basically used one water glass in the house, and we all just shared it, a Mason jar, 'cause we didn't have a whole lotta dishes. So then, with our water glass we would take a drink, and then pass it to the next person with this little ditty, "Crystal water, pure and fine; first it's yours, and then it's mine." *(Micki)*

Bathing, maybe you were trying to picture that. Wait a minute! You were?? Bathing could be spur-of-the moment casual.

One day it was raining real hard outside but it wasn't thundering and lightning, so Wayne stripped to his underwear and ran out and took a shower right there. It was simple, but it was funny. Glad nobody drove up. *(Sandra)*

In the summer a creek is for bathing and for just cooling off.

I just ran into a lady the other day, and she said, "Yeah, I remember sitting in the creek with you, and you taught me how to make baskets." You have to keep the vines moist to bend them and use them in baskets. Dale had made a really nice area where he would take his baths, and there was a little waterfall there, so we could just sit and put our feet in, or if it got too hot, we could just go sit right in the middle of the creek if we wanted to, so we used to go down there and sit in the creek, and make a lot of baskets down there. *(Sherri)*

Here's a simple bathing method and warmer.

Put two gallon-jugs out in the sun during the day, and they were warm enough to bathe with in the evening. *(Robyn)*

Clinch Mountain Girls

There were many versions of the outdoor shower.

> In the early years, we had an outdoor solar shower. We would fill the tank with the garden hose, and then take our showers about five in the afternoon in the summer. The water got very hot. Sometimes it'd be too hot, you'd have to turn it off! You kinda want to time it so it was warm but not scalding hot. *(Beth)*

> We had a gravity-flow shower, which was nice. You'd heat the water up, and then we had a bucket on a pulley system. We had like a metal shower stall. We'd pull that water up, and then we had a sprinkling can [head] on the end of it, for a shower head. You'd use the pulley and bring that warm water up—you'd have five gallons. Then you'd turn that sprinkler can end, and you had a nice shower. *(Janet)*

Your guest might like to take a shower—your mother-in-law, for example.

> We'd take a hose and we'd hook it up to the spring water, and at that time, too, we had a faucet. We'd throw [the hose] over the roof, and heat it with the sun, and then we had an outdoor shower. We always had dogs, so I generally knew if someone was coming, and I could run inside. I can remember my mother-in-law coming, and she asked me about bathing, and I told her. At first she thought it was too funny—too odd—to do that, but I fixed her up, and I put all that she needed on the picnic table outside, and pretty soon I could hear her whoopin' and hollerin' out there that this was great! She really loved it! She just had never bathed outside before. *(Dianna)*

Or your dad.

> In the summer time, when it was warm, we had a black plastic pipe that we stuck into the spring, and it was under a big, beautiful group of sycamores. Now, you always knew when someone was taking a shower 'cause you could hear the hollers all the way up and down the "holler." Honestly, I never perfected the art of showering without screaming, because it was so-o-o, freakin' cold! If I washed my hair I was going to get a headache from it because it was frigid. But, the end result was a clean body and clean hair, so that was fine. I'll never forget when my folks were visiting and my dad really wanted a shower. I don't know if they didn't stay in the hotel that time, or if Dad had gotten dirty from helping us in the mater [tomato] patch. Maybe he just decided he wanted to have the experience, I don't know. But he never repeated it after that! I could hear him hollerin'. He just couldn't believe it. *(Micki)*

Just for fun there is the "hillbilly hot tub."

> That "hillbilly hot tub" was a fifty-five-gallon drum [cut in half], sitting on top of one or two [courses] of cement blocks where we would build a fire underneath the drum, fill it with water. So that wasn't very successful. The water was way too hot on the bottom. You'd burn your feet! And it wasn't a very satisfying way to get clean. We also bought a big cast-iron tub, which we had out on the back porch, and we would just heat water and fill the tub and get in that. *(Beth)*

And then there's winter bathing as commonly practiced.

We had to haul the water and heat it up for baths. For a while, we had a big galvanized tub that we would pour water in, and people would take baths in the middle of the living room. *(Vicki)*

We had a Number 3 washtub, and we would fill that up and put it in the living room by the wood heating stove. [The] two [little boys] would bathe like that. My other son was older, so he bathed like we did. In the winter we probably didn't get as clean as most people do, but you know, we would just take a sink-bath in the kitchen by the wood cook stove—heat some water on the wood cook stove, and bathe like that. *(Dianna)*

There were two necessities for bathing: a convenient place, and, no waste of water.

One of my birthdays Mom wanted to know what I wanted, and I said I wanted a cast-iron bathtub, so she came down, and we went shopping, and found a cast-iron bathtub at an antique store. We put that right behind the wood cookstove. Dale drilled a hole in the floor, and ran a pipe out to the gardens. We used the [waste]water for gray water. *(Sherri)*

After [the kids] were done bathing, then Joe and I would get our turn. We would take our baths in the leftover water from the kids. And then stand over it and pour the water over our heads, and help each other to wash our hair. Now you know, being hippies with hair, we had a lotta hair, and Joe's hair was very long. And then, you know, he had a big beard, too, and so that all needed washin'!

> We wanted to stay clean. We weren't really into being dirty, but we were uber-conservative with the water and how we use it when we bathed. So then a lotta times, our bathing water, if it wasn't like real soapy, would water house plants. So it was like reusing as much as possible. Water was quite the commodity for us! *(Micki)*

The waste water, or "gray water," is any water from sinks, tubs, and washing machines, but not from the toilet. Gray water can be let out onto the ground through a pipe, and with the use of certain types of soap, is just fine for the garden.

As for the toilet, in mid-twentieth century, outhouses were still common in rural areas.

"Indoor plumbing" did not necessarily include toilets. Most of the families had outhouses at first.

> We had an outhouse, but it was a deluxe one, two-seater. The bottom of it was rocked up around it. It was good, except we didn't have doors. Though, the day we got married, and my brothers were visiting, they finished the door and hung it on the outhouse. We just looked out on the woods [from the outhouse]. It was fine till we had many guests milling around. *(Nancy)*

> One time [Jerome's] nieces came to visit for several weeks in the summer, and I remember one of them using the outhouse and literally falling in, but her arms saved her from going all the way down. *(Vicki)*

> We had a toilet dog, the toilet was outside. The toilet dog [was Betsy]. We'd say to Betsy, "Would you come to the toilet with me?" So, in the middle of the night, she would go out, and if there was snakes, or whatever, she would be there, and she'd sit in the toilet with you. *(Alicia)*

Many appreciated the advantages of an outhouse for years. Besides water, it also saves time and energy.

> We had an outhouse for twenty years. I really enjoyed not having to clean a bathroom. I mean, I could sweep it. So for twenty years I didn't have to clean up a bathroom from anybody. *(Tata)*

An outhouse is durable and always available. No water, no electricity? No problem.

> I still have the outhouse, it's "grandfathered in." I'm glad of that because you just never know what might happen that you'd need it, like, not too long ago, something was wrong with our septic tank, and it come in handy. *(Sandra)*

It has its own kind of esthetics.

> The outhouse had windows in it, and overlooked the creek. *(Sherri)*

Once a family had a toilet, they needed a septic system, and even septic tanks became do-it-yourself projects.

> We actually did have a septic tank that my husband dug the hole for. I saw him slowly disappear, until all I saw was dirt flying out. It was very deep; he disappeared. So, we did have a septic tank, and we would use the gray water from doin' the dishes, to flush the toilet. *(Lauren)*

Some tried a composting toilet inside the house. It works without water.

> When my husband's parents came to visit, [we] put in a composting toilet for them. They decided to come for two weeks I think it was. It probably seemed like two weeks—everything was frozen. The steps were frozen. The water was frozen. Everything was frozen. *(Judy)*

At any rate, to get water for a toilet—or a washing machine—takes a lot of work. The free water from a spring or well comes with the responsibility of getting it to the house, whether by bucket or hose. In the early years there were recurring problems.

> We had water that came from a little spring, but in the summer it ran out. And in the winter it froze. *(Judy)*

> We said, "Well, we can't get the place unless it has running water."

> When we came back to sign the [real estate] papers, [the owner] had a black pipe from the spring, running in the house. We had running water—till it froze. I remember once, we had the faucet on, running so it wouldn't freeze, and it started to slow down, and it started dripping, and I said, "Oh my God!" I ran out to the first connection. It was freezing. I ran to the next connec-

tion, freezing. Freezing, freezing, all the way down from the spring. I said, "Oh my God, what am I doing here?" We'd take the pipe [hard rubber hose] and put it where the sun was, and we would melt the pipe. That's what we did all winter. *(Alicia)*

Besides a toilet, a modern person deems a washing machine a necessity, but most of these women started their lives here without them. Laundering clothes takes up a great deal of women's time and energy the world over. Did the mothers use cloth diapers? "Absolutely!" said Vicki (who had two in kids in diapers at once). At least ten of these washerwomen had a wringer washer at one time or other.

> You had to carry the water to fill up the washing machine, and then drain it, and carry [the rinse water]. Couldn't do it in the winter 'cause you have to have your washing machine on the porch. But I didn't have to kick it, though, like Loretta Lynn did. I remember watching that movie. She'd kick the washing machine and it'd start up again. You know, I did like that—that was a great washing machine. *(Carolyn)*

Winter meant a half-hour trip to town.

> After I had Jesse, by the time we got to town [in the truck] with his wet diapers, they were frozen, so I had trouble getting 'em in a washing machine [because] I rinsed 'em out in the creek sometimes before I took 'em. *(Karen)*

Drying laundry used solar energy or radiant energy from the wood stove.

In the winter we had laundry ropes in the living room from wall to wall. *(Carolyn)*

Lauren, who did her washing at home, marked a progression in her laundry processing as her six children came along.

I had cloth diapers. For a while we had an old wringer washer. There were times when I washed clothes in the bathtub. Then, we "arrived," and we got a small, modern washing machine that stood in one corner of our bathroom that was pretty small. It was right smack up against the commode. That was in our house; I didn't have to go outside. So I washed, and then, if it was good weather, it got hung outside. If it wasn't good weather, we had sixteen lines that traversed the width of our living room, from one end to the other. Sixteen lines! Every other day, it was diapers, and on alternate days, it was clothes. The pants and the long things got hung to the side, so you didn't go smackin' into them all the time. *(Lauren)*

It seems apparent that the main problems with pioneer water systems are winter and laundry. The improvements were gradual. At Janet's first house on the river she had no electricity or water when she brought her first baby home from the hospital that summer.

One baby is not too bad. Just took the laundry out once a week. Then, in the meantime, you just have to wash the diapers, because of course we used cloth diapers. But I was breastfeeding, so it wasn't like I had to buy baby food, or warm up stuff. I didn't have to worry about that. *(Janet)*

Clinch Mountain Girls

Then Janet moved to a house that had a spring.

> We put in a pump, and pumped it from the spring up to the house. So we had spring water. We had electricity and water, so we had it all! It was nice. And, actually, all those times we were livin' rough, we didn't have kids, except for the last six months. So that's how we got by as good as we did, 'cause it would be too hard with kids. I think it'd be really tough. *(Janet)*

> When we had enough money, we put in a well. I never had a washing machine till after Ellen was born. *(Robyn)*

One couple even tried to dig their own well.

> At first we tried to dig our own well. We shared in buying some equipment with neighbors, Zan and Gerry White. They lived close to the river, and way lower than us, but we went in with them on some equipment to drill for our own well with a carbide bit and all that. Little did we know that it wasn't possible. So for days on end we stood there in the sun, grinding with that machine, and, yuk! Anyway, finally we gave up and had a commercial company come in to drill, and they had to go to four hundred feet to finally get water! But, it's beautiful water. That is a very wonderful thing about living here. You get clean water, and no chemicals, nothing in it. It's wonderful! *(Yvonne)*

Bringing water into the house became a goal for all.

> By the time Alyson was born, we did have water inside the house. By then, Ron was able to find a spring up in the holler,

and was able to have the pipe buried. There used to be a shed, and I can remember when he was able to get the water right to a hose that came out of that shed, a spigot, and I thought, Oh my gosh, this is wonderful! You could go out there and take a shower, and you can get the water, whatever you needed. It was fine, it didn't bother us. And then eventually, it came on into the house. *(Linda)*

One of the pictures I have in my photo album is me pointing to water coming out of the kitchen sink because it was a pretty big event to have running water in the house. It was a big deal! *(Beth)*

There is just no denying the elation of getting running water into your house and the magic of the indoor spigot.

The first time that I ever had water running into my house, it was amazing to me, and it hadn't been so many years that I'd done without it, maybe two. But I never turned on the spigot that I didn't think how wonderful that was. And then—behold! Hot water, too! Even yet today, even though I have a lot of conveniences at my home now, I'm still so appreciative. I never take it for granted, turning on the faucet, and there's water right into my house, good water. It's just made me think about things differently for sure, and appreciating them, appreciating Mother Nature, honoring it. *(Dianna)*

Chapter Six

Growing Our Gardens, Growing Ourselves

Gathering wild berries and mushrooms and raising healthful, organic vegetables for their growing families was an important goal of the back-to-the-landers. Self-sufficiency was part of their ethos. The fertile "hollers" provided enough space for relatively large gardens, and there was a long growing season. They eagerly dug into their earthy tasks.

> The first year I just tried to grow everything I could think of in terms of vegetables: spinach, lettuce, cabbage, broccoli, cauliflower, potatoes, tomatoes, peppers, corn. I think we were reasonably successful for being greenhorns and not knowin' too much about what we were doin'. *(Beth)*

> We grow several plantings of cucumbers, lettuce, broccoli, cauliflower, tomatoes. I like growing numerous crops of lettuce, and onions, beets, snow peas, bell peppers, and the different kinds of squash, potatoes—Yukon Gold and sweet potatoes—as well as a lot of fruit, fruit trees, and asparagus. *(Tata)*

Raised beds could be a necessity. The sides of wood built about two feet high contain dirt, manure, and compost to increase nutrients and the soil's water-holding capacity. The rich soil enables planting vegetables close together.

[My husband] put me in a garden and I grew standard things, tomatoes and things like that. Then he built me—because he was gone so much working—some raised beds, because they were easier for me to maintain. I loved 'em, and that's how I still grow my garden. Besides tomatoes I grow herbs—I have comfrey [for wounds and joint pain] and lemon balm [for soothing skin or digestion]. I have jumping onions that come back every year. And I grew cucumbers and beans and strawberries. This is what's been put in over the years: cauliflower, broccoli, cabbage, spinach, grapes—we have grape vines out there—definitely squash, zucchini. *(Sandra)*

The first year we came down, we had to use a pick, all to make holes for our tomatoes, and they died right away. We knew a little about farming, not much, though. We had to build our own soil. We had about two acres of raised beds. Dale had built me some gorgeous raised beds out of cedar logs. We filled them with manure from Walt's barns, years and years of horse manure. We cleaned out all his barns and filled up those beds with all that fabulous soil. [I grew] just any kind of vegetable. I tried everything, from popcorn to all kinds of squashes. We planted apple and peach trees. I had strawberries and raspberries and blackberries, and black raspberries and gooseberries and elderberries. I had lots and lots of berries. *(Sherri)*

Beth, Vicki, and Alicia grew shiitake mushrooms on logs. Many people gathered berries and other wild foods, even poke (pokeweed), which is poisonous so that only the young leaves in spring may be used and must be boiled and rinsed at least twice.

> I did gather a lot of greens, a lot of poke and lambs quarters, and sorrel. So every day those were growing wild, I collected that and would make up a big "mess o' greens." *(Micki)*

> We have the [black] walnuts, and I have harvested some of those. And lots of raspberries and blackberries. I have picked those in my big boots, so I wouldn't get bit by a snake. *(Sandra)*

> One time we had gone mushroom hunting, and we had found some wonderful, wonderful locations, where we were just getting shopping bags full of morels. *(Linda)*

> John and I really learned our trees and our edible foods. We would go into the wood with our book, and actually pick a leaf or pick something and bring it back and then press it and have it be reference and really did teach ourselves. The old-timers too, teaching us how to find ginseng and all the different things that are edible. *(Lee)*

The newcomers soon found that tilling the soil is hard, but rewarding work.

> I used to do two acres by hand, back when I could do that. I would go and get Walt's manure. It was a lot, but I had nothin' but time. I like to work, I'm not good at doing nothing. *(Robyn)*

> I did have my own garden there, right across the road in the bottom, and I did it all by hand. I didn't have a rototiller or

anything, so I had to dig holes, and plant things, and hoe everything, hoe all the weeds. But we got a lot of food out of it!
(Carolyn)

All plants are not your friends, especially the one named Johnson. Introduced from unknown sources in the 1800s, Johnson Grass has spread nationwide, and is recognized as an invasive weed.

> I had to learn to plant a garden. I knew that mulch was a good idea. Somebody offered old hay bales. Some of the people at the hospital [where I worked] said, "You know you don't want that hay. It comes from down on the river bottom and there's lots of Johnson Grass in it."
>
> I said [to myself], Oh, so what? I didn't know what Johnson grass was. I had no idea. Wouldn't you have asked a few more questions if people are warning you? But no, no. I just said, "Yeah, I want those bales of old hay." So I got them and I shared 'em with my friends. We all had Johnson Grass, then, in our gardens, which is just this horrendous weed that doesn't care if you dig it up because it just breaks off and spreads, I don't know how we got it up. It was just horrendous. What a disaster!
> *(Joanne)*

There were also various molds, causing blight and other problems.

> We had about two hundred grapevines that we put in. We had those for probably four or five years. We made some wine off 'em, but then that was just too much work. There was just so much spraying involved, to keep the mold and the Japanese beetles off, that it became just too much, so we abandoned that

idea, and cut 'em down. The land was layin' too low. I think they do better on hillsides. Because, when that fog [off Clinch River] would come in, it was just too humid and, really, they wanted to mold. And we didn't really want to do that much sprayin'. *(Janet)*

There were animal pests, too, including small humans.

Corn, we never could grow much. We fought the raccoons and crows with everything you can imagine. Music, and scarecrows, and nothin' worked. *(Janet)*

We had some of the most beautiful Burpee Ambrosia cantaloupes that were getting ripe. We came down there one day, and something'd come along and taken a little bite of this melon, a little bite of that melon—totally ruinin' the melons! We found out it was deer, and we went to the Ag guy, and he gave us this blank gun to scare the deer off. You put it up on a pole and like once an hour, it'd fire off a blank but it eventually would run out. And the deer say, "Must be OK to come out and eat these melons now." *(Cece)*

We had one goat. We bought another goat. There was no fencing, so it was us and the garden, or the goats and the garden. *(Alicia)*

I remember when Melissa was real little, maybe two, taking her up into the tomato patch, and she would pick off the green tomatoes and take bites out of 'em. *(Cece)*

And then there was, as Lee would term it, "a garden terrorist."

It was this really very large rattlesnake! I cut its head off right up there in the garden. Chop, chop. Off the head goes! So then I bring the carcass with a hoe, draggin' 'm to the house where on the front porch I had a table set up where I did all my skinning of all the hides. I dressed out this rattlesnake. I sliced him and I took out his entrails and I chopped off his tail—he had thirteen rattles! The thing was about as big as my leg, I mean it really was big! So, the meat itself was now laying on the table and the entrails got into a bucket. I walk back up to the garden with my shovel to bury all this stuff and of course the head was still there. I take my shovel, and I put my shovel into the mouth of this snake that has no body on it. And the snake bites down on the shovel! I'm tellin' you the truth! All the venom comes running down, comes running on down the shovel! I thought, I gotta tell everybody about that—You know, a snake can still bite you with no body!

So [I] bury all that stuff, and I'm amazed by this whole thing, and I come on back down [to the house]. At the time we were milking cows and had a lotta cats being around 'cause they loved the milk of the cows and everything. I get down to the open porch where this meat was, and it's gone. I'm thinking, Damn cats! R-r-r-r! It was my catch! What are they stealin' my stuff for?

Something caught my eye and I looked under the table and there was the meat moving all around. The meat! It had no skin, had no head, no anything! So, I beat the thing, beat on it, got it sorta softened up, and we ate it that night. *(Lee)*

Whew! Let's go back to the garden. It's early spring, and the snakes aren't out yet. The crows are not a problem—yet. Time to get started. Seeds and some know-how are needed.

We usually got the seeds at the [Farmers'] Co-op, or [from] friends if they were sharing seeds. *(Dianna)*

[The old-timers] taught us about just saving your potatoes that you decided to grow. Save them [at end of winter], keep going with that. [That is, cut them up and plant the pieces with eyes.] Sweet potatoes—you made slips [small plants grown indoors from potatoes' eyes by soaking them in water], you planted them, then made slips [the next year]. The saving of bean seeds and all that: just make sure they were well-dried and put 'em in a jar with tobacco, ground-up tobacco, and then the weevils and things like that didn't eat 'em. I really did try to save every kinda seed you could imagine. I used to save a little section of the garden, like lettuce. I would let a little tiny section of it just go to seed, then save that. The same with the spinach and the smaller things. *(Lee)*

Besides friends and neighbors, they consulted Rodale Press publications and Agricultural Extension pamphlets, and their own observations.

It's experimental. One year I do this, and one year I do that. *(Alicia)*

One year we had a terrible blight with our tomatoes. So I thought, My dad had left me an old farmers' book. So I'm lookin' up tomatoes and blight and stuff like that and it said if you happen to be milkin' cows, [since milk is] just loaded with calcium, go and put it directly into the ground. I am telling you the honest-to-God truth, it made that blight go away instantly. The next crop of tomatoes came; did not have the blight any more! *(Lee)*

The women also raised herbs and flowers.

> With my herbs, I'm pretty knowledgeable. I never gathered them, I grew them. There was very few that I would gather, because you can just really make the least little mistake, and some of that's poison, so I just always grew what I pretty well used. Some of 'em I used for [healing], and I dried 'em, I used 'em cooking. *(Sandra)*

> And gourds, like the loofah, whose dried membranes could be used like a sponge when bathing. We raised all kinds of gourds, bird head birdhouse gourds, and loofahs. I came up with a soap that I could use in loofahs. I'd slice the loofahs, and pour liquid soap into it, and let it harden, and I'd have a loofah soap. I used to sell my soap and candles to Dollywood, and to the Museum of Appalachia. *(Sherri)*

Besides Sherri's loofahs, Alicia sold shiitake mushrooms, and others sold produce.

> We grew sorghum, and set up a mill, 'cause you grind it and make juice, and then you cook the juice. The old-timers showed us how to do that. We did that for several years, made sorghum [molasses] and sold it. *(Lee)*

> The second year, we planted strawberries and sold them. We advertised over "Swap Shop." People would come, and we would have the berries ready. "Swap Shop" was on the radio from Duffield [Virginia]. Every morning at ten o'clock, you could call

in. "I have strawberries for sale. Here's my phone number, you can order some." *(Alicia)*

We sold our own produce that we raised. That's really hard, intense work raising greenhouse tomatoes. Like if it snows you gotta go out there and beat the snow off or your greenhouse will collapse. If it's a warm day you've gotta make sure you open up all those doors, or you're gonna cook 'em and they'll die. And it's just every day, you can't leave 'em. *(Carolyn)*

All these young homesteaders were growing themselves as well as their gardens, learning to balance their skills, values, and need for income. Agriculture takes capital, tillable land, intense labor, and marketing skills. For larger-scale commercial growing, chemicals were a decision point. No matter what their ideals were, their bills had to be paid. Marketing itself proved to be a stumbling block for several families, and most gardened simply to supply their own households. "Market gardening," however, is a small business venture, tilling a few acres and selling a variety of veggies in local markets. While several families, like Carolyn's, attempted that, three families succeeded in earning a living in that way for a long time. Those families were the two Haverland brothers, Jerome and his wife Vicki; and Joe with his wife Micki; and Bert Lakin and his wife Cece. They all began their commercial growing with tomatoes.

At one point we had four thousand tomato plants all staked and strung. That isn't just all we had. We had corn, melons, beans, squash—winter squash, summer squash—green beans, watermelons, and cantaloupes. Our biggest crop was tomatoes, and then corn, beans, and watermelon. Those became the mainstays. *(Cece)*

Similarly, for the Haverland families, tomatoes were their first and main crop. After learning from neighbors, they grew thousands of tomatoes.

> [Jerome] started workin' with somebody in Poor Valley, and learned some things. Then, he and his brother Joe collaborated on greenhouses, and the first one was in Thorn Hill. They built several greenhouses. We had one up on the property we were livin' at, and I think Joe and Micki had one. At that time there were no furnaces; there were wood stoves in the greenhouses, and somebody would have to get up in the middle of the night all the time, and go stoke the stoves to keep the plants warm. (*Vicki*)

Micki, who had studied horticulture for a year, explains more about tomato, or "mater" farming, and the need for greenhouses, homemade with plastic covers.

> Initially we had two greenhouses. We built [them] out of the cedar poles and the big, long slabs we would get from the sawmill, and then covered it with plastic. I'm thinking we may have had five hundred plants in each of the greenhouses. That was our early crop to be harvested in May out of the greenhouse. That was more the money-maker—before people had 'em in their home gardens. It was really, really important to catch that early market. But then we would also start our summer crop in the greenhouse, get a jump start, so that even our early summer crop would have an edge over people's gardens. Half an acre is what we started with, with our field crop. Then we expanded that into another field to be an acre. Although the piece of property we lived on was quite large, very little of it was

tillable ground. So it wasn't until we moved to our next home that we were able to grow more. *(Micki)*

Shocked as we are today to hear it, Carolyn and Micki grew tobacco. Indeed, half the homesteaders grew tobacco. They could not raise or make everything they needed, but could could earn money while staying on the farm by growing tobacco, as almost every local family did. And in a period of fewer health warnings, social norms and campaigns against smoking, many of the newcomers had smoked cigarettes themselves when younger. Micki explains how they could afford expansion, and how the "tobacco allotment"—a right to grow a certain amount of tobacco with a government-stabilized price— aided small farmers.

After five years there, a place came up for rent, two miles down the road. The owners were looking for somebody to lease this three hundred acre farm with this very together house [described in Chapter Three]. Three thousand dollars a year, which was substantially more than twenty-five dollars a month, but we got the tobacco allotment along with it. That was when we expanded to growing "'backer" [tobacco] as well as maters because we got the tobacco allotment when we moved here. The prime growing field was this three-acre river bottom. But over the whole three hundred acres they had multiple fields, and so we really expanded our mater-growing operation. We started growing the backer, which helped—sort of a more assured [income]. Growing vegetables for a living is dicey, because the weather is unpredictable, you don't know what the market's gonna be, you've got pests, and the whole nine yards. So the backer was sort of the stabilized factor. It would be rare that your tobacco crop would turn out unsellable. And it was a good allotment, it was quite a bit. So that was sort of this little bit of stability when it came to income. So we felt that we could bite off that lease of three thousand dollars and feel that we could probably make it. *(Micki)*

Cece and Bert felt the land squeeze as well.

We ran out of space to grow. Well, we'd cleared the hillside and tried growing up on the hill there and that got to be really difficult, and we didn't have enough room. So we would rent land from other people that wasn't being used for anything. So up and down the road here, we might have two or three patches of things. *(Cece)*

They marketed their produce, arranging care for their two young daughters.

We would harvest it, clean it, all the night before, and pack up the two trucks, and then he would go like to Morristown, and I would go to Kingsport with a truckload of produce on Saturday. We'd get up like five o'clock in the morning! Usually I would arrange on those days for Carolyn or somebody else to take the kids. On occasion he'd take one and I'd take the other. They're easier to handle if they're by themselves. *(Cece)*

Cece managed childcare in the field.

When we went down to like pick tomatoes, I'd take a laundry basket full of toys and lunch bag full of snacks, and we would park the truck down at the end of the row so we could see into the back of the truck. The girls would play inside the camper with their toys and eat their snacks while we would work out in the fields. They were happy. They had their own little space there, and they'd have their little tea parties. *(Cece)*

Marketing is even more difficult with perishable farm products.

We were trying to talk Kroger into buying organic maters. We tried organic in the greenhouse and took a load up to Cincinnati. They made an agreement that they would take a load of maters and try those out, organic maters from Tennessee. *(Micki)*

Family connections had made a deal possible.

So we took those up there in this 1954 Ford [pickup]. We did purchase tomato boxes to take those up there; we really wanted to make a good impression. It's one thing to grow the product; it's another thing to market it. Maters are incredibly perishable, of course, so that really adds to the problem. The thing is, growing a mater to sell locally, the variety that you would grow that has the best taste is not necessarily the variety that is going to ship without being damaged. That's something that we learned, because when we took those maters up to Cincinnati, our truck didn't have good shocks. It was all we could do to get the gas money to drive 'em all the way to Cincinnati. It was a pretty big deal. By the time we got the maters up there they had been bounced and jostled around a bit, so there was significant bruising, unfortunately. They were wonderful maters. We got a lot of compliments on them, but we did not get a contract out of it. But really, to be honest, I don't know how we could have fulfilled a contract. I think that was one of the problems—we could not meet a minimum. To get a contract with their produce department would require growing a tremendous amount. They were talking numbers that were unfathomable to us. Also the maters we were growing were not appropriate for transporting those kind of distances. We learned all of this is just all interwoven. *(Micki)*

So if there is a problem, you may eat the profits, literally.

We grew purple beans. We were all into some of these more exotic varieties. Well, we found that the locals weren't interested in purple string beans. They didn't sell. We ate a lotta purple beans! We got a freezer, and what came back from market, or we couldn't sell, or was our culls, that would be ours. That'd be what we would eat. *(Cece)*

* * *

Tobacco does not help people grow physically. The newcomers debated the ethics of growing that formerly common Southern cash crop. Through the Seventies, Eighties, and Nineties, tobacco was a reliable back-up income for the full-time tomato growers. Each farm came with a tobacco allotment, or marketing quota, to grow tobacco. Landowners could even lease their allotment to other farmers, but to actually grow it was much more lucrative. For at least half of the homesteaders—who were land-rich but cash-poor—the allotment was was an unexpected, important income boost as they were getting established. Tobacco provided a good income for a long time for a few of our families. Besides hay, Anne grew tobacco for thirty years, she says, "until all the allotments were gotten rid of some years ago."

I used to grow tobacco, and I grew it for several years. Part of the reason of that, was I didn't even have a vehicle to drive, so I couldn't really work anywhere else. Also if you have young children, that's a good job if you need to stay home with your children. *(Anne)*

Growing someone else's crop for a share of the profits is called "growing on shares." Lee and her husband John owned land with a tobacco allotment and also grew some on shares for others.

> We did a lot of growing of tobacco. One of the old-timers, Maury Jones, he said, "If you kids really want to get ahead in life, you grow tobacco an' raise cows, and that's the way you get ahead in life." We said, "Let's give it a try." So we started growing tobacco, and then other people were saying, "Hey would you grow ours?" So then we grew theirs. Then my boys said, "Gee, Mom, we wanna grow some so we can buy a car." So we helped them grow a patch. *(Lee)*

The first task after growing tobacco transplants from seed was setting them into rows, usually done with a tobacco setter, a tractor attachment with a mechanical wheel and two seats for people to sit with a box of transplants between them, laying them into slots on the wheel as it turned.

> John Hoellman brought his tractor over along with the mechanical tobacco setter that attached to the back of the tractor. Ray and I sat on the back and planted the tobacco plants, which was hilarious because we had never done it before. The wheel comes around really quickly, and you have to stick this tobacco plant in the wheel very quickly because if you don't get it in you're gonna have to go back and set that by hand because it's spaced out too far in the row. It looks like a Ferris wheel. The reason it was hilarious was because about half of our plants we put in upside down. So we look at the row, and there's all these roots sticking up in the air! Then we started laughing so hard it makes it even harder to get

the plants in correctly! So I remember that as a really fun experience, and feeling really stupid, but it was funny because we made so many mistakes. *(Beth)*

The next tasks, hoeing and suckering, were not fun.

I hated the suckering 'cause you'd have to go in there when the plants were big [four to six feet], and sucker them, pull off the little branches. You'd get all that tobacco juice tar all over your body. It was pretty toxic, you know. *(Beth)*

Families helped each other, and neighbors helped the newcomers.

Kathy Robinson and her husband, Hugh Kyle, they showed us how to do tobacco. We would help them, and then we learned how to do it that way. It's a whole culture all itself, with its own jargon. *(Nancy)*

During harvest, people worked in pairs. One person cut the plant off at its base with a mini-machete, the knife, before handing it off to a partner. That worker, who shoved a four-foot stick in the ground every six plants, jammed each stalk down sideways onto a sharp-pointed conical metal cap, called the spear, that he or she was moving along to fit atop each upright tobacco stick.

[My children] would help set it. They *liked that*—they'd ride the setter with the tractor—not too much the hoeing. *(Anne)*

[My children] would help a lot with the cutting, the spearing, and the hanging; particularly my boys. They were teenagers then, so they were big enough to help with that. Then, mostly I would just grade it all, and bale it [when the children were back in school]. *(Anne)*

I did tobacco for Lee Lawrence, and I actually took Liz in a playpen, into the field. And I worked for Lee and John, cutting. *(Karen)*

After cutting it and leaving it to wilt in the field for three days, skewered six to a stick and looking like green and yellow tepees, they hauled the tobacco to the barn and hung those stalks to dry, or cure, by laying the tobacco sticks across poles nailed into the barn beams.

When we learned how to do [grade] tobacco, we stripped it in the barn. We [had] hung it earlier on; then you let it *come in case*. That means in damp weather it gets kind of limp. Then you can take it [off the stalk]. People come and help you, and they either drink liquor or coffee, and I made thermoses of cocoa. People would tell stories. *(Nancy)*

Cutting tobacco, and hanging it up on poles in the barn, were both dangerous.

One time, [my friend] Margaret was cutting it, and she cut a little too far, and got her leg with the tobacco knife. I think it was a trip to the ER. Probably about twenty miles, a little longer than thirty minutes then. *(Vicki)*

And some tasks were literally nauseating to some.

When I was pregnant with Adam, I said, "I am not doing this again." I couldn't even stand to do it at all, and I didn't want to hurt him, anyway, with breathing in the fumes. *(Nancy)*

> Sitting in there day after day after day grading tobacco, I was nauseous. You were just inhaling those fumes, and it was really toxic. So we did it for two years, made a little bit of money. I don't know whether we figured out our human hours to see how much we got paid. But it was a paycheck when you finally take it to market and get a little something for it. *(Beth)*

Tobacco growing, and especially grading, were social opportunities.

> Tobacco was a very, very big part of our lives for years and years and years. And learning how to do it and having other people show us and also the sharing. When it came time for gradin', hell, we'd go over to the Seals' and drink some moonshine and grade tobacco and time would fly! You had fun! *(Lee)*

Tobacco was an important part of the culture when the back-to-the-landers moved to the Clinch Valley and a vital part of the economy. The crop elicits strong feelings in all who grew it.

> I enjoyed workin' in it, and it never made me sick in any way. It's just a beautiful plant. You hang it in your barns, and it's just beautiful there in the fall with the sun. It's just golden and pretty, and I liked it. It helps you—at least you can pay your property taxes, and gives you some money to catch up on your bills and things. *(Anne)*

* * *

Whether growing a market crop or raising a garden, the families showed dedication to a lifestyle and perseverance. Gardening itself can bring joy.

I lived in Amsterdam, I lived in London, I lived in the cities. [But] I thought this was splendid! With some of your clothes off, hoeing in the peanut patch—yeah! In the sun in the middle of the day in the summer—I thought that was great! *(Yvonne)*

We planted all kinds of stuff. We planted stuff in triangles, and circles, and we made it so hard for us to take care of. It was really pretty! *(Linda)*

One year the plum trees came in, in such abundance it was shocking! *(Tata)*

Bert would tell me, "Okay, put the water on, I'm gonna go pick the corn." It was like the sweetest, best corn I ever ate in my life! *(Cece)*

Yes, there were weeds and pests, sweat and danger, and repetitive physical toil. The amount of labor in the garden was immense, especially for those growing for market; but there was also expanding confidence, fresh air, and sunlit beauty. Hoeing a seemingly endless row yields plenty of time to ponder events and relationships. Whether family garden, or tobacco or tomato patch, there were hard choices on the use of pesticides, chemical fertilizers, and energy-saving machines—and on the allocation of limited income. The families had to work out the division of labor among partners, spouses, and children. All the toil and decisions could result in tensions, but also in bonding and personal growth. The bright colors and fresh taste of the plentiful veggies and fruits produced a new challenge described in the next chapter—preserving all that glorious food for the lean season.

Chapter Seven

Good Food All Year 'Round

Why move to the country? To eat garden-fresh food, of course! As the warm seasons flew by, they needed to preserve enough of that delicious abundance for winter and spring. (Yes, spring. That is planting time, not harvesting time.) At first, the women canned almost everything.

> We didn't have a freezer at that time, so mostly everything was canned—beans, corn, tomatoes, salsa, [tomato] juice. I made spaghetti sauce. I made ketchup, green dilly pickles, pickled okra, pickles, squash. *(Linda)*

> Tomatoes, and more tomatoes, and more tomatoes. *(Lauren)*

As Dianna declared, using a flat-topped wood stove, which enabled her to slide heavy pots to the area of desired temperature, was "the easiest way I've ever canned."

> We had a kitchen that was not insulated, so the cook stove, the heat from that in the summertime, just went right out the

roof. So I didn't get really hot, so that was easy to can like that. Later on, when we updated the kitchen I found that it was too dang hot to can in a room that was insulated, in the middle of summer, so I didn't. I did some canning outside, and I did some canning on the electric stove. *(Dianna)*

Dianna was not the only one who canned outdoors.

I'd can outside in a big old washtub. We had a little stand that we built a fire under it, so you could do like thirty jars or somethin' at a time. Get them boilin' and do that for four hours, instead of a pressure cooker. We did never have any trouble. *(Janet)*

We canned out on the back porch. It was an electric stove, but we just plugged it in, and cooked on the back porch. *(Linda)*

Most of the women had to learn, somehow, to put up food for the cold months.

I imagined myself being one of the pioneers. Oh yes, quarts and quarts and quarts of food. In the beginning—I didn't know enough—I think I put some dairy products in with the vegetables and beans and stuff. And of course, like fifty jillion quarts started to rot! *(Yvonne)*

I was a greenhorn, a novice, but one of the books my mom gave me was *Putting Food By*, for canning and processing food, so I used that as my bible for canning. Also, the Ag Extension Office in Rogersville, you could get pamphlets on how to can and process food. We canned a lot of tomatoes and green beans, so pressure-canning. And water-bath canning—never done that before. That's what everybody else was doing. If you didn't know how to do something we did have friends who were doing the same thing so we could get advice or share a canner. *(Beth)*

Local women neighbors gave advice on growing, canning, and processing.

We had some friends, older [local] friends, that when we came here were still cooking with the wood stove. They did all their own canning and freezing and growing stuff, and I learned how to live here from them. *(Cece)*

Aunt Sarah [an old-timer], she liked to do everything in a galvanized tub. Because you could do, like, thirty-five quarts of beans in one of those little galvanized tubs. So, we did that one year. We got all of our beans ready, and I thought, Okay, this makes me a little nervous. We put the galvanized pot up on some kind of a grate, and then [my husband] Ron fed the wood under it. We put it outside on the ground. We would put cardboard in between all those jars, and that kept them from climbing [rising and bumping into each other]. It worked beautifully. You know, you're outside, and you're just feedin' your wood under there, and you're not gettin' your kitchen hot, and "whammo"! Thirty-five quarts of beans and you're done! It was awesome. Three-and-a-half hours when you do it with a water canner, with a water bath. *(Linda)*

While teaching school, Linda planted her early spring garden, and sometimes there was a little time overlap with harvesting and the last school work days. No problem—sharing work is natural in Tennessee.

> I can remember one spring taking a couple of bushels of peas that I had grown to school with me, on one of those last days. The kids weren't there, and everybody was just sort of hangin' out, gettin' the end-of-the-year things done. Now, the teachers told me to do it, and I was so young and naïve, so here I go driving these peas to school, and they all sat and broke [shelled] peas. They helped me break my peas! I don't think you could do that now. *(Linda)*

Neighbors shared their produce, and sometimes in such quantity, that the shared food should be canned, too. The newcomers appreciated both the knowledge and the extra food from the local women, especially as they began establishing homes and gardens. However, some veggie gifts are appreciated more than others.

> You bet we canned! People gave us stuff out of their garden the first year we were here. So we canned zucchini—if you can imagine anything more gross! We had quarts of it, because people gave us zucchinis that were huge! And, they taste so bad when they're that big, anyway. And then to can 'em! They were floatin' in water, you know, and just—ohhh! But we canned everything—everything we could. *(Pat)*

There are several advantages to canning.

> [At first] I really learned how to can everything 'cause we didn't have any electricity so there wasn't any freezing or anything yet going on. *(Lee)*

> I can more than I freeze because it lasts longer and that's better, more convenient. *(Sandra)*

Even with electricity, the frequent power outages back then made canned goods a lot safer than frozen. However, not all of these ladies appreciated all the aspects of canning.

> Denny [my former partner] was into canning. I was not. I helped by washing all the jars out, but—Ohh, there was just something about it. It was just days and days and days of chopping and stirring and canning. I didn't wanna do it. I just didn't wanna do it! *(Tata)*

All but two of the women got freezers as soon as they could afford them.

> Loads of sweating in the kitchen, with these big, old canner pots. But the day that the freezer came along, I switched to freezing. *(Yvonne)*

> We froze a lot of stuff. We had a big, upright freezer, right outside of our front door. *(Lauren)*

Besides food from her own garden, Cece put up leftovers and culls from the marketing of their truck farm produce, as did Vicki and Micki. Lauren and Carolyn's husbands each had a wholesale produce business, and they brought home boxes of vegetables or fruits that had to be preserved. All the culled tomatoes that weren't so pretty, or had weird shapes, or had a hole in 'em or something, I would can up tomato sauce, and can up tomato juice and made green tomato relish. *(Cece)*

Freezing was an option. I would just fill the freezer up with all this stuff, even froze cantaloupe. You can thaw it out and it wasn't too bad. As long as you ate it half-frozen it's pretty good, it's refreshing. *(Cece)*

The women tried other ways to preserve food, such as an age-old method—drying.

I did dry tomatoes and fruit for fruit-leather. I dried venison, too, and made jerky. Actually, I had a little dehydrator, and I tried drying everything. I can't tell you I was successful with all that! I used to hang beans up in the attic, and I'd read about them calling them "leather britches," so I strung the green beans, and that was fine, and that was fun, but that wasn't as good as canned beans. *(Dianna)*

We [used] a big needle, something that the string would go through. The [beans] were probably about six inches. You'd [work]—till the string broke or you got tired. So, you could make, like, a three foot string of beans. Neighbors talked about them, and they loved them, but I didn't like 'em that much. But, it was something to eat to eat. *(Alicia)*

We had excellent luck with the Fellenberg plums. We had so many of 'em. So we got into making fruit leather. You just barely cooked it at all to make it fall apart, put it in the blender, make plum soup, and then pour that into your drying trays, and we wound up having three driers at once. My partner at the time was hiking the Appalachian Trail in sections, five hundred miles at a time, four hundred the next year. So he was really liking having the fruit leather and then read more books about drying food to take if you were hiking. So instead of buying everybody else's pre-mixed this-and-that, you could make your own. So then we got into actually making soup, or rice and beans, and then dehydrating that, so he could take it on the trip. All he had to do was add hot water, and he had a nutritious, organic meal that he had grown himself. *(Tata)*

[My husband] had built me drying racks that had a little wooden frame and then we just put window screen on 'em. I can remember a couple times putting things on our tin roof to dry. I had all kinds of stuff drying from the rafters, constantly. People used to come to the cabin, and say, "Well, just give me about fifteen or twenty minutes before we sit down so I can look around first." It was just lookin' at everything that was hanging in the cabin, drying: garlic, onions; flowers; herbs of all kinds 'cause I had a little herbal business, culinary herbs; apples, carrots. Anything I could dry, I dried. *(Sherri)*

The homesteaders kept potatoes and other root vegetables in a root cellar; or more often in a "can house," an outbuilding dug into a bank to store food canned in jars. Several women improvised.

I have one of my bedrooms in my house, that's a cold bedroom, and I don't use it. So, I've kept my potatoes back in there. *(Anne)*

We experimented with picking the carrots, and putting them in sand and straw in a garbage can with a lid, leaving it out in the cold. Then one year we left the carrots in the ground and picked them as needed, and that worked. *(Tata)*

Cece preserved late tomatoes.

At the very end of the year before the first frost, we would go and pick what was left out there, wrap each one individually in newspaper, the green tomatoes, and put 'em in boxes, and we'd go through 'em periodically, and as they ripened we would have tomatoes.

The newcomers used sugar to preserve foods, such as jams, jelly, or "apple butter," a traditional fruit spread.

[I had] blackberries, and the reds [raspberries], too. But I don't like the seeds, so I put them through the [food] mill. I used to make a lot of strawberry jelly, and I would make it outside. *(Anne)*

Aunt Sarah wanted to make apple butter, because there used to be this old apple orchard; it had all kinds of apples I've never even heard of. She had a big kettle—copper kettle—and a big long [wooden] stirrer. We'd peel all those apples and she would just keep pourin' the bags of sugar in it. It was unbelievable. I never saw so much sugar in my life. I didn't care for it, but that's how she liked it, and she put her cinnamon in it, and she'd make all these jars of apple butter to give to people. It took all day. The apples were already peeled in the morning, just to get them in that kettle and going. I'm serious, I think we probably started at something like seven or eight o'clock, cooking. And, we probably didn't start puttin' 'em in the jars 'til about four. But I thought, That'll be a neat thing to learn how to do.

I did, I learned it, and I have never made apple butter since! I don't care for apple butter. *(Linda)*

Lastly, there's an ancient way of preserving food—fermentation.

I made pickles and sauerkraut, that I learned from my husbands, first and second. They had learned from their mothers. *(Alma)*

I would make flavored vinegars. I'd use a lot of my raspberries for my flavored vinegars. *(Sherri)*

Fruits can be fermented not only to make vinegar, but also to make—yes!—wine. This was not an all-work-and-no-play group! As you may recall, Janet and her husband grew two hundred grape vines and made wine. Others tried their hand at it.

We definitely picked berries, lots of blackberries, apples. I canned that up, and we made wine with that as well. *(Dianna)*

One time I had so many strawberries I made strawberry wine. I did one run. It turned out pretty good. A lotta work! *(Cece)*

Margie and I came up with a "mountain tonic," we called it, and it was like a one hundred ten proof wine. We did have to buy brewer's yeast for that, but it was pretty good wine! My favorite was peach, but we'd make it out of everything. She even made some cantaloupe [wine], and she used to make a lot of dandelion wine, and so we made that. *(Sherri)*

Though considered an essential part of simple living, growing and preserving food was complex and challenging. In the summer, for most of these women, those chores were all-consuming.

We always had gardens and we always put up food. We had freezers and we canned. It's pretty much a full-time job. I had three children when I came here and [later] I had four. So taking care of those kids and gardening was pretty much what we did! *(Judy)*

Despite the chopping and stirring, the heat in the kitchen, and often caring for babies at the same time, these women were committed to raising and preserving food for their families.

I always enjoyed that, and the best part of all is being able to eat your own food out of a jar that you know where it came from, and it's made with love, and you know it's going to be good. It was something I always wanted to do, and I got to do it when I moved here! *(Robyn)*

* * *

Over half of the families followed a vegetarian diet, but their gardens did not supply all of their nutritional needs.

Rice and beans were staples, as well as the local popular fare—beans and cornbread. We ate a lotta burritos and of course, we had the [food] co-op at that time, so we were eatin' good food. Yeah, rice, and beans and some vegetables, mostly. *(Janet)*

I decided when I was seventeen that I would be a vegetarian, and I remember announcing it at the dinner table to my parents' great dismay. I didn't know anything about how to be a vegetarian then. All I knew was, I was finished eating meat. So I just told them, "Well, I'm announcing I'm becoming a vegetarian. Just so you know, don't pass me the meat." At that time I had no idea how to handle the nutrition of being a vegetarian. So I was not a very healthy vegetarian until after I'd read *Diet for a Small Planet* and that taught me how to combine proteins, et cetera, et cetera. *(Micki)*

The "whole foods" concept has been around for a long time, and these women were early adopters. Preparing all of those nourishing foods demanded much of the women's time.

I made all the bread, all the tofu. We were vegetarians. Made all the tofu, soy milk, everything. It was a busy time. *(Carolyn)*

We were vegetarian. Soy-based, and beans and rice, and the vegetables from the garden. Most everything from scratch. Bread from scratch. Made some tofu—well, that was a very long process for a very little block of tofu. *(Vicki)*

I learned how to make soy milk and tofu, and soysage [vegetarian sausage]. We had very, very little money, and so we would buy a bag of soybeans at the Farmers' Co-op. But they had food-grade, that were, well, food, that they would feed to pigs. They weren't sprayed [with pesticides]. We knew that much to make sure to look for that. *(Micki)*

They learned tofu cookery in several ways. Vicki learned to make tofu from *The Farm Cookbook*, while Cece learned at The Farm itself, the intentional community established by Stephen and Ina Mae Gaskin in Summertown, Tennessee.

My job while I was at The Farm waiting to have the baby was to work in the soy milk factory. I was stirring the large vats of soy milk that we would cook. You grind up the soy beans, add water, and then cook it. When all the soy is infused into the water, then you strain [the soy milk] out, and you're left with the grounds of the soy. Some of that would become tofu. My job was kinda not letting the soy milk scorch on the bottom. *(Cece)*

Families bought fifty- to one hundred-pound sacks of soybeans and of whole wheat flour or wheat berries—the seeds in the wheat head that are ground to make flour.

Soybeans were an important piece of the diet. Even the desserts—my kids loved the frozen peanut butter tofu pie. We kind of expanded into other grains, like we ate a lot of millet and brown rice and got some lentils and black turtle beans, started varying our diet more. Maybe Jerome, somebody, would go all the way to the food co-op in Knoxville and buy the twenty-five-pound bags of wheat berries. I had the hand-grinder mounted on my counter that we made, and so I would grind the wheat berries and make the flour, and make the bread, or make the tortillas. So we would have bread or tortillas and soybeans for kinda the staples. *(Micki)*

> We all baked our own bread back then. I loved to bake bread and the girls, I would give 'em each their own little blob of dough, and they would roll it out and play with it. I would give them cinnamon sugar and butter, and they would make little rolls and then bake it with the bread. And I made a lotta different pies! Lotta pies and cakes. (*Cece*)

Food co-ops became the source for the wheat berries, flour, and dried beans. First, a few families united to travel to a co-op in Knoxville, an hour and a half away. Then a group formed to order from a health food store closer by. Meanwhile, yet another group of families had food shipped in.

> I think it was just us, and one or two other families for a while, because we were ordering from a Seventh Day Adventist place up in Battlefield, Michigan. We had to have a three hundred dollar order, I believe, and the man would meet my husband in the old K-Mart parking lot. And then later, we became part of the co-op. (*Lauren*)

The co-op that Lauren referred to is the Little Pumpkin Valley Food Co-op. Eventually all the groups united in that cooperative. Within the co-op and in all the work the women did, there was camaraderie, good eating, and pride in their effort to feed their families.

> We made all our own food. We grew and canned tomatoes and vegetables, and froze vegetables. We bought wheat berries and we had a hand-grinder. We would grind the wheat berries for flour to make bread. We had soybeans for making tofu. We had cashews and almonds to make different kinds of milks and gravies. We had potatoes we would store—and [winter] squash—

under our bed 'cause that was cool under there and dark. So we were pretty self-sufficient as far as food goes. *(Carolyn)*

It is an accomplishment to prepare healthy food from a garden and a sack of beans and bring it to your table, nourishing your family and holding to your principles while doing it. Although many of these homesteaders were vegetarian, after a year or two, almost everyone elected to use some animal products, such as dairy and eggs. Later, several families chose to start eating meat, while others were already confirmed carnivores upon arrival in the valley. Consuming food from animals led to more choices. They could buy their meat, eggs, and milk, or they could own animals, controlling how the animals were raised, what feed they ate, and how they were treated.

Chapter Eight

Some Creatures Wild and Small

The lure of fresh eggs and butter was strong for the new arrivals. Though they had arrived with their own food customs and convictions, the local country culture offered appealing options.

> When we came to East Tennessee and Pumpkin Valley, we were vegetarians. We didn't eat any dairy. We didn't eat any eggs or fish or anything like that. Then, I met Lilian Holt, a local lady, who milked her own cows, and sold milk and this fabulous homemade butter that was to die for, and also buttermilk. So we started going back to eating eggs and dairy. *(Cece)*

It was easy to obtain eggs from neighbors who raised chickens, but before long, most of the back-to-the-landers opted to raise their own poultry, and some even sold eggs.

> We got eggs for the first little while from the neighbor, but then we went to the local flea market up there in Tazewell, and got ourselves some chickens, a variety of types of hens, and there was a shed on the property where we kept them. We had to do a

little work to the shed because of the weasels and other critters that have a tendency to get after the chickens and the eggs. They ran free during the day. They would have a tendency to roost in the cedar trees in the evening unless we could coax them down from the cedar trees into the shed, their coop, where we would then close them up for the night. *(Micki)*

I loved our rooster! Some roosters are mean to hens, and some roosters are like veritable knights! *(Yvonne)*

We had run-of-the-mill chickens. At one time we had all these little banties [bantam hen chicks], and they would go off, and come back with a whole lot more little banties. The little babies would get stuck in the sticky weeds. We had a proper chicken house at one time, with proper chickens—bigger chickens that would lay their eggs in the nest and you could go in there [and get the eggs]. Black snakes went in there, too! But these little banties would just go off and lay about ten to fourteen eggs in a nest somewhere and then show up some time later with all these little babies. Really cute, but they're everywhere! They got in everything, and finally we sold them, like fifty cents apiece. People would come over and we would run around trying to catch the babies. *(Trudie)*

And then there are the top-knot chickens!

I had these two black top-knot roosters that I found. [They] would attack me in the barn. I was milking once, and something hit me in the back, and it was one of these roosters. He looked like a vampire with a cape on! They have fluffy little feathers just sticking out of their heads. *(Karen)*

We had those silly top-knot chickens. They don't have a lick of sense. We had like a chicken-roost in the barn, and they could get in out of the rain. [But] you would see 'em sitting on the top of a gate in pouring-down rain, and the top-knot feathers hanging down like that [over their eyes]. You would say [to yourself], What is the matter?! They're gonna die! It's gettin' cold, they're all soppin' wet, and then it'll freeze, and they'll be sick! You'd have to go out and catch 'em. They wouldn't see you coming, 'cause they couldn't see. Then put 'em in the barn on a roost or something, and tell 'em to stay. Not a brain in their heads! *(Trudie)*

Not all top-knotter stories end well.

One time we were going to sell baby pigs so [an Ag] Extension Agent had to come out, and he got to the barn. He's supposed to check it for cleanliness, and this and that, and it smelled awful! It smelled like death, and I was really embarrassed. So we look around, and way up in the top of the barn in a crack in the siding one of these [top-knot] roosters hung himself! He got his head in a crack and got hung in the top of the barn. So that was the excuse for the bad smell. *(Karen)*

Trudie did have a more sensible chicken at one time.

We did have a chicken that would come in our house and sleep. We had a wood cookstove, and she would go under it because it was warm. Dianna and Bill [Young] were over here one day, and Bill says, "You know there's a chicken under your stove?" And we're like, "Yeah, yeah. She does that." *(Trudie)*

Besides chickens, Sherri had geese, and even a "guard turkey."

Had a turkey once. He didn't like men very well, and I can remember he was a better guard dog than dogs were. He'd sit right on the patio and guard it. The UPS man would come, and he'd deliver anything down to my door, which was down two hundred fifty foot. We lived kinda right in the middle of the side of the hill, and he would carry anything down there, but I had to come up with the broom so I could keep the turkey from flogging him, 'cause he got flogged a couple times by that turkey, and that doesn't feel too good! He'll bite you and hit you with his wing, and they can hit hard. It can bruise you pretty bad. Those wings are pretty strong! *(Sherri)*

Horrible things can happen to your charges.

I had a favorite chicken, a white chicken. She was like tame. I went out the back door one day, and she was there. I had no sooner gotten out the back door, than a hawk swooped down and got her, and it took her up in the air, and it broke her neck. He dropped her, and she fell down dead. Killed my pet chicken. And then just dropped her! It was terrible, it was terrible! *(Trudie)*

The only animal I remember threatening our chickens was a black snake. I found him one day right in the chicken house, getting the eggs right out of the nesting boxes. I knew black snakes are good snakes to have around, but I didn't want him in my chicken house so I picked him up and took him down to the garden, which I thought was far enough away from the house. But like I said, I really didn't know much about these things. So the very next day he was back up. Only there were little doodles, little baby chicks. These were all free-ranging; we would put 'em up at night, but they would be all around the house and the yard during the day. So the black snake was going after one of my little doodles, and may have already eaten one, I'm not sure. But now I'm a little more agitated so I went after it, and I'm thinkin', You had your chance. I actually killed the black snake, which I still feel bad about to this day, because black snakes are good snakes to have around, because they eat rodents, mainly. So I have nothing against black snakes, but when they were eating my eggs and my little doodles, I made an enemy. I think I just grabbed a shovel, and went out there and chopped it's head off, and that was the end of that snake! *(Beth)*

Oh, but there are more critters than chicken hawks and snakes that will pursue your poultry!

We had more trouble with animals from the creek. We had weasels, and an otter one time. They were snapping off the feet of the baby ducks. And they were snatchin' the eggs, because the geese liked to lay 'em close to the creek, for some reason. But that didn't last long. We got the dogs after 'em, and they took care of that problem. *(Sherri)*

Sometimes the enemy comes from within.

I had some chickens that a friend of mine gave me, and they were great chickens. They each laid an egg a day. They were very sweet, very personable, and I had a dog—for fun—chase 'em and kill 'em! She didn't want the animals. It was just a little game I guess. And they were big fat hens. They were big fat hens! So I haven't had chickens since then. *(Robyn)*

A family gets attached to its chickens and the delicious fresh eggs. So, then, does that family slaughter them and eat them when they get too old to be dependable egg sources?

We didn't eat the chickens. Probably we weren't really into killing the chickens. I mean we weren't vegetarian, we bought meat from the grocery store, but I never did the whole experience of slaughtering the animal and then eating it. I didn't just go that far with it. *(Beth)*

Didn't [slaughter] a lot of chickens—that whole thing about Adelle Davis saying, "You are what you eat"? But we thought, Well alright, chickens—let's chop its head and we're gonna do this chicken thing. So you know how they talk about a chicken without its head on? Do you know that chickens, when you chop their heads off and you let them like run away, they actually run around without their heads on?! Then, you dress them out and the smell of chickens used to make me gag. So, if it's true ya' are what ya' eat, I didn't wanna be like that! *(Lee)*

[I killed] chickens and rabbits. I don't remember killing the turkeys, but I guess I did, baby turkeys that we raised up. A block of wood, a hatchet. Oh! And then they run around. Oh, I was young; it was a challenge. And now, I give the roosters away, and I don't want to do it. It's a lot of work. *(Alicia)*

There are some parallels between raising chickens and raising rabbits—the joys, the challenges, and the harsh realities. Several of the women raised rabbits for fun, fur, and, yes, for food.

> [We ate] a lotta beans, a lotta rice, and then as we got going, we learned the hunting, and the raising of food—not just the vegetables, but the raising of the meat. Especially rabbits were a very big part of our diet. They're a really good meat—lean, more of a white meat. *(Lee)*

> We had the rabbits. We got rabbits started, so we could eat them—which was a terrible thing. Well, we didn't wanna kill 'em. We'd raised 'em from little bunnies. But we did, eventually. We had the horrible day. I don't think we used the skins. We weren't very good at getting the skins cured. *(Pat)*

The "horrible day" occurred for others, too, and here's how one woman handled that.

> I told [my husband] Dale and [our friend] Walt, "I'll do all the raisin' of the animals, and you guys have to do the middle part, and I'll do all the cookin', but when you guys are doing the middle part I'm going to town!" So I'd go to town, or go somewhere. And I said, "When [the meat] comes back, I don't wanna hear about it, I don't wanna know about it, I just want it to look like it came from the grocery store. Then I'll cook it." *(Sherri)*

Lee raised rabbits for meat. She also learned to tan the hides. The hides were fantastic!

I taught myself how to tan the hides and did everything, made everybody a blanket with the hides. I covered a couch with the hides. Whoa, it was cool-looking! I mean, it was really cool-lookin'! Also the hides were great for weather-stripping. You can put it all around your windows and your doors, and boy, I'm telling you, we needed them living in this cabin. Made coats, made everything out of rabbit. I can remember a wonderful hat that looked like I was living in the Arctic or somewhere. I made my daughter a muff. You know the old-timey muffs? She loved it because it wasn't mittens. It was just a pure, white rabbit fur muff, and she just thought that was great, with a little blue velvet string to hold it on to her coat. *(Lee)*

While Lee tanned rabbits' hides, four women plucked Angora rabbits' hair carefully, and spun it.

We used to raise rabbits. I had two kinds of rabbits. I had a big, meat rabbit, and then I had Angora rabbits, and I would pluck their hair to spin the wool. I have Angora rabbits, and I can take the wool off that Angora rabbit and spin it. I would go to craft shows and I would demonstrate, and I would also sell some of my things at craft shows, or I'd sell even some things around here. Usually I had five or six [rabbits], for the shows. I would make scarves and hats. It was fun. I really enjoyed that. *(Sandra)*

And how about dog hair?

I have spun dog's wool before. Actually I did a project for my daughter-in-law. She was keeping her brother's dog who was overseas, I can't remember what war it was at the time. The dog was basically old and was not going to make it, so she would send me all the sheddings, and I would spin it up. I blended it a little bit with [sheep's] wool. I made him a hat with it, a toboggan. It wasn't a dog that you would usually do that with. That's why I had to blend a little wool in with it. It was more of a stiff-haired dog. My Pyrenees dog out there, you could spin its wool. *(Sandra)*

Dogs and cats, and even geese are useful in other ways, such as preventing predation.

I had lots of cats named after herbs and spices. I had three big dogs. I don't remember seeing too many mice because of all the animals we had. The ducks and geese would take care of them, too. I was a basket-maker, and I would go to honeysuckle patches in the middle of nowhere, tall grass. I'd take my cats with me, the geese would follow me, and you just put the cats and the geese in those patches for about five minutes. I never saw a snake. Never, ever saw a snake. *(Sherri)*

Sometimes, even with dogs and cats around, it seemed as though wild creatures were taking over. A constant concern was keeping food and small domestic animals safe from predators.

I feel like when you're in the Land of Raccoons, you gotta do so many things to prevent the raccoons from killing your chickens. I've gone round and round with raccoons, let me tell ya'! Two years ago we used a live trap. We were keeping cat food in a metal garbage can with a lid, inside a giant parrot cage in the barn. One raccoon found out about it, and went and told everyone, so that year we caught twelve raccoons in the live trap, just one right after the other. It was just Raccoon City around here! We had them come up on the porch. [My partner] Bobby would open the door real slow, and shoot 'em if it was a right alignment. I can only take so many raccoons, and then I go nuts! *(Tata)*

Mice could be pesky. We just had dogs and cats, always, plenty a' dogs, plenty a' cats, and chickens. That was all the livestock there was—oh, well, lotsa mice, lotsa mice! They helped us eat the food I put in the cupboard—that I didn't properly store. They ate some of the insulation, or made nests out of the insulation. They did have a nice home! *(Dianna)*

Yes, often pests were inside homes. For example, snakes.

It was corn season, and my two oldest boys were shuckin' corn all the time. Sometimes we'd use banana boxes; the shucks would go in there. And then we'd feed 'em to the cows. On this particular day I was going to my daughter's bedroom, because there was a large banana box under her crib that had a lot of material in it, and also a stuffed snake that I used in my Sabbath School class at church. I wanted to go through that material and get rid of some, but I was doing it while she was taking a nap, so I was being extra-special careful. On the top there was, sure enough, the large, stuffed snake. I took that out, but next to it was a snake skin, which was not unusual in my family, because on any given window sill, there would be birds' nests, there would be turtle shells, there would be raccoon skulls. There were these two holes in the sides of the banana box, and [a snake] could've gotten in through a hole. I finally came to the inevitable. If it got in there, and it shed its skin there, wonder if it's still there? So then, I'm pickin' up material, like there's teeth. But I get down to the last piece, and everything looks smooth as light, and I really don't think I have a problem. I pick up that last piece, and there it is. Coiled, very neatly coiled. And looking at me.

Now, very near and dear to my heart, is the fact that I want this child that's sleeping, to stay asleep. So, I control this scream. I pushed the box and got to the steps. I went down the steps and across the kitchen. Then I had this awful thought, Wow, let me try and put this snake in a container, and I'll show it to the kids in Sabbath School. But it got away from me, and it got under the upright freezer that was outside the front door! I'm trying to coax it out, but I don't see it. I'm satisfied. It's gone, and it's gotten away.

The next day, my three-year-old and my five-year-old are shucking corn on the bottom step. The baby is waking up from her nap. I'm goin' up the stairs; I'm turnin' the corner—with the snake! He was also headed to the bedroom! I screamed bloody murder. The snake went down a hole next to the chimney onto the floor next to the boys, who took flight. The snake went into the bathroom and got under the washing machine. The [boys] went and got my husband, who told Timothy, "Go and get the hoe out of the shed." So Timothy comes with the hoe. Where am I during all this? I'm on top of the commode, and I'm not getting down. [My husband] gets it out from under the washing machine. The snake goes back into the kitchen, and he gets the hoe on the back of his head, right behind his eyeballs. And he's not going to kill it. Why? Because it's a black snake.

They eat the mice. They eat the rats. And, that's not who we are! The corn tongs were right there on the table. [My husband] said, "Get the snake right behind the hoe, and grab him pretty good." So I did. I did! I mean, that poor little guy's eyeballs almost were bolting out. And he says, "Okay, well, I'm gonna let go. Are you ready?" No, I wasn't ready, because I did not expect what was gonna happen next. He coiled around my arm. It was about four feet long, and his entire body was wrapped around my arm. We decided, go down the long driveway, down the road to the creek. Well, [the snake] wasn't goin' anywhere. The circulation might've been cuttin' off on my arm, but we were good. It wasn't a boa constrictor. We get onto the road, and here comes a car. I wanted to jump in the ditch. I just didn't want anybody to be privy to this scene, but there was no time. I just said to my husband, "Just relax. Just act like we do this every day. We take the snake for a walk." So, I just looked straight ahead. Anyway, we got down to the creek, and my husband unwound him from my arm—which took some doing. He let him go, and it slithered along the creek, and we never saw it again. *(Lauren)*

I was raising parakeets inside the house here. Back in the old days it was pretty open and pretty loose, and it wasn't anything to see critters inside the house. So I come home one day and I'm hearing, I'm hearing all this squawking going on with my parakeets upstairs in this very large space that I had them in. And there is a black snake with three good-sized bulges in him. He had taken down three already and was goin' for more. So I went and got a hatchet and opened up the door and I would strike at him, he would strike at me, and I won and then sliced him open, thinking that maybe I could save these poor parakeets. But lo and behold, no, I couldn't save them. But, it's ah—you know, snakes are somethin'! *(Lee)*

Or large rodents.

We had a rat in our house at Alum Well. He would take bars of soap, and hide them behind the washing machine, and first I was saying to Steven, "What did you do with the soap? Why are you taking the bars of soap?" And then we found 'm. We could hear him, at night. We slept in kind of a loft bedroom, and then [below that] there was the kitchen, and then downstairs the living area, and we could hear him. So Steven got this bright idea. He took an ear of dried corn, and tied it so it was kinda like hangin' down on the stairs. Then he got our pistol. At night he would sit up in the kitchen area—there was a couch up there, too. He's in the kitchen area. He's going to be shooting down. Thank God, since I was in the loft. So, I went on to bed, and he had gone down, and he's on the couch, and evidently he heard the rat. I think the plan was he would turn on the flashlight, and shoot the rat. So, anyway, I'm asleep and I wake up to gunfire in the house, and that thing is *loud*, I'm not kiddin' you! So, he's fired a round at the rat, which he missed. We have a really nice, antique oak bookcase that now has a bullet hole in it because he shot the bookcase and missed the rat. I think, eventually—his parents came to visit, and maybe we had a rat trap by then—but his dad ended up, somehow, stompin' the rat to death on the front porch. But I preferred that to Steve shootin' up the house in the middle of the night. When the rat wasn't around any more, then he couldn't steal the bars of soap, which you really don't want to use after the rat's had 'em, you know. It was a very tidy rat, I guess. *(Trudie)*

Clinch Mountain Girls

Oh my gosh, I was pregnant with April. This was like 1980, and this house has all these stone ledges [projecting from the walls]. We didn't have electricity but we did have a little gas stove, propane, and so I had this kerosene lamp sitting [beside it], on one of these stone ledges. It was evening in the wintertime, and John was off milking the cows, and so it was just my son Jung, up in the loft, and myself, and all of a sudden I'm there cookin' dinner and I'm lookin' up, and there is this huge, huge rat the size of a cat comin' down the wall. That year we had decided we were gonna grow corn for our cows, and make our own feed and everything for the cows. Rats tend to be drawn to large containers of corn. So here's this rat comin' down the wall and I'm thinkin', Oh my gosh, what am I gonna do? We heat with wood and we had this homemade stoker that had a tremendous point on it for moving wood around inside the fireplace. So I went over and got that and I yelled to Jung, "Jung, Jung! Come on down here!" So he comes on down, and I said, "Alright, now I'm gonna take this poker and I'm gonna stab this rat and then I'm gonna bring him down to the floor, and you're gonna take this iron frying pan, this huge iron frying pan, and you're going to whack 'm right on the head soon as I bring him down to the floor. Are you ready? Okay. Here we go." So I stabbed this thing into the stone, and he's like screaming and with his big yellow teeth gnarling at me. And I said, "Alright, here we go!" But as I lifted him down, his huge tail hit the kerosene light and threw it onto my propane stove, so that caught on fire, and I caught on fire but nevertheless threw him down to the ground, and Jung smashed him down and killed him! And I then, you know, peeled off all my clothes and stopped the fire from going. So it was a real adventure! *(Lee)*

The dream of many back-to-the-landers was a peaceful home in the country, perhaps with charming animals that they could feed and care for. The truth became apparent—tame animals were not always adorable; they might even decide to kill and eat those animals. Small wild animals were persistent pests, and with those, too, there may come a time to take a life. All who raised animals delighted in their favorites. The work, the schedules, the ailments, the fears, and the deaths were real, practical, and daunting to the naive but stalwart women. Nevertheless, the animals brought joy, and also a new, down-to-earth maturity.

Chapter Nine

Sheep and Lambs and Goats and Kids

"No goat ever got upset about riding in the car," said Pat, one of the two Goat Ladies you are about to meet. First, consider the characteristics of goats and sheep. While not as small as chickens and rabbits, the charming medium-sized ruminants, sheep and goats, are relatively easy to gather, pen, and feed. Goats forage on brush, vines, and weeds as well as grass, so they were immediately helpful in clearing overgrown pastures.

Before we even had a house, we had goats! *(Beth)*

While the popular goats yielded milk and milk products, sheep are valuable for their wool, and are also good grazers, eating weeds as well as grass, keeping fields "picked down" and appearing picturesque roaming over the green hills.

When we first moved here, there was nobody back there [on the hill], so my sheep would range the whole area back there; I didn't have a fence up. They would just stay there. Every now and then we would have to shoo 'em back, because they'd hear us down here, they'd hear my voice. I had Romney Sheep, and they were dual purpose. You could eat 'em, the lambs, and we'd sell 'em, or I could sell some of the wool that I got. I just spun the wool. I never was a weaver. I spun some of the wool, and made things with it. Even before I got sheep or any of that I liked to crochet and do that kind of thing. It's probably what got me into it. I've made mostly toboggans [caps], hats, and scarves. *(Sandra)*

Sandra had goats as well. In fact, half the homesteaders kept goats.

I didn't have to worry about anything with [my first goat]. We got her fenced in, for her safety more than anything, but [she] would even follow me. It was funny when I'd walk down to get my mail, you'd see I had two dogs and then the goat just following me down there. They'd follow me everywhere! It was funny. The barn was up there. And there it was—just one goat. So, when I would be down here, she would follow the dogs down here, and she would get under the porch with the dogs! It was just fun! *(Sandra)*

Kids and lambs are cute. Of course the families would name them. We had goats. Milked goats every day. We had Daisy and the Daisyettes, her babies. *(Sherri)*

We had Sneezy. And Monica. We started naming the baby—the baby everythings—after people. So, we raised our friends. *(Pat)*

Sneezy loved to ride.

Sneezy was a purebred goat, so we got her bred. Got to know goat people. There are a lot of people that raise goats, all the way to North Carolina. And that's where we went to breed her. The goats would ride in the car. We had the Volkswagen, and the back seat was down, so it was like a little truck—we had hay in the back—the Volkswagen bug, but they're bigger than you'd think. So, we would have a goat in the back, and people would see this goat lookin' out in this Volkswagen. They loved to ride. No goat ever got upset about riding in the car! *(Pat)*

Soon a male kid was born, and Pat and Alicia started building their herd.

You keep one male, and [we'd] keep him across the road, and then the females would be over here. We gradually got enough goats to have enough milk to make cheese. The cheese turned out to work, and the cheese sold. [The herd] just kept increasing. I think we were [at] about twelve maybe, at the most. And then their babies. When they were all bred we would have a good number of babies, because they all had twins, triplets. A lot of people would enjoy coming to see the babies. People stopped here all the time, so we'd sell 'em anything we had to sell. Then we got some friends that kept coming back over the years. First they came to buy whatever we had to sell, and then they just came to visit. *(Pat)*

Pat and Alicia came to be called the "Goat Ladies." They sold their goods, provided advice and laughter, and became well known in the valley.

Yes, we got to be known that way! We joined a couple of co-ops, and of course, we met a lot of people. When we met Carolyn and Rick [Novkov], we were still feeding [goat] babies. They all had those little children. Cece [Lakin] was there, and Margaret and Eric [DeVos], and others. Their kids liked to feed the baby goats, so we fed 'em all on bottles. There sometimes were twenty baby goats to feed, so we were always glad to have the help. So they would come over and do that, or see the goats. Goats are always so friendly—the baby goats had been handled since birth. A lot of those people had goats, too. Margaret and Eric had goats. Beth had goats, and she came over one time to get them de-horned. *(Pat)*

Pat explains de-horning and the complicated ethics of raising goats.

Oh, [de-horning] is a difficult thing to do. We had to learn to do it, because we couldn't take the goats off [the farm] and get someone else to do it. You burn [the horns] off when they're just little, so they're just little buds. They heal right away, but it does hurt, I'm sure. Well, you do a lot of bad things when you're a farmer. Raising chickens, and you kill 'em and eat 'em. Goats—we ate the baby goats. We tried to sell the baby goats, the males. But, they get mistreated so much. People think it's so cute when they're little—they love to get the little baby goat to fight with 'em. You put your hand out like that, and a little baby goat will come along and butt you with their little heads, and it's so cute and everything. And they learn to butt people. So we tell 'em, "Don't do that, don't do that!" And they'd do it! And then it'd get to be a big goat doin' that. That's very dangerous. So we wouldn't sell them as pets unless we knew the people really well. *(Pat)*

Instead of being sold, those baby billies became food for Pat and Alicia.

We would just butcher them. Somebody came and shot them for us, and then we would butcher them ourselves. We were pretty good at it. Somebody came over and asked us to show them how to skin a goat, because they were gonna skin their deer. We were the experts on it 'cause we would just hang 'em up, and we'd do 'em all the same day. *(Pat)*

Goats brought income for Vicki and her husband Jerome and their four children, though she had regrets.

Jerome thought he'd try cattle for a while, but that didn't work out. And then we had goats and had them for quite a while here on this farm. Probably the most we'd ever had was sixty. We did not [milk them]. Jerome would sell them, sell the young ones after a while. I don't even like to think what happened to 'em because I'm a vegetarian, and they were probably born to make somebody a meal. But I loved watching the baby goats. They're the most joyful little creatures in the whole world. *(Vicki)*

Most families raised goats for their milk.

We built a goat barn and had an area fenced off that the goat barn was in, and we built a milking stand, that was partly from pictures I'd seen. That was a pretty neat contraption. The goats would just hop up on the milk-stand, and you had a board that would come up around their neck, and [another would] kinda lock them in there, and they didn't mind it 'cause they were eating sweet feed, chowing down on some really good sweet grain. My goats were always real good as far as standing there. I don't remember having any difficulty learning how to milk 'em. Of course I learned how to milk goats when I lived out in California. It was fun! *(Beth)*

How many goats a day did the women milk?

> Probably the most I ever milked was like maybe three or four at a time. I kinda did a half-and-half system where I would milk the goats out when they were still nursing their kids. I would save half the milk and then bottle up half the milk and then feed the babies. I had the mothers in a separate stall at night, so the mothers' udders would fill up with milk at night, and then I would milk 'em in the morning. Then during the day I would put 'em all back together so they kinda got both [nursing and bottle-feeding]. *(Beth)*

> Alicia always did the milking, but I can't think we ever did more than eight at a time. If we had eight females what I'd take up to the cheese house every day would be four gallons, take it up to the cheese house and make cheese out of it right away. Every day. Sometimes they're milked twice a day, when they're really full, coming in strong. *(Pat)*

All who milk—goats or cows—face the exigencies of schedule. Modern urban life has its alarm clocks and rules, but so does the farm.

> When you're milking, you milk! I mean you hafta be there—you hafta milk. There's no gettin' around it. They are dry [not lactating] for a while, a couple of months, but sometimes not all at the same time. Sometimes you'd be out at night and have to get [home] to milk the goats so they'd be later than usual. But I think even when the kids were on them, there would still be some milk left in the udder, so I would still milk in the evening 'cause you would want to really empty it out, 'cause otherwise there was more danger of them getting mastitis. *(Beth)*

Clinch Mountain Girls

There is intense seasonal labor.

> You have to get them bred for the next season, so that they'll have the milk. Then we were always there for their births, and always went out to check 'em every night. No goat had her babies without us being there! *(Pat)*

> You just had to be there, and that was the hard part with the barn being up there. There was many a time at kidding, I was jumping in the car, running up there to see if they were okay or not, up on that hill. But usually you were there just in case. I did have one goat that had four babies. That was kinda unusual. *(Sandra)*

Attendance was necessary to ensure successful births and an ample milk supply from the nannies.

> We wanted to get the babies away from the mothers right away. It seemed kind of cruel, but— *(Pat)*

So what about that schedule, those chores, over the long haul?

> When it's your own choice, you're free to quit any time. Nobody made you stay. Nobody made you do anything. *(Pat)*

The families could consume their animals' products and maybe even make a little money!

> We drank the goats' milk, but also made some soft cheeses. I made yogurt. Then you could make yogurt cheese from it. There were different recipes that I would either get from a *Foxfire* book or Rodale Press stuff. *(Beth)*

> I make my own yogurt. I make cheese, I make ice cream. I make ice cream out of the yogurt, and that works very well. It's just nice to have fresh milk. I cook with it—scalloped potatoes—there's just a lot of good stuff you can do with it. Just follow the recipes, and it's very easy—in a lot of good books, and the magazines too [like] *Mother Earth News*. Any kind of products you buy, like the vegetable rennet and things like that, they'd come with recipes. *(Anne)*

> Yes, [I made cheese] the real easy kind like ricotta or something. It was good! We sold goat's milk. I think we may have sold some cheese, and goats. *(Trudie)*

Alicia made soap from goat's milk, but the Goat Ladies' main business for quite some time was cheese-making. She describes the outbuilding where they started making cheese.

> It was above the root cellar. It was a little one-room thing. We made that into the cheese house. We had a stove and a refrigerator. A man came from Nashville to inspect the place. We asked him to, we wanted to sell the cheese. And we had, I think, three rounds of cheese in the dairy, aging. He laughed. We had put linoleum down on the floor—I think it was cement—to make it look clean. We put up tile board so it looked clean, and shelves. He said he would grandfather us in. So we made cheese and we sold it. He gave us a license. *(Alicia)*

They talked, and the inspector offered more help.

> We got the cheese house fixed up, so [the inspector] came out here, and he sat on the front porch. Alicia made him apple pie,

and he got charmed. He sat down on the porch and we chatted. He said, "You got to meet this man that's making cheese and has a cheese plant. I'll take you there." And so [later] he took us there. We toured the guy's cheese plant, and he told us everything he did and how he did it. *(Pat)*

They worked hard to get their cheese business going.

For ourselves, we made mozzarella, [and] some kind of a hard cheese. Then we made—for sale—feta, and *chèvre*, which was cheese balls in olive oil with herbs in it. This was probably twenty-five years ago [or more], and nobody ate goat cheese. We would go to fairs, and little markets and try to sell it—and couldn't. People would say, "Ooh, goat cheese! The smell!" Then we had a coupla' stores in Knoxville—one restaurant, one store [that bought it]. We had a store in Johnson City, a natural food store. We had two in Johnson City. And, we had a store in Jonesborough that bought it. Then we sold it at our food co-op. *(Alicia)*

Meanwhile, some people continued to come for milk. And Alicia still sold soap. Then, success came to the Goat Ladies!

The guy [with the cheese plant] was making marinated cheese, in a little jar. So I liked that; that was a good idea. He gave us some ideas, and how he made it. First I tried it with yogurt [cheese] balls, marinated with some pepper, black peppercorns. I bought the jars, a big load of jars, wholesale. The cost was [the concern], but when I went to sell it down in [Knoxville]—I started to go out to places to sell it—these health-food stores, and gourmet shops and stuff, they would pay eight dollars a jar, so then I could do it.

> People came to the farm all the time and bought it. I never had so much I couldn't get rid of it. I never could make enough! I could've found more people, especially gourmet restaurants. One restaurant used a whole wheel just on one dish. It put salmon caviar on top of it, and then a couple of more delicate things on the plate. We went there one time, just to see what it was like—to see the cheese! The cheese went places we couldn't afford to go! *(Pat)*

Then, success went away.

> We paid for the license every year. Until it got—it got terrible! The rules changed. They wanted us to get a calculator on the homogenizer, or pasteurizer, so that we could keep—it was a computer, it was supposed to be computerized. It was gonna cost us like four thousand dollars for this instrument, and we said, "Forget it!" So, we made cheese for ourselves, and gave it away to our neighbors. *(Alicia)*

Since cheese-making was not their only income, Pat and Alicia did not "lose the farm." On the contrary, their financial success with the cheese helped them to pay for it.

> Alicia was still makin' all the quilts, and so we got the place [paid off]. Some friends helped us, and loaned, too. So we got the house paid for, and then we didn't have to come up with that payment every month! *(Pat)*

Besides cheese-making and licensing problems, there can be unforeseen incidents with goats.

> We had [the goats] in sort of a corral, with cattle [fence] panels. But, you had to still tie them up, 'cause they managed to, somehow,

get over six foot of cattle panel. One time I got there, and a goat was lying there on its back—with, with only a rope around his neck—just about choking. It was just in time! *(Yvonne)*

They [the neighbors] had goats. I was pregnant with Jesse. We were having a Fourth of July party at their house. They had a goat, a pregnant female goat, tied under a cherry tree, and a little girl was feeding leaves to the goat. They say wilted cherry leaves are poisonous to goats [due to a chemical conversion to cyanide]. While we were there the goat started screaming, and so we all gathered around the goat, and it died.

I said, "Run, get a knife right away!" I then handed it to Rick [Arvo, the goat owner] to do a Caesarean, and he said, "I can't do it."

So I did it. Cut the goat open, and got the baby out. [Rick] actually did mouth-to-mouth [resuscitation] on the baby, but it didn't live. So the cherry tree leaves, I suppose, is what killed it and probably the baby, too, at the same time.

It was a big, beautiful baby. Doing that when you're pregnant is not really, not really good. *(Karen)*

After that sobering and heroic tale, you may be ready for lighter stuff, like some stories about the dogs who care for goats, sheep, and their owners.

We did have more farm dogs like Border Collies, and Shepherds. Then we got Great Pyrenees, and that's what basically we've had ever since. They're guard dogs. They guard the animals, and basically they guard me, too.

There's coyotes around here, and there's other animals, and they [the Pyrenees] will keep any predator away. Just their bark alone keeps 'em away. Just the bark, it's such a deep thing. They guard me, too. I can remember my very first Pyrenees, if somebody drove up in the yard, [he] never growled at 'em, didn't really do too much. Well, he put many a man, grown man, back in their car! *(Sandra)*

We had the dog before we had the goats, or right at the same time as the first goat. But, we loved that dog, Jenny Wiley. Our original Border Collies were pure-bred, and we bred Jenny. That's another way we made money is, we sold the babies—puppies. They brought in a pretty good amount. *(Pat)*

Pat and Alicia raised the Border Collies primarily to sell, though they had sheep for a while. The dogs tried to help with the goats, too.

They're very intelligent dogs. But a lot of people don't like 'em, 'cause they've got that working instinct, that just drives everybody crazy if they don't have work to do. Jenny thought she was working all the time. The day she died, she went out to work the goats. We were gonna have to have her put down because she was so bad, but when Alicia went down to the barn, she followed her, and did her work. She'd crouch. She thought she brought the goats back and forth to the milking room. But of course, it would've been easier if she wasn't even there, because the goats knew where they were going. They would come in one at a time and get milked. The big thing was, the dogs should have some sheep to put away, because [to] the Border Collies [sheep] were everything. They needed sheep, because they don't work goats—they just mess up with goats. *(Pat)*

Working dogs are vital on many farms, and their owners feel a great attachment to them. I've just got two [goats] now, two females, to keep the Pyrenees company—the big guard dog, beautiful, wonderful guard dog. They do their jobs very well and are very nice animals. *(Vicki)*

Bruno was faithful and heroic. We had a little bum lamb. The mom rejected it, so I had to bottle feed it. I did bottle feed it, but finally I wanted to put it back in the back [pasture] there to get it used to the other sheep so it'd kinda hang out with them. I put it out there, and it seemed okay, but it wasn't. It took off, and I didn't realize it. It went from here straight across the woods over there, to Clinch Road and somebody recognized my dog [Bruno]. My dog would not leave that lamb. See, they're trained to do that, to just stay with their [charges], to take care of them, and he stayed there. So they called us because at the time we were the only ones who had a Great Pyrenees in the area, and they knew it. They called us, and Wayne went and got both of them and told Bruno to get in the truck. Well, Bruno would not get in the truck until Wayne took the lamb and put it in the truck, and then Bruno jumped in there. Those dogs are so good, they're so good! *(Sandra)*

The mutual bonds at the homestead are clear. In return for safety and food, the goats and sheep (and guard dogs) offered much in return. The women and their families were grateful for the companionship of the goats as well as their milk, cheese, and yogurt. Wool was at hand for spinning and crafting. And, the homesteaders' pastures were greener, graced with the brown and white grazers and their small bounding offspring.

Chapter Ten

Some Creatures Wide and Tall

Many of the families raised creatures that are large—for various reasons. The meat-eaters raised cows and pigs. Over half owned riding or work horses. But, ownership could sometimes seem accidental.

I inherited five cows with that farm. They just came with [the farm], and I didn't know anything about how to raise cows. *(Nancy)*

Dan, which was an old [horse], he came with the farm. He wasn't even fenced in, he just lived there. I think he originally belonged to [our neighbor] Walt. Dan was an old black Percheron. My husband Dale learned how to harness him up and plow our eight-acre cornfield. Walt taught us all that. Dan just stayed around our house, and he was still alive when I left. He was always there. *(Sherri)*

Or animals were just there as grounds keepers.

Everyone [in our house] was vegetarian, but for some reason the [steers] were there. They were bein' raised mostly to clean up

> [eat grass and weeds], where you have animals to clean up your property. *(Anne)*

Or they appeared in conjunction with refrigeration.

> After we started gardening we ate a lot of garden food, and then, of course we got the refrigerator and the freezer and had meat all the time. We started raising hogs, and chickens, and a few cows. *(Karen)*

Of course, some newcomers raised animals to earn money, like Anne, who raised milk-stock calves destined to be dairy cows.

> They were just babies. You get 'em so young, the little Holsteins, mostly just to re-sell, because that's one way you can make money if you have land. *(Anne)*

Lee raised veal calves, usually the male calves of milk cows. They are fed only milk and are marketed when only a few weeks old.

> Back in those days we had milk cows, and what we did with the milk cows—we had Guernseys—we would raise veal calves off of them. They'd have a calf, and then we'd raise it up to veal size. Then we'd then take it to the market, sell it, and then buy a little baby, like three days old, back. Then put the [babies] on our milk cows, and then we'd continue doing that, raising veal calves. It was a very good little business for us. We didn't make a lot, but the market was there. We took very, very, good care of them, sort of like little babies, always a very clean pen that they lived in. *(Lee)*

Nancy Withington Bell

Nancy and her husband raised beef calves.

> We would go to the stockyard and buy feeder cows—little calves that had just been weaned. We also had a milk cow, named Miss Pretty. We would bring a calf if it hadn't been weaned and put it on her. Some of them were ready to go [already weaned]. You just fattened them up in the summer, and sold them in the fall.
>
> Later, we raised cattle for food as well as for market. We would have a steer killed every year, and butchered. You can take 'em to these little mom-and-pop butcher places. They're very clean, and they'll butcher the beef for you. So we put it in our big freezer. *(Nancy)*

Several women milked cows. To prevent mastitis, a cow's udder must be emptied completely—no matter what.

> Had my first milk cow, which was an experience. I went and bought this milk cow. She was so big! Her name was Olana. She was so tall, and of course I was learning how to milk, and of course the first time I milked she kept stepping in the bucket. I'd run back to the house, wash the bucket, come back up, try it again, mess up again, run back to the house. Finally I said, "I give up on this milk, I'll just milk the cow out!" Finally got her milked. And threw the milk away 'cause she kept steppin' in it. *(Karen)*

> We made a little stanchion to milk Miss Pretty in. I didn't have it so good when I moved to Jones Road 'cause I remember milking Miss Pretty in the field. I didn't mind so much, but for some reason, our cows were mixed in with our neighbor's at

one point—maybe because we were trying to get her bred, I can't remember. But their bull was kind of feisty, and he would paw the ground. So I was always nervous, and I would look for trees that I could run around and get behind. It was a little nerve-wracking. She got mastitis and I had to give her a shot in the neck. Lee taught me how to do that. That's a daunting thing, to take [the syringe] out and you're holding it like a foot away, and then you go "pow," right into the neck of an animal. *(Nancy)*

Once human and animal adjusted to each other, milking was a peaceful activity. Next was processing into delicious dairy products.

We had a cream separator in the basement of the house, and we milked a couple of cows and eventually it was primarily one cow, a Guernsey, that gave a lot of milk. They're noted for that. Anyway, I made cheese, hard cheeses, Gouda, and a lot of cottage cheese and had a little butter churn, and we made butter and sold it to neighbors very reasonably. All of this was done for the pleasure of doing it. It wasn't any big farm operation. It was a desire to live in this area, in the mountains, and have land. *(Alma)*

We were milking cows so we had this fresh butter, made everything. Made cheese, made even hard cheese. Made yogurt, made it with just whole milk—we didn't pasteurize or homogenize or anything. But you talk about delicious yogurt! Just putting it in this crock with the culture and then putting that into another crock of warm water and just covering it over with towels. You just cannot believe how delicious! How really unbelievably delicious! And then buttermilk—we of course had buttermilk left over from the butter. *(Lee)*

Churning the cream causes it eventually to gather into a small mass—the butter. The liquid that is left is the buttermilk. When making cheese from milk, the remaining liquid is called whey.

> I was growing pumpkins one year, and just thought to myself, I'm just gonna try sump'n'. So I took a nail and made a hole in the stem of the pumpkin, and then put a piece of string, cotton string, into a jar of whey—'cause I was makin' cheese. Man, you should have seen that pumpkin! I mean it was huge! I just kept the thing goin', feeding this pumpkin, feeding this pumpkin [wicking the whey into it through the false stem].
>
> We were raising a hog for ourselves at this time, and then I'd feed the hog the pumpkins. I fed it the whey, too, but talk about a delicious tasting hog! It was good! *(Lee)*

Not only did Lee's family enjoy milk products, but as she has said, she had "a lotta cats around 'cause they loved the milk." The cow manure enriched the soil of fields and gardens.

> We always felt that the whole cow thing was like the cornerstone of our barn and of our farm because it was like all the milk products all fed everything. They fed everybody, not just the pumpkins or the pigs or anything like that. *(Lee)*

People develop a real fondness for their gentle cows. Karen cried for her cows twice in one day.

> Olana was our first cow and she was a beautiful cow. Eventually she got into staggerweed and died [toxins caused nerve and paralysis]. I was pregnant. Olana didn't come in [to be milked].

[My ex-husband] Ellison went looking for her, said she was down [on the ground] at the top of the hill, sick. And she was pregnant, too. So my neighbor, Lon, sent me to the store, Earl Hardin's Store, to buy eggs and mineral oil. So I come back, run up the hill. We're pouring all this stuff down her throat, which is supposed to make her pass the poison out, but she didn't. So she died with her head in my lap, this huge cow.

Then, the same day, we go down the hill, and Lon says, "Oh, your other cow is in heat. You should go get her bred."

So we put her in the truck, and I'm crying, and we take her off to find a Brown Swiss bull. The bull was out in a field, and the cow laid down in the truck on the way there, and Lon says "Well, she won't get bred today."

But we got there. We went out and brought all the herd in so the bull would come in. Had her [standing] tied to the back of the truck. The bull went to breed her, and broke her down. She fell down and Lon says, "Well, broke her back."

So I'm crying again. But, she was okay, and she got bred...That was a bad day! *(Karen)*

Alma, the eldest Clinch Mountain "girl" and her recently retired husband Sid, both physically fit and enthusiastic, created a full-fledged farm, Alma having been raised on one, and Sid with experience in his youth. A lush, green spring day on a farm can still hold danger.

My husband had this favorite milk cow he named Myrtle, a Guernsey with horns, but they were curved in, not sticking out. He had taken me to the airport to fly to Minneapolis to visit family and friends, and he came back and he saw that his pet cow had calved. It was springtime. He went out and he thought, Well, this year I'm going to separate the calf from her—take the calf away and just milk her once a day. Put her in the barn and separate the calf at night, milk her in the mornings and in the daytime turn the calf out in the pasture with her, and the calf would suckle the cow, milk her. Well, the problem was—he was in his seventies already—he found he really didn't have the strength to carry a pretty big calf up hills to the barn. So he set the calf down and picked up a little stick and was poking the calf along in front of him. The cow was tagging along of course, and when they got up to the barn, she turned like a mad bull, came at him, rammed him up against the side of the chestnut-sided barn, and he fell. And then she didn't stop. She came at him again and again and again and trampled him. Broke literally about half of his ribs, and two lobes of the lung were punctured. Then she left him laying there, and backed off with her calf.

So, he lay there and he thought, Well, one neighbor up on the hill—didn't think that they were going to see him. It was too far away, and then, the husband and wife there would go to work, and maybe they were gone. So he lay there in great pain and he decided, Well, I'm just gonna lay here. I'm gonna die here.

Then he decided, despite everything, he would crawl up quite a slope, up the pasture from the barn to a gate, and be able to get through the gate and across the road. The house was sitting there, a little rise up to the basement door—and he'd go in the house and he'd call. [When he reached the door] he thought, I'm not going to be able to climb the stairs to get to the phone—

So, he crawled back outside to our small car and he managed to pull himself up into it and he started it, but it was a shift and his shoulder had been so damaged by the cow that I guess it was dislocated, and his arm was swelling up like a balloon. So he just put his foot on the clutch and let it roll down the grade to the road.

He thought, Well, nobody's gonna see me in [the car]. So he let himself out, laid on the ground at the side of the road. One car came by, and he was kind of calling out, "Help!"

They slowed down but they drove right on. A second car came by, a van, and it slowed down, but it didn't stop. But it did go on down the road [to] a small house with a couple there, and the young man, Bill Frost, came out, and the man in the van said, "There's an old man laying on the road up there, and I think he's hurt bad." So the neighbor ran to our house, found Sid laying there. Then he ran back, got his wife to call an ambulance. The ambulance came and carried Sid about a half a dozen miles to the local school, and then they called a helicopter from a Knoxville Hospital, and he was airlifted to the hospital.

He was there in the hospital for at least six weeks. He was an older man, in his seventies. He had a lot of fight in him. Otherwise he probably would've died. He managed to recover. He came home. I still had that cow, Myrtle, out there, and I said, "Well, we really need to sell her, Sid."

He would look out the window but he wouldn't look at the cow. And I'd say, "You know, we really—" and he wouldn't hear of selling her.

So, that was quite an accident, but Sid did recover. One of his daughters came and stayed with me, and we nursed him back. He came through it. *(Alma)*

Moonie and Beth liked each other.

We never had any cattle, except one time Ray was out somewhere visiting a local guy, and one of his cows had calved and then died. So there was an orphan calf, and the man asked Ray if he wanted the calf, so Ray brought home this calf, and she was a pet, really. I bottle-fed her for the first six or eight months of her life. Her name was Moonie, she was born in the full moon in the month of May. She came to her name. You could go "Moonie," [making a mooing sound] and she would come running. She was a really, really sweet animal. She was like a dog, she would lick you to show affection, and they have these really rough tongues that are really the strangest sensation when she'd lick you, but you knew what it was about. She was just really, really sweet. We didn't keep her and we didn't slaughter her. We didn't have enough pasture, so we gave her to our neighbor, who had a bunch of cows. He'd have his cows on one field for a certain amount of weeks or months and then he'd move 'em.

I hadn't seen her for probably a couple of years. One day I was out behind our barn, and I saw that he had his cows in a bowl-shaped area at the edge of our property. So I walked out to the fence line and I was looking at all the cows, and I thought, I wonder if Moonie is still alive.

She could have been taken to slaughter a long time ago. I didn't have any idea, but I just thought, I'm gonna see if Moonie's there. So I started calling. I said "Moonie," and at first several cows looked up and they kinda looked at me strange. You know, What are you doing? And then they'd go back to eating. So I just stood there and I kept saying "Moonie, Moonie!"

Eventually there was this cow that was way up on top of the ridge, at the top of the bowl, and I was in the bottom of the bowl, and this cow came running down the holler, right up to me! It was Moonie! She started licking me; she remembered me! I had no idea that cows were like dogs in that sense that they would have a memory for that attachment. *(Beth)*

Horses were an important part of many lives. The women enjoyed riding them, caring for them, or just seeing them in the pasture. Horses worked on several of their farms, and breeding them brought income.

We had a Morgan stallion, beautiful animal, and I also had a Morgan mare that I had bought as a yearling. We raised some Morgan stock out of them. We also had work horses because we did farm with the horses. *(Lee)*

We had the pony and the horse. The pony was Diamond, and the other one was Bernie. She was an Arabian that [my daughter] Alyson won in an essay contest. The thing about it was, as beautiful as the horse was, it was not trained. So we had to take it somewhere and pay some money to get it trained. We didn't have much money back in those days, and it took a lot of money. It was expensive to keep that horse. It got its "nails" done—I've never had my nails done! But it was beautiful, and Diamond was sweet too. *(Linda)*

[With] my last paycheck I got a horse. It was a three hundred dollar paycheck; I got a horse with a baby. Well, she was a big, roan-colored mare. She was very tall and it was hard to get on her, and I didn't have a saddle for her. I really couldn't get on her very well. I'd take her out, and our hillside was "terraced" [from cows traversing the steep hillside], so I'd get up on the terrace, on one of the "steps," and jump on her. *(Karen)*

[Local quip: The terracing is why cows have shorter legs on one side.] So Karen sold the roan mare.

She was a little bit wild, so we took her to market. I sold her at First Monday [Market, in Morristown], and I got a smaller pony-type horse with a saddle, and then also a calf, and a bag of feed for the horse.

So I had the horse, his name was Wildfire, and he was shoed, so I could take him out on the road. He was somethin' you could just jump on without having to step on something. *(Karen)*

Sandra and her husband loved their horse Duke, and Duke loved them, but also their neighbor, Miss Lemons. Duke was gettin' out all the time, my big horse. He was one of those horses that was gonna make us not nice neighbors because he kept gettin' out! We'd fix fences and we'd do everything we could, and he'd still find a way to get out. But I think that was because he was by himself. Duke loved Miss Lemons down there. He would go straight to her house and stay, and it drove that poor lady crazy. We had a Great Pyrenees, and if Duke took off, the Pyrenees went with him to guard him. Duke was like sixteen hands high. He wasn't needing guarding, but— *(Sandra)*

Horses were capable of doing a lot of work, such as logging and tilling.

We had first a mustang. They would have these round-ups and they would gather up a bunch of [wild] mustangs and ship 'em across the country, and I think they shipped 'em by train to middle Tennessee. Ray, my husband, had to drive quite a ways to pick 'em up. That was the horse we used for logging the hills to get our lumber, and also we used the horse in the garden for plowing and disking. We had an old-timey manure spreader, and the horse pulled that. We had a tractor, but we did use the horse for a lot of those things in the early years. Later on we got another mustang. *(Beth)*

The mustangs were courtesy of the Bureau of Land Management's Horse and Burro Adoption Program, which still exists.

Some homesteaders had work animals.

We had a pony, Buddy, a work pony that would pull a plow. He'd pull a skid to pull logs, or stones and stuff. He was a really neat animal. I ended up using him as a lesson pony. He was just the world's greatest pony! He was a good little pony. [My husband] Steven had a bit of a problem with him. He would get on, just hop on and [ride] bareback, and Buddy would take off and scrape him off on something. Yeah, [against a tree], or a fencepost or most anything. Some people came to visit us once. They had all these little kids, and they all wanted to ride the pony, so I was lettin' 'em ride him. There were two of 'em on him at once, and I think I had a bridle on him. They were all bareback. Evidently he got tired, 'cause he'd just swing right around the corner of the house and just scrape them right off—but, they were okay. The main reason we got him was 'cause he would pull a plow. He was very good. He skidded logs. He hauled rocks on an upside-down car hood. The only complaint I had about him, we had a television antenna that was up be-hind our house, and it was actually in his pasture. We didn't get very many stations, and sometimes we'd be watching something and the picture would go. He'd be up there scratching his butt or something on the antenna, and it would be going like that [waves arm]. It was, "Buddy! Stop that!" *(Trudie)*

Kate worked but had an attitude.

We started out with a pony, and the pony didn't work well for pulling the plow. Then we had a mule, and working with a mule is a lot of work. You're on the ground and traveling and geeing and hawing and all that stuff. [My husband Bert] had a turning plow and a disk and everything that was horse-drawn. Well, Kate the mule got real stubborn and wouldn't go, wouldn't work. She would just lay down. A neighbor made a sled out of huge hickory runners for us that we could actually get up the hollow with before we actually got the road built up the hollow. Kate would lay down on those rocks, behind the sled, in the middle of the hollow, and she wouldn't get up. Would not get up! We'd have to go and round up some people, round up some guys, and help get the mule off the ground—make her, push her up 'cause she wouldn't "giddup"—literally. *(Cece)*

What's next? A horse, of course!

Bert kinda had it with the mule after that last episode, and he sold the mule and got a wonderful, sweet workhorse he named Otis, after Otis Redding. But we did get a tractor. So we had the horse and the tractor. The horse was really great for cultivating between the rows with the cultivator—at one point we had four thousand tomato plants. *(Cece)*

Besides being smart and strong and stubborn, mules can be dangerous—like Raymond.

Well, this one morning, for some reason Raymond just turned around and just whacked me in my ribs, and threw me. I mean the kick just knocked me across the barn floor. It was a kick that I knew was bad. I was finally able to get myself up and put him in his stall and close the door. And with that I pretty much just collapsed. Luckily within maybe a half-an-hour, forty-five minutes, John did come down to the barn, and he loaded me up, and we went to the emergency room. At the emergency room he was answering for me 'cause I really could hardly talk. Finally they're rolling me into my own little room and then loading me up to get an MRI 'cause I was hurtin' really, really bad. This nurse is wheeling along with me, and she's being so sweet, and she said, "So, what happened?" I said, "Well, Raymond, [whispers as if in pain] Raymond ended up kicking me in my ribs." She patted me very kindly and said, "Is Raymond related to you?" *(Lee)*

Words for creatures that are wide: hogs, pigs, piggies, piglets. Those words make most people smile. But swine have a dark side: ponderous, voracious omnivores; intelligent but wily; and heavy, weighing up to eight hundred pounds. For the homesteaders raising pigs was a practical matter.

I raised pigs, from the goat milk—the whey from the goat cheese. *(Alicia)*

> We had hogs, raised hogs, sold piggies. Once a year we'd butcher a hog. *(Lee)*

To raise hogs and market piggies, they first had to transport the sow to be bred.

> Yeah, [it's hard to load a pig into a truck], because she doesn't want to go. We put a rope around her foot, and then tried to drag her [walking], to get her to go the way you wanted her to go. We would get behind her, to scare her—push her along. *(Pat)*

> After breeding, the sow farrowed, or gave birth. She needed a farrowing pen. That whole pig project was fun, and we didn't know anything about it! We read the books; that's what we always did. Then we'd start to try to fix a place where she was gonna have the baby in the shed across the road. We built this farrowing pen, from the Boy Scouts' [pamphlets]. *(Pat)*

Neighbors gave advice and relatives helped.

> Once [the sow] was in labor, she started making a nest, and broke the farrowing pen. The neighbors said, "She'll try to kill the babies." So, I stayed with her till two o'clock in the morning. Pigs come out—baby pigs come out—running. They don't come out like a puppy or a kitten; they come out running! So, I'm trying to gather up all these pigs. She eventually had twelve. And she wasn't trying to kill the pigs—she was trying to kill me for holding her pigs! My family were here visiting. The neighbor said that the baby pigs would follow their mother. She didn't say they had to be a certain age. So, we opened up the pen. She

came out. We started driving her and the babies over here, to the big pig pen in the back. And then, all the babies wouldn't follow. So we started, my brother-in-law and myself, trying to pick up the baby pigs, and they started screaming. So, she came back ready to kill us! So, he says to all his kids, "Get on the porch!" So anyway, we eventually got them all in the back, but that was his pig story, I'm sure, for the rest of his life. *(Alicia)*

Once Alicia bought a baby pig to raise. It was a frequent escapee.

A couple of times we went and got the [runaway] pig, put it in the little pen, not realizing that the pig was tiny, and could run through the [large-]mesh wire. And then I'd scream because I'd spent forty dollars on a pig, and it's gone! Then I'd come back, and there—there was the pig! So, I put it across the road in the barn, and locked it in a stall. Then it got so big, I couldn't get it out and carry it back to the pig pen. So this man, very innocent, came by, and I said to him, "Could you help me with a pig?" He was all dressed up in city clothes, and he said, "Well, I never touched a pig!" He helped me catch the pig in the pen, and I carried it by its back legs, and we put it half in a wheel barrow. I held the legs, and he wheeled the wheel barrow down to the pig pen. I'm sure that was *his* pig story! *(Alicia)*

Karen took little piggies to market.

When you take 'em to market, you have to cut their tails off. You have a bottle of alcohol, and you have some scissors—and you cut 'em, and they squeak. You just cut it right off and clean the scissors and cut. When they're in a big truck together, and they're waggin' their tails; if one bit the other, it would bleed, and they would attack it. So, a little mob thing goin' on there. So, you just did that ahead of time. Yeah, like a week ahead. It would be healed. A usual animal auction house would have really tall fences and gates, and everything. Well, in a pig auction house, [there are] baby pigs, and there are tiny fences. It looks like a miniature auction house, and all these little pigs stream up and down. Yeah, like in a maze. They're so cute. But [the dealers] just buy 'em, and pay you, and that's it. Then they put 'em in a big truck and that's where the tail thing comes into play. *(Karen)*

Not only did Karen like raising pigs, she kept a pig as a pet on two occasions.

Now one time I kept a little pet pig. It had been cut in the shoulder by either its mother or something, and so I called Doc Slaughter [the veterinarian, really!], and I said, "I got this pig. He's cut. Can you come out and stitch him up?"

And he said, "No, just slap some Vaseline in the hole, and put him back."

And I'm like, "I can't. They crawl all over each other."

So I couldn't put him back, we actually stitched 'm up, and I kept him as a bottle-fed pig. I'd just run out and call, "Pet Pig!" and he'd come out, and get his bottle. Then one day, we were gonna take the litter off to the market, and he was not eating and he was not drinking. I picked him up to carry him down to the pond to cool him down, and he walked out into the pond and drank and drank and drank and died. I carried him back to the house. He sounded like a little water bottle. He sloshed around. It was terrible! I'm not sure whether we might have given him tetanus, by stitching him up ourselves. But that was the story of Pet Pig.

Karen's second story about a pet pig is not for the faint of heart and/or vegetarian.

> One time I kept a little boy pig, and I gave a little girl pig to my neighbor, Lon. I took it down and put it in his shed on Christmas Eve, so when he woke up Christmas he'd have a new pig in his shed. And his wife [Anna Rae] said he went out there, and he was talkin' to it and said, "Where did you come from?" Lon raised that pig. She was Susie Sow, and I had Spanky. And last minute before butchering he wanted Spanky instead of the sow. So I gave him Spanky. He was a big ol' pig. And came time to butcher 'm, he had [his son] Hugh Matt kill 'm.
>
> We're sitting there butchering him, and I cut my finger. And it just—I don't know whether—I don't know—They had Spanky's head sitting over in a bucket lookin' at me!
>
> Anna Rae called me in to have some breakfast. She had made some tenderloin, fresh tenderloin. Yep, pig tenderloin. Fresh! I go back out. Spanky's still lookin' at me! His head's in the bucket. And I actually turned green and got very sick.
>
> But yeah, Spanky was mine. Hmm. So we had Susie Sow and raised her. No stitches in my finger, it just cut the tip off and it grew back. *(Karen)*

The last step in the pig-raising process is butchering. Not all the families, even stalwarts like Karen, did the butchering themselves. "We sent 'em out and had 'em slaughtered, or sold 'em, just sold 'em," she said.

> My neighbor helped me two or three times, and then other times I brought [the hogs] to a slaughter house. I cried, "Please, take good care of my Red." *(Alicia)* ["Red" was the Red Duroc she raised.]

> I've always—not entirely—but mostly, been vegetarian since I was about sixteen or so. Beef, I would eat not much, but maybe a little bit. Then I was with a man that was from here, and butchering is pretty much standard here. I did [help him] as a matter of practicality. It's just more a matter of getting something done that needed to be done, and the need for food. I know that's why I've raised hogs here, a lot of it. The last one we did, my dogs got all of the bacon, and they got all of the ribs, and there was a whole lot of that meat that went to my dogs. I'm very happy to have my dogs to have it. Very healthy for them. They love it, the bones and stuff. *(Anne)*

> Killing a hog is a mess. We didn't do it ourselves. But, the first one, we were gonna hire this man that does that here. They'd hardly charge anything in those days. But he couldn't do it, so he sent his nephew, and his nephew wasn't quite the expert that he had been. You have to get the water a certain temperature [just hot enough to scrape the hair off]. We had sold some of the pork already. There were these two nuns that we knew, and they'd ordered some pork. And there was a couple down the road that were sort of "gourmets," and she wanted to make her

own pork sausages, and she wanted to use the intestines. So that was a whole-day thing, and went into the night. But we finally got it done! *(Pat)*

Rendering the lard is part of the process in which nothing is wasted.

The whole beginning of doing hogs was helping the locals do theirs—the killing, the gutting, and then the shaving of them, the rendering of the lard. They have these five-gallon buckets that they call lard buckets. We would render this lard and it would be just this pure white lard. I'd put it in this five-gallon bucket, and put it in the root cellar. There was no preservative in it. There was no anything. And it would just stay as white and clean and not ever rancid or anything. I'd use it for everything. It was great! *(Lee)*

You just put all that fat in your big pot—and you just cook it down for a long time. You just keep stirrin' it, and eventually, it just turns this beautiful, very light golden liquid, and then you pour it into a jar—like a half-gallon jar—and keep it in a cool place. Well, back then I used it, so anytime I cooked cornbread, I would use the lard in it, and I would just use it generally, 'specially if I was out of a different kind of oil. It just makes delicious gravy. *(Anne)*

In general, butchering animals was economical.

When you butcher, you utilized everything. You certainly tanned the hides, but I sure boiled a lot of bones in my life, made all the stock, and canned meat, too. You name it. We tried a beef;

we did a hog every year. Wild meat, too. I guess I've tried just about everything—not rats!—possums, groundhogs, snakes. *(Lee)*

Some women simply removed themselves from the slaughtering and butchering stage, as when Sherri told her husband she would, instead, go to town. The carnivores among them recognized the benefit of raising one's own chickens, cows, and pigs. As Karen said, "You know, we had a lotta meat in the freezer!" Most of the women who arrived here were young and inexperienced. The penning and fencing, and feeding and breeding of animals was hard work, and terrible events deeply affected the homesteaders. Managing animals can be exasperating at times, too, but the affection of the women for their animals is clear. The integration of the care of animals into their daily routines, not to mention lessons learned from adventures with animals, challenged the families, but also—from Moonie the cow to Buddy the work-pony and Pet Pig—enriched their lives.

> I am an animal lover. I really think I like animals most of the time better than people. *(Lee)*

Chapter Eleven

"Just Somethin' to Get Around In"

Living twenty miles from the nearest grocery store, Pat and Alicia were quite isolated, especially in the Seventies and Eighties.

> Well, this road was a dirt road, and it was rutted. I remember our mailman, he kept saying, "Write to your congressman, please! My back is killing me!" He came from Clinchport [Virginia]; that was our post office at that time. So, anyway, it was rutted. The first winter we were here, it was horrible. I mean, we never got out! The neighbor came and said, "Whadda-ya need?"
>
> We said, "A candy bar!" *(Alicia)*

In the 1970s, the only paved roads were (1) three state highways that crossed Clinch Mountain, and (2) Clinch Valley Road, which ran parallel with the mountain on the north side for about thirty miles. In winter, there was no maintenance by county highway departments to keep the gravel roads open. The bumpy tracks took a toll on the vehicles that the women's families could afford. Hardly anyone had one of the newer four-wheel drive vehicles. Some women were especially isolated.

The would-be homesteaders had arrived in vehicles that included Volkswagen vans, a school bus painted metallic blue, a school bus painted gold, and a van pulling a pickup with a dog and her four puppies. As they began their homesteading life, if they could afford it, their first vehicle was likely to be a practical pickup truck, unless they just used their VW bug for goat-hauling. So what were their vehicles like?

> Mostly, at first, old trucks; then, old cars. Old cars and old trucks. None of them were my favorites. They were just somethin' to get around in. *(Janet)*

> For the longest time we had only one vehicle. It was really like the situation with the wife barefoot at home with the children. And Bill going out to work, in his pickup truck. *(Yvonne)*

> They were like the "Clinch Mountain Specialties." Many different kinds—whatever John could sort of jury-rig together. We had a Dodge truck, but it was missing some letters on the front, so we called it Dog. We had a big, white [Plymouth] Belvedere station wagon, that we got for three hundred dollars. The fender was all crashed in, but it was great. It had a [V-8] 318 engine in it, and we could load up the soccer team into the thing and off we'd go. We called it "The Ambulance" 'cause it was white with red interior. That was a great vehicle! Three hundred bucks! We never paid more than three hundred dollars for a vehicle, if that. At one point we had nineteen vehicles—extra for parts—hanging around. My poor mother—who did not really think that I was living up to my potential living here in the hills of Tennessee—she came to visit and was just appalled. But listen, you could get a radiator out of one, you could get the top end,

you could get the block out of another. All this stuff that you could get! *(Lee)*

Cece and her husband would pack up their produce for market in their two pickup trucks, and each drive to separate markets. They probably had the most reliable pickups.

We had a white sixty-five GMC pickup truck and it was "Betsy." Then we bought another, I think a GMC Sierra. It was gold with the brown wood like on the side and we called her "Goldie." They were in good shape, but back then there were no seat belts or carseats or anything. I would let the girls sit down on the floorboard of the truck while I was driving, 'cause they would get thrown the least from that space. *(Cece)*

Oopie and Doopie were a pair of pickups. (Convenient for parts to ensure that there is at least one running vehicle.) Gary had two rusted Toyota trucks, when I first met him. And the dogs would ride in 'em, and their heads were out either side. He bought 'em real cheap from the Florida Keys, because the saltwater had rusted out the bottoms. Those were the first trucks that we could see the road running by underneath as we went along. Then there was the Falcon station wagon. Gary had it repainted from this kind of an old red, to a sea-foam and white, and it looked wonderful. The only trouble was, the inside of it had this cloth ceiling that kept coming down, so we would have to duct-tape it back up. It was only in the summer it would come down. Then we would be on our backs, in the back of the station wagon, boiling in the sun, trying to stick the duct tape up, stick the ceiling back up there. *(Nancy)*

Vehicles had their quirks.

> No heat in that old truck, and I remember just absolutely freezing to death. *(Janet)*

> [Moving from California] we were packin' up all our goods in this Volkswagen van that you had to have a bungee cord to hold the shifter in fourth gear and we started heading east. *(Cece)*

No brakes?

> Can you imagine, driving around with no brakes? How about ones that had no doors? Or ones that had no floor boards? "Maiden of the Mist"—when it would rain, it would rain inside the truck. You had to have windshield wipers on the inside of the truck, not the outside! *(Lee)*

> I remember one [truck], I went over to Pumpkin Valley and stalled going on a hill, and you had to lift the hood, open the carburetor, stick a screwdriver in it, and start it again. But I was on a hill and didn't think of backing down the hill, till—You have to scotch it! [Put a wedge behind the back wheel.] Did that a lot. *(Karen)*

> Rick and I had a Chevy—those big Chevy SUVs. They're like the first SUV ever, and they're really good cars, and we brought it from California. We would use that 'cause we could fit everybody in it. 'Course it didn't have seat belts or anything, but, who needs seat belts when you're packed in like sardines? *(Carolyn)*

Clinch Mountain Girls

For one family, no seat belts? No problem.

> When we first moved from California to here, we moved in a bare-bones Land Rover. We had a two-by-six nailed down in the back with three car seats screwed into the two-by-six, bolted to the board. That was our first transportation. *(Judy)*

A missing part? Maybe it was simply relocated.

> One thing we couldn't get [a part for] was this Dodge Dart. The gas tank started leaking. So John took the gas tank from out of it and put a gas tank—from a totally different car—into the trunk. He forgot to tell me. He told me it was fixed, but he didn't tell me that you had to open the trunk and put the gas into the gas tank in the trunk. So I'm down there at Charlie Burton's [country store] gettin' gas, and I realize in the first minute that there's this "shhhh" sound, and there's gas being poured all over the ground. Charlie Burton's freakin' out you know, and I'm goin' like, "Oh my God, what's going on here?" *(Lee)*

One truck was a prize winner!

> We had a truck which we got a really good deal on. It ran really well, but one time Bill entered into a contest in Rogersville and he got the first prize for Ugliest Truck. It was a hazard to drive, but we did it over the mountain and anywhere. It was a big truck and hauled a lotta wood. *(Dianna)*

Some trucks had plenty of room, even for livestock in the cab.

> We picked up calves from the market in that four-door truck. We put a piece of plywood between the front seat and the back seat [the calf was too young to ride standing in the truck bed by itself], and this one calf didn't like it at all. The whole way home we could hear the drumbeat of its hooves. A lot of calves do settle down, but that one was feisty; it didn't. *(Nancy)*

Some cars were basically pickups.

> We once went to the stock pen over in Greeneville, and brought back two calves in a Maverick, two little milk-stock calves to raise. They were just peaceful, and quiet as they could be. They just stayed there. *(Anne)*

> We'd go in our little Volkswagen and pick grain up, get the feed. *(Alicia)*

However, sometimes a load is too bulky for a Bug.

> I know we gave [people] a laugh. I grew soybeans, or soy hay, for my goats. And I cut the stuff, and I dragged it home—on a shower curtain. Along the road, hauling a shower curtain. So, wouldn't you laugh? *(Alicia)*

Back then the VW was popular, but not with Joanne.

> I had a truck for a while, it was kind of a "hybrid." Looked like a Volkswagen car from the front, but it had a truck bed in the back. I was afraid that I would have some kind of malfunction. I could get to Rogersville—that was twenty or thirty minutes—and

get the groceries and do the laundry and do the errands. But going further to get better prices on food, or sales? No, no way! *(Joanne)*

Trading up is an ideal that sometimes just transforms into a deal.

We bought a great big Oldsmobile in Morristown, Tennessee. I think we paid seven hundred dollars for it. [Then] we realized that car was way too big to traverse a lot of the roads around where we lived, so we ended up taking that back up to Ohio and selling it for fifteen hundred dollars, so that gave us an extra income for the month. *(Dianna)*

Lauren's first car, ever, hits an unexpected bump (or two).

It was a sweet little car. It was older, but it was in perfect shape. I drove it home, but I diligently parked it. I didn't have the money to get a license plate for it, and to get insurance for it, so I didn't touch it for a couple of weeks. Then I had the money to do that, and got the license [plate] put on it, and went to visit my neighbor, Pat Grimsley, who was a great friend. We visited for a couple of hours, and as I was about to leave, she had her head poked into the window, leaning down talking to me, and she said, "Oh, Lauren, didn't you need to make a phone call?" I said, "Oh, yeah." I didn't have a telephone. She says, afterwards, that she saw me put the car in Park. I went and made my phone call, came back out, and here was Mrs. Grimsley to greet me, and she's coming towards me, saying, "Oh, Lord. Oh-h, Lord!" I didn't know what "Oh, Lord" meant, but I didn't see my car. Now, Mrs. Grimsley lives on top of a very tall hill. And my car had, apparently, jumped out of Park, and had gone down that hill. So, I followed what I could, because there were trees down. It was a hillside full of half-grown cedar trees. I followed where those were down, but there must have been long sections where it must have just been flying through the air. But it came down on all four wheels, at the bottom of this—it was a very great distance. I felt sick. I felt, probably, that it was one of the worst days of my life. I finally found it at the very bottom of this very steep hill, and behind a barn that was down on a whole 'nother road. Boots Greer came with his tow-truck, and was able to get it out, and it drove! It was totally out of alignment. But afterwards, we took it to Michigan twice. We took it to tree-planting down South, for a whole winter, and it was a good little car; it served us well for several years. *(Lauren)*

As in the case of the dwellings they started with, the women's fortitude and sense of humor helped them cope. But was there a limit to the abuse that the vehicles—and the women who drove them—could take?

The dump truck tipped toward one side [at the pond's edge], and [my husband] went and got the bulldozer. He said, "Now, I'm gonna pull it this way. Now, you just get in there, and when it starts to come—" And I'm like, "I don't, I don't think I wanna do that." I said, "I'll tell you what, this is the best I'll do for you: I'm gonna stand here on the running board and reach in, and the minute it's lookin' shaky, I'll jump off." Which actually, in retrospect, I think, was the worst plan. But, it's been like that a lotta times: "You can do it! Just hop up there, and steer the dump truck when I get it flipped back up." I was relieved we were both alive. I said, "We're okay. We came through that unscathed." Because he has gotten the truck or the tractor or something wedged up against a tree, or stuck on a rock, or something down, all over this farm, and if we didn't have the bulldozer to pull everything out, guess we'd still have equipment all over the farm. *(Trudie)*

Where is that limit?

One truck we had, John said, "I'm gonna put a new engine in that one." So, he says, "Lee, you drive it on up here." Had no engine, there was nothing in this thing! It was just a shell. So he said, "I'm gonna pull [tow] this truck to the top of the hill there. I've got it set up that I can put an engine in it." So we're cresting out at the top of the hill. Oh, let me back up. This is a truck that the doors, they wouldn't open, so we had to climb in and out of the back window. We had no back window [glass]; we climbed in and out of the back window. So we're cresting out on the hill, and all of a sudden the chain breaks that's pulling me up the hill! There's no brakes! There's no brakes on this vehicle! There's no engine! There's no anything, except the drive shaft is like laying in place. So he's yelling as this thing is going down backwards down the hill, and he's yelling, "Jump, jump!" And I'm going like, "What, what? Out the back door, out the back window? How do you jump?" Oho-o! Jump for joy, here. So I went—I, I, I crashed pretty bad. And this, this drive shaft came through—and took a piece off my elbow—and into the back of the seat. I mean, if I had been sitting where it's—it would have, like, gone through me! Those are the vehicles we had—but we're alive to tell those stories! *(Lee)*

Chapter Twelve

A Woman's Work: Childbirth

The stalwart women who managed livestock and drove old vehicles showed their strength in another way—childbirth. They moved to the country to experience a natural, simple life, raising their own food organically, heating with wood, and drinking spring water. Many aspired as well to a natural birthing for their children. That concept included home birth.

> I didn't know anything about pregnancy! I didn't know anything about childbirth, how that worked. But I knew that I wanted to be the one to have control over that experience for myself, and I just didn't want to go do that in a place like a hospital. *(Micki)*

Of the two dozen women interviewed, six were childless, and two already had all their children before moving to Tennessee. Of the remainder, ten actually experienced home birth. The rest gave birth in hospitals—some by choice, others by necessity.

> [My daughters] were both born in hospitals. I really didn't know some of the midwives around at that time. Hadn't crossed their paths yet.

But then, too, I was an older mother "by standards." It might have been safer for me to be where—if somethin' could happen. *(Linda)*

I had decided, since I was already thirty-eight years old, that I was not gonna take a chance on anything, and I was gonna have my son Adam in the hospital. *(Nancy)*

Cece wanted a home birth, and started her planning on the way east. She visited The Farm Midwifery Center, founded by Ina May Gaskin, in Middle Tennessee.

We went there and I was checked out by the midwives. We stayed there for several weeks, and we decided we had to start going, looking for a place [to live]. We had several months before I really needed to be there. They want you to be there about six weeks before your due date. And of course they wanted me to keep up my prenatal care, which I did with the [Hancock] County Health Department when I came here. *(Cece)*

Sometimes the best-laid plans—

[My first daughter] became Melissa [May] because of Ina May. I wanted to honor her in helping me through my birth, which was not the easiest. Ended up having a Caesarean, taking me to the hospital. I rode an hour in the ambulance, holding the [midwives'] hands, and the actual doctor that did the C-section permitted the midwives, Ina May Gaskin, and a lady named Cara, to be in the operating room with me. I was allowed to stay awake. I had a spinal [epidural anesthetic], and I squeezed their hands with all my might the whole time. I thought I must have broken both their hands, because I was so petrified and afraid the baby wasn't going to be okay. I wanted to know right away if she was okay, so I wanted to stay awake. They were very kind to let the midwives, who had been with me through my twelve or fourteen hours of labor by then, to come in the operating room and be there for the birth and support me emotionally. That was very unusual. It was Vanderbilt University Hospital, Dr. David Acker. *(Cece)*

For Vicki, The Farm Midwifery Center was a secure and happy first experience with birthing.

We decided we liked the philosophy of the home births at The Farm, where we had gotten married. So we contacted them. They were very liberal, and it was free, as long as we worked while we were there. So, we went to The Farm and had [our baby]. It was a good experience. At the time, the midwives would just come to the house that you were staying in, and deliver, with help. [We went there] probably a couple of weeks to a month [before the due date]. I don't remember accurately about that. Jerome worked on the wood crew, and I helped in the kitchen. My second child, Annie, was also born there, and that was like twenty months later. They were good experiences. Very, very nice. I never did want any medication or anything like that. I wanted to fully experience my births. The midwives were very sweet and helpful, and my husband Jerome was there. *(Vicki)*

The Farm had an environmental and human rights program, Plenty International. While away for a while from her own farm in Clinch Valley, Yvonne availed herself of its services.

> With Sabino, I had a home birth. When we lived in Tacoma Park [Maryland], in D.C., there was a sort of a small hub of "Plenty people," who did midwifery. Mary Beth, I think was her name, who had learned her midwifery from Ina May [Gaskin] from Plenty, I had my birth with her. I visited them regularly. So, in Tacoma Park, Sabino got born, in an apartment on the seventeenth floor. It was a good birth. *(Yvonne)*

Back in the Clinch Valley, Nancy, Robyn and Lauren received prenatal care from the Hawkins County Certified Nurse Midwife, Ellen Hartung, who also assisted Nancy and Robyn in the hospital.

> [My daughter] Ellen was born in the hospital, Holston Valley. I think it's about fifty miles or so to Kingsport [Tennessee]. It's about an hour drive. There was a midwife from Rogersville who helped deliver her and there was an intern, really good guy. *(Robyn)*

In preparation for her first baby's hospital birth, Nancy saw a lay midwife, too.

> Carolyn was my birthing coach, and she was a lay midwife, and helped birth many children.
>
> When I went into labor and my water broke, I said, "I've gotta make a call, and find out when I should get Carolyn to come over here." Our phone was out of order. Of course it was! So I had to go to my neighbor's house, Dianna's, and use her phone. Then Carolyn came to my house and waited with me, and my labor went on, and on, and on. Finally we decided I wasn't progressing enough, so we went to the hospital, and it still was many hours. A

> Nurse Midwife came in, a credentialed midwife [Ellen Hartung]. They eventually decided I probably needed to find out why [the labor] wasn't progressing. So I had an x-ray, and they determined that my baby was too big [for a normal birth]. So they scheduled a C-section, which did not happen for an hour and a half, because it took that long for the anesthesiologist to get there. *(Nancy)*

Some women had had home births before they arrived in the valley.

> They were all born at home—our three in California were born at home—and then my fourth one was born at home when I was in Ohio. *(Judy)*

Carolyn also birthed her son, Joseph, with the midwives in California. Most of the rest of the home births for this group of women in Clinch Valley were attended by Carolyn as the midwife, but there were a few other midwives in the area.

> April was born here in this house. I loved being at home and having a birth at home. She was born on April twentieth, in the springtime, very good time to have a baby, very good! I also had my dear, dear friend Joanne being the midwife for it. It really was wonderful to have friends. So it was John, and myself, and Geri Lou [Kitchens] and Joanne [Irvin]. With my little team, yeah, it really was [a good experience]. *(Lee)*

Joanne worked as the only Registered Nurse in the thirty-two-bed Sneedville Hospital including in obstetrics. She had had a midwife at her second daughter's birth, at Holston Valley Hospital and later became a Certified Nurse Midwife herself. Joanne was present also at the first of Karen's birthings.

> Jesse was born on Shortt Road. We had that small house, and Joanne [Irvin] and Marthine Thomas delivered Jesse, and Lee [Hoellman] was there, and a girl named Sherry Arvo was there. I had the baby, but I retained my placenta, and we had to go to the hospital. So we left Lee alone with the newborn baby; went into the hospital, Joanne went in also. The doctor was not very nice to me and actually stitched me up without anesthesia and got mad at me. They tried to put gas on me and I didn't want it. So, anyway, they gave me a shot of ergot of rye, and so the placenta came out. Went on home, and there's Lee, sitting in the rocking chair with the newborn. And so, that was the first one. *(Karen)*

Despite the attitude and reprimand by the doctor for attempting a home birth, Karen was determined that the next birth also would be assisted by a midwife. Fortunately, she found Etta Nichols, a lay midwife of some renown, about whom stories later appeared in *National Geographic* and *People Magazines,* and on NBC's *The Evening News with Tom Brokaw.*

> Elizabeth was born [in 1981] four years later [than Jesse], and she was born with a midwife, Etta Nichols, and that was in Del Rio, Tennessee, so we had to travel there to her house, and my sister-in-law took me. It was about forty-five minutes [from my house]. She was back in a country area. She had a birthing room, and that had a sink and a toilet, and an incubator, and two single beds. She said the only baby she'd lost was, um, the mother rolled over on it—she was big. She lost that baby. But otherwise she delivered like two thousand babies. Etta Nichols

was eighty-six. She charged fifteen dollars to deliver a baby, and we paid her double. She insisted on putting a belly-band on the baby [to prevent umbilical hernia] and dressing it in clothes that she already had. And feeding you breakfast. She put on a big spread on a big, round, oak table with all this food and then peaches in sweet syrup, and white bread. And Chippy, who's Elizabeth's dad, kept saying, "I think that's bad for her." And I said, "I think you better leave her alone, because she's eighty-six years old and she's fine." She had a lot of goats, so in between this-and-that delivering the baby she'd go out and feed her goats and come back and make breakfast. And charged fifteen dollars! To do it in her house! Her dad was a doctor and she went with him on some runs so that's how she learned how to do it. I retained my placenta, and she said, "Well, just sit on the toilet, and we'll shake the cord every once in awhile." And it came out fine—by itself. Yes! But she really calmed me down, didn't make me nervous. *(Karen)*

As these baby boomers in their child-bearing years landed in Clinch Valley, it was fortunate that one of the newcomers was herself a midwife in the making. Micki reintroduces her to us.

We moved here on October first of '77. The very next month I became pregnant with Zack. It was wonderful when I met the group of people that I met down here. That was perfection because here was a group of people who were also embracing things like natural childbirth, and a number of them wanting to have their children at home. One of them was Carolyn Novkov, and she had not yet acted as midwife, or caught any babies, but she had, out in California, done some studying, and was interested in it. When I knew I was pregnant, then I began seeking out, Who can help me with this?

So she and I began to talk, and there was another friend of ours who was also pregnant at the time whose baby was due a little bit before mine. Carolyn also agreed to help her, so we were the first two that Carolyn was working with. I was glad that there was somebody who was going to go before me! So I got a chance to hear about her experience, but I also read. My bible at the time when it came to the childbirth thing was *Spiritual Midwifery*, by Ina May Gaskin. I never went to The Farm, but many of my friends had been, and had had their children at the Midwifery Center there. Their information, coupled with what I was reading in *Spiritual Midwifery*, was basically what I had to go by. So, when the time came, Carolyn came and she was accompanied and assisted by Margaret [De Vos]. The two of them came over to the house, and guided me through that first long labor and childbirth. *(Micki)*

Carolyn had some training, although not hands-on, and had witnessed births. And she studied on her own.

Going back to Joseph's home birth [in California], that's when I became interested in lay midwifery 'cause I had two lay midwives. So, then I took some classes with them, and worked with them a little bit. Not enough, but a little bit, before we had to move, because Joseph was three months when we moved. I did [go to some home births] with them. So I got to witness them, but I didn't participate. I don't think I ever met [Ina May Gaskin]. I used to read her all the time. Her book, *Spiritual Midwifery*, was my bible, but I never did meet Ina May. I went to a couple classes in Nashville with some midwives, but I don't think she was ever there. I met some other midwives from The Farm. *(Carolyn)*

But learning-by-doing sounds hair-raising when human lives are in the balance.

The first time I had to deliver a baby I had to go to Copper Hill [Tennessee]. Where Patty and Oliver went. She was my first. So I had to leave home, and leave [my daughters] Sarah and Rachel with my husband Rick; took Joseph 'cause he was only a year, and went to live with them until the baby was coming. Then the baby was way overdue, so I was gone for like six weeks from home and very homesick. I was really missin' my kids so much. But I was committed. I'd promised I would do this, so I had to do it. This baby was probably at least ten pounds. He was a huge baby and [had] some dystocia, which means he was a little stuck. We had to turn him, and the mother had to stand up! She actually had to stand up to get this baby to come down, but he was okay. Yeah, it was really scary. Mm-hm, my first solo. You'd think I would have quit! Just spurred me on. A sense of adventure! A rush! And ah-h, at the end of it all there are so many stories. Some of 'em went so smoothly and beautifully—*most* of 'em—and people very happy and grateful. *(Carolyn)*

So, was that a typical home birth?

A typical one? There's no typical one. Well, gosh, they're all memorable. Just pick any of them. I mean the ones that you remember are the ones where you didn't know how this was going to turn out, be a little scary. We did have some emergencies in home births, but fortunately we never had to call—well, 911 didn't exist.

> I don't know what people did, but we just threw people in the car and took 'em! Took 'em to the hospital. *(Carolyn)*

The Clinch Valley itself is isolated, and the drive to a hospital took at least a half hour. Carolyn lived at the east end of the valley, while many of the mothers-to-be did not. Because most people lived on unpaved, narrow, winding back roads, it could take much more than thirty minutes for Carolyn to reach a woman in labor, or to get her to a hospital in an emergency.

> Most of them were remote. You know, Micki lived out on the Clinch River. Because they were all back-to-the-land people, most of them, they were pretty remote. Vickie and Jerome [during one birth] lived out in Washburn, up in the mountain there; some people lived on the river. *(Carolyn)*

Micki's third child was due in the winter, when driving could be dicey.

> Luke was born here in this "mansion" house that has the running water and the insulation in the walls. He was born on New Year's Day, so it was a good thing. But Carolyn almost didn't make it to that birth because the roads were so icy, and [her husband] Rick had to drive her out in the middle of the night. Really, really icy roads, and the roads around here, when they're iced over, you generally don't go, so it was one of those when nobody would have gone anywhere, except for an emergency.
>
> So I'm deeply indebted to her for coming out. We were all being watched over somehow, someway, because everything turned out wonderfully. *(Micki)*

Confidence and experience go a long way in dealing with a dangerous situation and turning it around.

Moriah, I was having at home at Green Road, and Lee, and Nancy, and Carolyn, and my friend Earline were there, and that's why Moriah's middle name is Caroleena. Carolyn said her heart rate was slowing down a little bit, so Lee took us into the hospital. It was Father's Day, and the doctor was out to eat. He came in and said, "I gotta change my suit." While he was changing his suit the nurses delivered Moriah, and I always say that I had Carolyn in a headlock because it was so bad. Moriah was nine pounds two ounces but I had broken my tailbone in between the two births and I think it made it harder. So she was a rough one. She was born, I tell her, as blue as a Smurf, and as soon as I touched her, she pinked right up. She sorta had her cord around her neck a little bit. Then I spent the day in the hospital and my parents came and took me home. So that was good. *(Karen)*

Calm, sure judgment and firm words can save lives.

Timothy was my first child, and I didn't know what to expect. One morning I woke up—and gushed. It was two months yet before he was due. So, I went to Carolyn Novkov's, because she was my midwife, and she looked at me and she said, "I don't do preemies; you're going to the hospital—now." *(Lauren)*

Lauren was sent to Knoxville, but turned down an ambulance with some regret because of the expense. Although not in labor, she knew that she and the baby were now open to infection. The year was 1981, and Knoxville was in a frenzy of preparation for the World's Fair.

All the roads were different because of the World's Fair. So, we were terribly lost, and it had started to pour cats-and-dogs. Finally, my husband is right behind a cop car at a stop light, and he jumps out in the pouring rain, and says, "My wife's gonna have a baby!"

The policewoman turned that siren on, and we were at the hospital in probably less than two minutes. Then we just had to bide our time. At seven months, the baby is just starting to manufacture something called surfactant that is going to allow it to take its first breath, and the lungs' alveoli to stay open. And, I wasn't in labor, so I just lay there, and waited. So, that was Monday. [My friend] Patty had come with me. [She] brought me food. I don't know what I would have done without her, she was so good to me. She dropped everything. They were waiting for me to have a temperature, because that meant that I was finally starting an infection, and now it was time to take the baby. So, it gave him a few days to manufacture [surfactant]. *(Lauren)*

Patty came in on Wednesday. Feeling that the pains Lauren was having may have been true labor pains, not Braxton-Hicks contractions, she insisted Lauren's temperature be taken, and demanded to know what the result was. It was over one hundred one degrees. At that point, the hospital staff checked her, wheeled her into the labor and delivery area, attached monitors, and started a glucose drip, as well as Pitocin.

Well, they put me on Pitocin because they wanted the baby to come quick, to encourage the labor that I was already in. Labor on Pitocin is very intensive, but I had no strength. I had zero strength, because I was almost in a coma. The sugar was doing me in 'cause I never ate sugar whatsoever.

Patty held Lauren's hand while she experienced severe pains. When she thought she felt the baby emerging, a nurse claimed it was probably an effect of the internal monitor.

Patty went out and got somebody ASAP, and they checked me, and that baby was on its way. They wheeled me across the room. I had a cheerleading team screaming at me to push. And, with what strength I had, I pushed—a mighty push. And, they cut me, from here to next year—into my sphincter muscles. It was an intern. Ellen [Hartung], the midwife saw me four years later, and she said, "Oh, my word, who did this to you?" But, anyway, that's why I screamed so loud with [my second child] Aaron. Because I have had pain ever since. *(Lauren)*

Timothy survived and was healthy. After Tim, Lauren had Aaron and four more children at home with a midwife—Carolyn. Contrasting those five births with the hospital birth, Lauren says, "They were a piece of cake!" She describes the atmosphere at her home births.

Oh, well, it was wonderful! And I always wanted to see a baby being born, so I wanted to let other women see my babies being born. The Haverland women—Micki and Vicki, [were there] and Margaret [De Vos] and, let me think, Kathy Esperito. Kathy Esperito would write beautiful things, beautiful testimonies of the birth. It was—it was a party. And my husband would always pray afterwards, that the Lord had blessed the delivery. And it was always a good day. Very different than a hospital, yeah. *(Lauren)*

Childbirth was an experience that was shared. It was usually immediate family present—like their mom might be there, the mother of the mother-to-be, and the dads were always there. I don't remember any dads not being there and not being a big part of it. And, siblings. Usually if the siblings were there, and they were young, there was somebody there to take care of them. *(Carolyn)*

> Eli's was a home birth, and Carolyn Novkov and Margaret were there assistin' me. It was a somewhat easy birth, it seemed like. [His brother] Woody was three years old. Eli was born on Woody's birthday, which is the day before my birthday. So, that was exciting. Of course Woody was there. And I had another friend there, to kind of be with Woody, so that it really went smooth. It was a night-time birth, and Carolyn got there in plenty of time. When she got there, it was maybe another five hours or somethin', till he was born. It went really good, and everything went smooth, and he was healthy. It was in the bedroom, and I was laid down with Woody, for him to go to sleep, and then I could tell, you know—and Carolyn could hear—that I was about to give birth. So, then we went on, moved on in to my bedroom, which was right next to his, and then Eli was born probably thirty, forty minutes later. So yeah, that last bit of labor, I spent laying down with Woody in his bed. That's sweet. *(Janet)*

There were many circumstances of birth, but for all their relative poverty was a factor.

> The first two kids, Zack and Seth, were both born at the first house, the shack-with-no-water house! We did have the proverbial big kettle of water on the stove. Zack was born in August, so it was plenty warm, actually it was too hot, but what can you say. Seth was born in the middle of March—so luckily it was not cold for either of those births because it was such a cold house in the winter. *(Micki)*

> People whose babies were born at home didn't have any money. They were friends most of them were friends, so we would trade, like a load of wood or canned goods or whatever, for my service. That was fun. That was a great, great time. *(Carolyn)*

The rewards were many for all.

> Giving birth, for me, us, was such a—I talked about empowerment earlier, and growing up. Pivotal parts of that were giving birth, and learning that I could do such a thing. That was just tremendously empowering. *(Micki)*

> The setting? My bedroom. A loving atmosphere. I was not hooked up to any machines or anything, and I felt loved and encouraged and felt like it was a real blessing to be able to do it like that. I'm very grateful to Carolyn for taking that chance. *(Vicki)*

Many grateful friends expressed their thanks to Carolyn, but it is difficult to pin down the number of home births where she presided.

> I don't know. Probably twenty-five or thirty. I don't really know. Margaret might know. She probably has a better memory than I do. Sometimes she went with me, sometimes Dianna went with me. *(Carolyn)*

Carolyn and these mothers were not interested in counting, but simply in treasuring their childbirth stories.

> They were such awesome experiences. And being able to do that at home—with my friends, and my husband, and having my other kids watch if they wanted to, was an amazing experience—to be able to welcome those people into the world that way. And I am so grateful to Carolyn, and to my friends, for being there. They were very spiritual, wonderful experiences. *(Vicki)*

Chapter Thirteen

Working at Home and Away

Being a homesteader and being poor were mere abstractions when the women began their lives in the Clinch Valley. Soon almost all the families were struggling to raise their food and pay the rent or mortgage. Some even had to work out-of-state for a while. Local Appalachians shared many of the same concerns. Poverty was relative.

> [The house] was cold, but it was twenty-five dollars a month, although we had a terrible time making that payment. That was a tremendous amount of money for us. I really have so much gratitude to my grandparents and to my parents, who from time to time floated our rent payment because we just couldn't cut it. *(Micki)*

> We had some money with us when we came, but it didn't last very long. We were living with other people and nobody had money so we were all living off of what money we brought. But we had brought a lot of food with us, fifty-pound bags of rice and beans, and we really didn't have to spend a lot of money. People would send us money, like for birthdays. My family always sent

really nice clothes for my kids, so [my daughter] Sarah had good clothes to go to school in. Nobody at Kyles Ford School was dressed to the hilt, so she was fine. *(Carolyn)*

Some women worked outside the home from the beginning. Linda got hired the summer she arrived in Tennessee, but found the low salary shocking.

They didn't pay teachers anything back then. You made four thousand dollars a year. That was in the Seventies. I made more money working in the grocery stores in Ohio, than I did teaching here. It was outrageous. Of course that has changed, but it was tough! *(Linda)*

Joanne had a job, but had become a single parent.

I had to pay for a babysitter. I wasn't making very much money. I was working as an RN at the hospital on the evening shift. Well, I was the *only* RN at the hospital. It was a small hospital, about thirty-two-bed, with an emergency room and a delivery room. I think I was making $4.50 an hour. It was just amazing, but that's what I made. That's what we lived on. The kids, I don't think they knew we were poor. They said they never realized it. Everybody was pretty poor around here. And we had enough food, and we had a roof over our heads. The girls would play out in the woods; they would make up their own little houses. What pretty much was my focus: try to keep the car running and build a house. *(Joanne)*

The women adjusted to their new situations.

Yeah, I made our own clothes a lot, just because it was fun and you didn't have to buy something. I mean the whole thing about being self-sufficient. [Making clothes] hit every aspect of it. Okay, let's see how we can do this? And material—people would just give away scraps, scraps of material. You just learned how to do everything. *(Lee)*

I don't know where we ever got any money, maybe twenty dollars here and there. But I put up and canned lots of things, so we had food. *(Carolyn)*

Yvonne, raised in Amsterdam and later a resident of London, elaborates.

We lived below the poverty level, for a good long time, but we absolutely didn't care. Living here, you don't need anything, because, well, there is nature, and it is so plentiful. If I ever went to the supermarket, I never bought like kiwi fruit because that was too expensive. You just spent very, very little. But, it was OK. I never felt like I was poor. *(Yvonne)*

Pat and Alicia, former nuns, philosophized.

I guess because we took a vow of poverty, we never did have any money! So then, when we didn't have any money, that was just what we admired. Not having money was kind of an ideal! *(Pat)*

The self-sufficient life proved to be incredibly labor-intensive, and women's roles were vital.

Mostly it was gardening, and looking after household things. Oh, yes, I cooked a lot and I think in those days I also made tofu at home, so, extra, extra jobs. Our days were like, working in the garden, and that took hours and hours, actually, hoeing and digging and schlepping. And then sewing—I sewed all Sabino's clothes also. I sewed all those clothes! And then cleaning. And, for the rest, I didn't even watch TV. *(Yvonne)*

A lot of the time you're just workin' and slavin' seven days a week. We'd go to the markets on Saturday. On Sunday we were just exhausted. We'd have to have Sunday to recuperate our strength so we could go back to work on Monday and do it all over again. Some stuff had to be done anyway, like takin' care of the horse, and certain chores you have to do every day on the farm. *(Cece)*

It was back-breaking. It just killed me sometimes. I aged real fast, doin' all that. But it was fun, and it was invigorating, and I learned so much that it's funny that when the world turned, [to] this millennium, 2000, we were afraid all the computers were going to go out, and there wasn't going to be any electricity or water or anything. I can remember my mom saying, "Don't worry about Sherri. She'll be able to survive. She knows how to do everything by hand." *(Sherri)*

Tomato farming was arduous.

We worked from sun-up to sun-down, and even later. It was very tiring. I had four kids. Breakfast with the kids. Go out and work, string the tomatoes, pick the tomatoes. I would leave the field about eleven o'clock to fix a meal for all the workers. I think that was taken from the way old-timers had always done here, that they would always feed their workers. Later on, when I got my [teaching] job, the people that Jerome hired would have to bring their own lunches. The kids would be doing their own thing, and that was good for 'em, the girls were older at that time. The workers were some friends, and kind of laid-back people—and we were, at that time, kind of laid-back about it—[and they] took hacky-sack breaks, and basketball breaks. If it got too hot, we would walk down to the river and take a dip. Then, back to work. Worked till late. Made supper, washed the dishes, read to the kids. Maybe didn't do a whole lot of house-cleaning, at that time. That was kind of a typical day, when we were tomato farming. Just roll into the bed at night. *(Vicki)*

I was extraordinarily busy, all the time, because if it wasn't with the [breast]feeding, I made three complete meals every day, from scratch of course. Having the children, and taking care of them without running water also adds an extra dimension to it. Then also being responsible to help working on the farm. As we expanded our operations, and began to grow more, it became more important for me to become a more integral part of that, to help provide the labor. It took us five years of farming to start turning a profit, so we really could not afford to hire any help, so it was just up to us. It was a busy life, and I'm really glad that I was young! Farming is a seven-day-a-week occupation. You can't take a weekend off. Plus, a lot of our marketing was done during the weekends. So it was really like having children is a constant twenty-four seven; if you're farming, for a living, that's the same. *(Micki)*

Bartering and sharing can go a long way to support a cash-poor economy. For example, Robyn traded her handmade jewelry and Carolyn traded midwifery service. Others traded handicrafts, garden produce, services, or other labor.

> I love to trade, and I will trade just about anything. Food, absolutely. I traded for fudge, at a show. I've traded for food at a restaurant before, in Abingdon [Virginia]. It's awesome. I'm always up for a trade. *(Robyn)*

> I don't think we sold any eggs. I may have traded eggs for something with people, "You give me this, I'll give ya' eggs." *(Alicia)*

> I bought hay from other people. Because I'd been a massage therapist for a long time, and met many people, I even got to where I could trade massage for hay, and they'd deliver it. *(Tata)*

Sometimes trading is just the neighborly thing to do.

> I've been very, very lucky since we've moved here. I've had neighbors that knew how to milk, like when Lou lived here. She would milk for me when I wanted to go to Georgia, and I would milk for her when she would go. I'd take care of her farm and stuff, and we just would swap back and forth. *(Sandra)*

> I helped [my neighbors] plant tobacco, pull up the young plants. I did get paid for sorting, grading the tobacco. But, we traded. I mean I gave them stuff. People would give me fabric for my quilting, and, if there was something that I didn't feel I could use, I would give it to my neighbor who made quilts. Not for a living, but we shared. *(Alicia)*

Not everything could be bartered for or shared. Inevitably, a need for cash to pay the mortgage or to buy a tractor, a chainsaw, water pump, or other supplies forced the homesteader to make hard decisions about working outside the home-place.

> We had a couple of guys [who would work for us] when we were ready to have somethin' done and we had the money to buy the materials. And, we were thinking, You know, maybe one of us should get a job. We said, "No, that would be the end of the farm." We didn't wanna. Neither one of us wanted to, so we didn't. We made it, but it was very, very [difficult]. And, it would have been a long drive. *(Pat)*

Pat explained that it was ten miles to a paved road, taking over forty-five minutes to reach a town. She and Alicia built a successful goat cheese business despite the challenges. Others faced similar decisions about outside employment. Sherri was selling soap, loofah sponges, and candles to Dollywood to supplement her husband's earnings.

> That [craft business] was how I contributed. Dale was a cabinet maker and carpenter. So he made a living and I did most of the housework and homesteading stuff, all that. *(Sherri)*

Making a living off home-grown animal products proved difficult, and not all ventures ended well.

> We got into Angora rabbits. That was a mistake. We had got a good deal from somebody we had met, and they had these Angora rabbits. They were leaving, and for sixty dollars they sold us about eight Angora rabbits, cages, all the equipment.

You pluck their fur. They're constantly shedding this fur. Then you spin it into Angora yarn, and you make caps. A lot of people were doing it. There were clubs of knitters that were making their own [yarn]. You have to pluck 'em right from the start, so they get used to it. But she [previous owner] had kinda let it go and so they weren't real used to it. We tried to sell just the fur. There was no market for it, so finally we sold the rabbits. Yeah, the [crafters] were raisin' their own; they were spinning their own wool from their own rabbits. *(Pat)*

One or both partners in a couple might have to find outside employment. Financial survival was a balancing act.

I wasn't working at all other than on the property for quite a while. Money was an issue, so I took a job as an aide at Clinch School. I also did some substitute teaching at Clinch School. *(Beth)*

We thought that we would have a cow and goat, and so forth, but we kinda soon realized that we were probably gonna have to leave the farm to work. So it was hard to think about milking twice a day, and all the other things that we thought we would do when we moved there. In Ohio my husband had a snowplowing business, and we had a really big, nice truck there, and we sold that truck. The person that bought it paid us monthly for two years to pay off that truck. So that was our income, five hundred dollars a month. During that time, I went back to school for nursing, and I knew that I had to be done in two years. We did not have a regular income except for the payments that they sent. And then Bill earned some money here and there building some things, and I think he went to Sneedville and worked in the furniture factory for a little while. Just some odd jobs here and there to earn some money 'cause we were tryin' to add on to our own house and improve our own living situation. *(Dianna)*

Dianna earned an R.N. degree in two years. "I did start working right away, and I could not believe having a paycheck! It was great! I started out in a nursing home, in Kingsport—an hour drive from where I live." After two job changes and hour-long commutes, Dianna explains that she settled into a better situation. "Then I did Home Health nursing for a long time within a twenty-mile radius of where I lived."

It was common among these families to find a hodgepodge of part-time jobs and occasional work.

> The jobs I had before I had children—CNA and waitress. My husband, for eight years got the produce for the school system in Hawkins County. He would go to the farmers' market in the early morning, twice a week, and he'd pick up what had been ordered [by] the ladies in the different cafeterias of the seventeen schools. *(Lauren)*

> We had the little country store—I think we had that for four years—which used to be Alum Well Country Store. We did that for a while and you don't make any money doin' that, that's for sure. You put a lot of time in. *(Linda)*

There was a sawmill that Joe and Jerome [Haverland, husbands of Micki and Vicki] both got jobs at to provide an income.

> They had two different jobs. They hung drapes for the Drapery Boutique, which was an establishment in Morristown that sold high-end draperies custom-made to high-end homes, and Joe and Jerome were very tall men, and so they were the drapery hangers. So they did that when they would get calls to do that, and they also worked at the sawmill in Springdale. The sawmill had left-over slabs that they would sell, that people could take home for firewood. We burned a lot of that slab wood. *(Micki)*

Searching for a job can be difficult. Widowed soon after arriving in Tennessee, in her early twenties, Anne had no partner to share the financial burden. Her previous experience as a horse trainer was not helpful.

> Just wondered what kind of work I could do. Trying to keep a vehicle and just trying to keep going. But mostly I just didn't see any work options in the area that, if I wanted to work with horses, the horses here aren't the kind of that you can be employed to take care of. You need to go somewhere where there's more money, and people have those kinds of horses and stables. *(Anne)*

Tata went looking for a horse but found a job.

> When I decided what kinda horse I wanted, I went on a go-to-here-go-to-there-talk-to-people in the communities between here and Morristown, and Kingsport and Johnson City, looking at horses, going to horse shows, meeting people that had horses, talking to them, and telling them who I was as a massage therapist. And those people hired me to do house calls. So for a year and a half, I drove here and drove there, went to people's homes.

> Then one day Ann Russell said, "I hear you're [a massage therapist] as well as an artist, and I'm opening up a new hair salon and there's a separate room. Would you like to come work there?" I was tired of doing house calls, lugging all the stuff around, so I said, "Yay!" *(Tata)*

Janet's husband Jesse worked at the Phipps Bend Nuclear Power Plant construction site (never completed). Before he drove for over an hour, he had to cross a river to get to his car.

> We bought twenty-five acres on the [Clinch] River in Hancock County. Moved over there into an old house. At that time, my husband was workin' at Phipps Bend. He had strung a rope across the river. He'd stand up in the boat and he'd pull himself across to go to work. He had to park his car on the other side, 'cause it was such a rough road getting' into where we were livin'. It's just easier to pull yourself, with the currents and the rock [ledges]. I would imagine it was probably before six a.m. [that he left]. It wasn't easy. But that's a super-shallow part of the river. It's a lot of shoals, so it wasn't a deep part, so that was good. He actually did that! But, it was only for three months. It was [only] in that summer. Then we bought the place on Swan Creek, and I don't know what he would 'a done in the winter. It would've been difficult. We weren't thinkin' that far ahead. We were just enjoying bein' on the river. *(Janet)*

In contrast, Sandra had only a half-hour commute, and no ropes were involved.

> When I moved here, I worked for Debbie Beal. She had a pottery shop downtown [in Rogersville], and I was her assistant. I did the cleaning of her greenware [unfired pottery]. Sometimes I

did take care of the shop while she went somewhere or she was at a show. [Later] I started taking care of senior citizens, people that were bed-ridden, and they couldn't help theirselves. I did that mostly at night because I could get enough sleep at night, doin' that, and then I could come home and do what I needed to do here, farm and whatever. *(Sandra)*

One day at Beal's Pottery, Robyn walked in, and Sandra told her she was soon leaving so her job would be available. Robyn was yet to earn her living entirely from jewelry-making.

> I worked for Debbie Beal at the pottery shop. I worked for her a lot. I did everything but make the pots. That was a great job. She would make the pots, and I would mix the glazes, where you had to measure everything on a triple-beam [balance], all the chemicals and stuff like that, and then after she threw the pots [formed them on a potter's wheel], I would load the kilns with the greenware, and then clean the pots and glaze them, and reload the kilns, but I signed her name on the bottom of the pots. She was a whiz. She was a master at throwing pots, she really was. *(Robyn)*

Other homesteaders met each other through their jobs.

> I was workin' for Joyce. She had a health-food restaurant for a short time. I worked there, six months to a year, worked in the kitchen, bakin' bread, and fixin' the salads and the sandwiches and stuff. And that's where I met Cece, too, for the first time. She came in as a customer. *(Janet)*

And jobs came with extra benefits.

> After I had [my first baby] Erin—we had met someone in Morristown who had opened up a health food store, and a health food restaurant—[my husband] Jerome, and our friend Janet [Hechmer], worked at the health food restaurant. And—so nice!—Jerome would bring food home to me. *(Vicki)*

With just two exceptions, all the households in this story had a member who worked outside the home. Moreover, some folks worked way, way outside the home.

> Almost all but five years of us being married [my husband]'s been an ironworker. He just had to travel on some of it. *(Sandra)*

> [My husband Ron] did a lot of jobs where he worked away from home and would be gone and then be back. But one job he had working for United Geo-Physical Oil Company, we got to travel. When Alyson was a baby, eighteen months old, we lived in the state of Nevada one summer, which was a very good experience. Then the next summer, we lived in Tulsa, Oklahoma. Hot but dry, but fun! It was like bein' on vacation for me and her. Ron had to go to work, but we managed! It was fun! Went out and got ice cream. Or beer—I got Coors. Couldn't get Coors back here. It was fun. [In] Nevada we actually lived in a tent for six of those weeks that we were out there, which was pretty interesting. We were staying in a ten-by-ten-foot tent. Of course in the daytime, she and I would walk around the Humboldt National Forest, or we'd go into the little town, and we'd hang out at the park. *(Linda)*

Besides Linda and her husband, six other couples traveled out of Tennessee to work. Janet and her husband Jesse moved to Florida for a year.

We had met some people that said they were buildin' condominiums in Florida, so we moved down there and worked. We lived in a little, tiny motel half a block from the beach, so that was nice. That was in Briny Breezes, Florida, which is near Boynton. We lived there for about a year. Then we got laid off; we moved back to Tennessee. That was '76. *(Janet)*

Yvonne and her husband moved away for a couple of years to the Washington, D.C. area in the late 1970s.

We lived in Tacoma Park [until] Bill quit his job with the National Council for the Traditional Arts. *(Yvonne)*

Two couples went to the Florida Keys to work for the winter.

[Gary and I] got married in the spring of '79. He was already going to the Florida Keys for the winter, and he had had his eye on a restaurant across from the campground that he stayed in—a canned beer bar, just really the pits. But he thought he could make it into a restaurant. We got married and six months later, we left with a school bus, pulling a rusted Toyota truck. We had a lot of pedestals of tables, all piled up on racks on the top of the school bus. We had lumber that was still green, that we had cut down the trees ourselves on our property, some beautiful oak, and some walnut. We ripped out the plywood bar and put in an oak-topped bar. It was very beautiful. It warped here and there, but anyways—we started [Mangrove Mama's Restaurant]. We took down some people with us, and so it was very fun. We'd go there [for] four, sometimes five months, and we'd be back here for the rest of the year. We did that for nine years. My son Adam was born the end of October, and we went down in November that year. Then when Marissa was born, that year we sold the restaurant. When I would go to the Keys, I was so homesick for Tennessee for about three weeks. I was so busy during the day, but, like if I had a spare moment—we lived right next door—I'd go back to the house, and start thinking about the people and the hills. The other thing I didn't like about the Keys was that I wanted to live a self-sufficient life. The water was piped in from Miami. The electric came down on wires all the way from Miami, which resulted in very big problems. The water pipes lay on the ground, and they would get broken. They would rust, there were leaks all the time. They would shut the water off. If someone hit a pole two keys up, all the electricity would go out. That part was exciting. That part was like Tennessee. But the rest of it—not being able to grow your own food, and to think that you're just kind of living off tourist money and not producing your own stuff— *(Nancy)*

Two of the people that Nancy and her husband took with them were Lauren and Joe Freire.

I was a baker at their restaurant, in Sugarloaf Key, Florida, at Mangrove Mama's, for the first winter [they] were open. Joe was the cook, along with another man, Mark. [When Mark got married] I baked them a carrot cake, because they thought I could. I said, "I've never baked a wedding cake in my entire life." But, I followed a recipe, and people ate it, and it didn't kill me [or them]. [We lived] across the road, in a campground in a fifth-wheel that Mark got out of storage. We got to live there, and it was a very nice place. *(Lauren)*

Another winter Lauren and Joe left the state to work.

> We went tree planting, and lived kind of like in an Indian village—a number of people in campers and tents, on hillsides or in a Seventh Day Adventist campground [in] South Carolina. We also stayed at a chicken farm the same winter. We also stayed—on a hillside somewhere—where somebody had set up some bathrooms, somewhere in Georgia. When we would have everything accomplished at one place, then [we'd] go to the next place. I was not doing [the planting], my husband was. I'd just had Timothy. And while I was there, found out I was pregnant with Aaron. I think Vicki and Micki were both there, if I'm not mistaken, with their husbands. I loved doin' it. I loved livin' just small, with all these people around. I liked it. I thought I would've made a good Indian. [If] it was winter, we did have actual [no-work] snow days. Neither did we work on Saturday, which was Sabbath, because the people that ran [the business] were Seventh Day Adventists. When it rained, they worked. They wore ponchos, and they worked. [I was] cooking and being pregnant, and wondering what motherhood was all about, taking care of an eighteen-month child. *(Lauren)*

Vicki and her husband Jerome also migrated every year to plant trees.

> Every winter for quite a while, we would hitch a travel trailer to the back of Jerome's vehicle, and we would go down south to plant trees, which was a whole other adventure. We met a lot of people on the road, and got close to a lot of the people. Two [girls the first winter], and then Molly was a baby and a little girl for a while. [Our fourth child] Jared went tree plantin' for a few years, but not as many as the older girls.

Vicki estimates they went for ten years, three or four months each winter.

> We lived in a twenty-two-foot trailer. Kind of a closed-in space, but it was the South, and the kids got out a lot, and yeah, it was very—I keep saying things are interesting experiences—but it was! Met a lot of interesting people. I had home-schooled for a long time, and I did [take their lessons on the road]. I planted trees one season—there was another woman there, and we would take turns watching the kids—that was very hard work, about the most physically demanding work I've ever done. But, [other years] the day was, just go with the flow—make breakfast, do some school work with the kids. We would hike. We would go to any historic site or museum that was in the vicinity. The kids would play. At night, usually there was a bonfire, and the tree-planters would gather around the bonfire, and tell stories, and it was a great time! Challenging, too, sometimes being closed in, in a small space with the kids for a great length of time, when the weather was not good. Some of the places we had to access were pretty challenging to get to. Even drivin' the car up some of the places was "iffy." I wanted to stay home, I didn't want to work, because I wanted to stay with my kids. But as long as I was with my kids, and with him, the tree planting aspect of it I think I saw as an interesting adventure, and, a worthy challenge. Yeah, I wouldn't change that. Came home [to Tennessee] and got the tomatoes ready, and the greenhouses, and all. So yeah, [the two occupations] worked out well together, and [the routine] worked out by itself in the summertime, planting and picking and stringing, and grading and selling tomatoes. *(Vicki)*

Micki's husband Joe also went tree-planting for several winters, but Micki accompanied him for only one of them (when Lauren was there). Nursing her second child at that time, Micki did childcare for others instead of planting trees herself. Sherri's husband also went, but she did not.

Some families recognized the need for outside income right from the start. After she described her gardens, chickens, work-pony, and goats, Trudie responded about whether she felt like she had been homesteading.

> Pretty much, except I was working full time in town, so it wasn't just that was all that we were doing. He made a living by surveying mostly, and then me working in town at different places—County Executive's office, Industrial Board, lawyers' offices, youth program, different places like that. *(Trudie)*

Education and work forced Lee and her family to live half the week in Clinch Valley and half the week elsewhere for several years. And three other women—Joanne, Cece, and Karen—had to move away for two decades. We hear those stories in the chapter, "Back to School and Other Changes." During the early years of establishing the farm and feeding a young family, the newcomers worked hard to make the homesteading dream become reality, and immersed themselves in the delights as well as the toil of tending gardens, animals, and small humans. The families dealt with their relative poverty, limited job and marketing opportunities, low pay, and intense physical labor by calling upon their coping skills, their sense of adventure, and their feelings of accomplishment.

So, all-in-all, did they enjoy their new lives in the country? Sandra expresses here what most have said and you may already have guessed.

> It was fun! Even when I look back, and realize how hard it was, we just didn't care, we were doin' what we wanted to do. We never went hungry. Everybody thought we were nuts! But then they'd see how happy we were.

Chapter Fourteen

The Creative Life

The aspiring homesteaders brought a few practical skills with them, some modern ideas about freedom and self-expression, and a significant amount of creative talent. Some supplemented their income with hand-crafted items. Twelve women sold their creations. Four women arrived here with art degrees, while others grew into their art.

"I was born to be an artist," said Sherri, who received her Associates Degree in Interior Design immediately after she graduated from high school and then earned a Bachelor of Fine Arts from Herron Art School (Purdue and Indiana Universities' art school). After college, she worked at a shop and gallery in a living history museum named Carter's Conner Prairie, near Noblesville, Indiana. There she showed her paintings in the gallery and her creative cooking in the deli.

> People were wanting my recipes, so I started putting them down. I was working as an illustrator for *Organic Gardening [Magazine]* and *Farmstead Magazine*, and a couple other Rodale Press magazines. They were buying my illustrations originally, and then they started using more photographs, so in order to get my illustrations published, I started writing articles about making

my own food. I started compiling the recipes into a book, and when we moved down here, I got the book finished. It's called *This Homesteader's Garden, Kitchen, and Herbal Primer*. I started selling that. The original copies were all hand-lettered. A guy would rent me his Xerox machine for a whole day, and then I'd collate them myself. I bought a little binder, and bound them myself. The Museum of Appalachia used to sell them for me, and then Dolly Parton, the first year she bought [what] used to be Silver Dollar City [soon renamed Dollywood], sold my books for me, but the first, I think, thousand of the [copies], were all in my own hand-lettering. *(Sherri)*

Sherri explains how she gained more income from her craft business and—a nickname.

We did pretty good once we got all that goin', and I lived off of that for many years. Even when I was on my own then, I still sold my candles, my herbs, my potpourris, and my books, and booklets. The Old Mill use to carry 'em in Gatlinburg, Pigeon Forge, and some other places in Tennessee. A lotta tourist places like that kind of little book.

Yeah, [I sold candles, vinegars, and soap]. Lots and lots and lots of soap. I went down to Dollywood one time to take an order. We went down the midway and came up to the old soap lady that they had there, that used to make the old lye soap in the kettle, and she knew me. She'd met me several times, and she said, "Oh, this is the fancy soap lady." So she called me the Fancy Soap Lady. Yeah, and it stuck. *(Sherri)*

Sherri also made baskets.

> I made willow baskets and all kinds of baskets back then for all kinds of uses. Later on I started making artsy kinda baskets that were more for fun, but they were even usable if you wanted to use them, but most people just bought 'em for fancy decorations. I made a lot of big baskets. A melon basket. I used to make baby cradles. All my baskets were rib baskets. Most of the ones I made to sell were honeysuckle and grapevine and Virginia creeper, and they were round. I made some odd-shaped ones, too, but they were all out of those same vines. *(Sherri)*

Charming, well-executed crafts did pay the bills. Sherri sold her paintings as well.

> I sold prints. I don't sell my originals very much. I did in the beginning when I really needed some money, but then I was really sad that I ever did, so I made prints, then colored pencil paintings. I call 'em paintings because some of them are done with watercolor pencils. I made those into cards and prints, and sold those for several years. *(Sherri)*

Yvonne also arrived with an education in art; she attended the School for Applied Arts and the Academy for Visual Arts, in Amsterdam. When her children were very young, she spun and died the wool from her Angora rabbits and made scarves and hats.

> I stayed home, but after a few years—Sabino was maybe four or five, I started to do art classes in the Rose Center [community cultural center in Morristown, Tennessee]. I did art with the

little kids, first graders, second graders, something like that. So, I didn't make much money, of course, with that. And actually, all the money that I earned—I also taught yoga in the Rose Center—I did not have to put anything into the house, in the food or anything. I put it in my own bank account for "education." *(Yvonne)*

Soon Yvonne spent more time in developing a new art form, and showing her creations in art galleries.

Later on, with all my [teaching and] yoga money, I made a bunch of doll-like figures [termed "porcelinas" at her son's suggestion]. That took a lot of my time. I sewed the work in my [home] studio. So, I made these faces; porcelain takes a lot of time, a lot of intricate work, sanding and carving, because you pour a head, but when it comes out of the mold—which I had made myself—it's rough. It's a little bit coarse looking, so, you have to refine it and sand it and carve it. Then you give it a real filing, and then the painting. And then, it turns into a figure! So, you want to sew the clothes and embroider them, and each piece of clothing became a sort of an artwork in itself. I did a lot of sewing at night. *(Yvonne)*

Tata started earning money from her art at an early age.

I've been selling art since I was nineteen years old. I had moved to Riverview, Florida. I got a job operating a snack shop on the ninth hole of their golf course. There was hours where nothing was happening, so I asked the management if I could bring watercolor papers and watercolors to the job, and I'd paint in my free time. They agreed. The men coming in there took an interest in what I was doing. Whether they really liked it, or they just wanted to support a budding artist, I don't know, but those guys bought my paintings. That fueled my interest in furthering my art career, 'cause if I could do something I loved on paper, and someone would give me money, why not? But that was my first I-sold-some-art experience.

After a stint painting signs in Jamaica, then studying art at the University of New Orleans, Tata realized that depending on those skills to make a living was not the best plan. After becoming a licensed massage therapist, Tata established a practice first in Florida and then in Tennessee. Meanwhile, she says, "I just did the art and didn't worry about selling it."

I have been primarily painting in acrylic and watercolor. I also make reproductions of my work on canvas [and] on greeting cards. I consider my photography an art form. I like doing trees and landscapes, unusual anything. There have been so many times I've looked out our windows here, and seen the ever-changing faces of Clinch Mountain. With fog, without. With green leaves, without. So I feel like I've been a recorder of the landscape around me as it changes. I love being able to have reproductions of everything I do. It makes it easy to be generous, and share my art whether it's for money or a free gift. *(Tata)*

A third of the women in this book were able to earn their living in part or whole using their creative talents. Robyn tells how she got her start while at the University of Florida.

I started to do [jewelry-making] when I was in school. I started to do like seed beads, and hippie beads, and three-dollar strands of beads. Those people didn't have any money, either, just like me. Then, one of my uncles had a fine jewelry store in Ohio, and he took me to this woman who used to work for him. [She] was doing beaded stuff, but she was emphasizing it being *big*, because people with more money want bigger things. That's who you wanna look for, right? None of *us* have money to buy jewelry. She gave me some stuff, I guess—and I started to do some different things, and took off. Started selling to museums and doing shows, things like that. My first show I made five hundred dollars, which was just awesome, in Gainesville–Micanopy. That was exciting! So that got me going, and I started doing chimes. I used to sell at the food co-op in St. Augustine or I'd consign there. Then somebody saw my work, and she was opening a shop, and she started sellin' my stuff in St. Augustine. From St. Augustine we came here.

A small inheritance enabled Robyn to visit Bali where she gathered new ideas and materials. After a short stint working at Debbie Beal's pottery shop, Robyn has earned her entire income from her jewelry and wind chimes business.

I just started doing all that, and hoping that it would work out here and, knock-on-wood, it did when I moved here 'cause I was the only one doin' it. People appreciated what they saw, too, being Bali beads, and hand-made glass, and stuff like that. That was [my primary source of earning a living] when I came here. *(Robyn)*

Clinch Mountain Girls

Other women, influenced by local culture, discovered their creativity while in Tennessee. Lee started out in a fun but practical way with scraps of material people gave her, making the so-called crazy quilts. Then she added something new.

> Made quilts, but they weren't the traditional quilts that everybody makes around here. It was more with the fur. I just liked a different kind. *(Lee)*

The birth of Lee's daughter led to new inspirations.

> After having this beautiful little girl into my life, when she was about two years old, I said to myself, God, it'd be great for her to have a cute little chair. She was always trying to climb up into one of our big chairs. She needed a little chair. So I made her one, and so many people said, "Oh, that's so cute! Would you make me one?" So it sorta started a career. And the same with my rocking animals. I really wanted her to have a rocking horse. A hefty one, too, 'cause we had this front porch that was covered and that was like her giant playpen, [so] that I could still do all my canning and she had a play yard, but I knew where she was, but yet it was fun. So I built this horse. Again, people just went, "Oh my God, would you build me one? Will you make one for me?" So that was fun, wonderful—and I was very proud of that aspect of my life—of the woodcarving. I really was. It seemed natural to me. I enjoyed it. It was creating things; it wasn't just copying somebody—it could be my own thing. People gave me some ideas what they wanted for their chair, or for their this or that. It really gave me a little bit of like, Go for it, Lee! And I liked that. *(Lee)*

Lee describes the various rocking animals she made, and other carved creations.

> Oh, you name it! I mean the obvious one was the horse, but I've done pigs, I've done giraffes, zebras, dogs. I did a rocking dog for somebody that they really wanted. So alright: 'coons, you know Rocky Raccoon, so that was a good one; rabbits, one of the best sellers were rabbits; well, dogs. I did two beautiful black panthers. Oh, God, they were beautiful! Lions, did a couple lions.
>
> Then I actually got into doing some furniture, too, some [kitchen] islands with carved vegetable legs. Did some crazy-looking animals that were tables that a friend, acquaintance, took down to Key West, and had them down there in his shop. They were fun!

As in Lee's case, other women's artistic efforts evolved into work that found both recognition and some commercial success. Janet, a successful basket maker, says, "I did craft shows, and so I made a little money doin' that. It was a good hobby, and I had fun doin' it." She describes her creative journey.

> Sandra Taliaferro, and [her then husband] Lonnie were makin' baskets at that time, so I went up to their house. At that time they lived way up on the creek, where ya had to hike in there. Hiked in, and she taught me how to make a basket. From there, I just, you know— books. The internet, of course we didn't have it at that time. It was mostly just books, and learnin' on my own. Just practice. I used a lot of grapevines, and honeysuckle, and made, like, an abstract basket. I sold in Gatlinburg. I sold

'em at G. Webb Gallery and I sold 'em at Arrowmont Store in Gatlinburg. I sold a lot there. Those were the two main places. Then I always was at the Mountain Makins Festival [Morristown, Tennessee]. I did the TACA Show in Nashville—Tennessee Arts and Crafts Association. They were all juried shows. I was also a member of the Foothills Craft Guild, which is a juried organization. The Foothills is out of Knoxville, and I did their show several years, with baskets. No, [I don't make those baskets anymore]. I started usin' a lot of wire in the baskets. Then I started realizing that I really liked playin' around with that wire, and so I started makin' wire jewelry—wirework jewelry. *(Janet)*

Originally keeping goats in Colorado, Sandra brought her love of animals and her skills in spinning and crocheting with her to the Clinch Valley. Sandra's rabbits and sheep and her spinning craft are described in Chapters Eight and Nine. Like Robyn, Sandra also sold her crafts at fairs and shows, where she demonstrated the plucking of her live Angora rabbits, and the spinning of Angora and sheep's wool.

Angora's high dollar wool. It's not something cheap, so you can't make something too big with it; it wouldn't sell. It's too hot to make a sweater with it. You'd have to live in Alaska to wear that, you really would, 'cause Angora is like eight times warmer than sheep's wool. So the hat or the scarf is good, and affordable for people, too. They would pay me for doing demonstrations, and then I could sell my stuff, too, so that worked out really good, and it was fun. I really enjoyed that. *(Sandra)*

For Pat and Alicia, crafts were a serious enterprise.

Alicia started making quilts, and I quilted 'em. And, so between us, that brought in a chunk of money if she sold a quilt. That would pay the rent [that is, the mortgage] for that month. *(Pat)*

Karen, a hard-working homesteader with four children, who majored in art at Bennett College, found little time to practice her art in Clinch Valley in the Seventies and Eighties. Now she throws herself into interior design and landscaping.

> Well, I could always crochet or knit back then, and did a little bit of weaving. Painted things. I remember painting just things around the house. I majored in art in school, but did mostly sculpture. Liked sculpture! When I was in art school I thought, I don't want to be an art teacher and I'm not good enough at art. Actually, my teacher went and got me a scholarship for half my tuition. I thought I always wanted everything in my house to be made by me, and then I realized other people did nicer things. So I got used to, maybe, collecting other people's stuff. Met Sandra [Taliaferro], did a little bit of basket-making after she showed me some things. I know how to crochet, and knit, and tat [make lace]. I crocheted a dress for [my daughter] Liz, sewed a little bit, did a big quilt. *(Karen)*

Micki, a mother of three boys she homeschooled—and a tomato farmer—squeezed in a little time for personal pursuits.

> I started learning how to do some beadwork, and did some jewelry-making. I somehow found some time—I guess it was my outlet, because I've always had a strong spiritual drive—so I was doing some studying with an Iroquois medicine woman, and was learning the traditions of her lineage. I was learning about

herbs, and medicine, and natural forms of healing—but also integrating the spirituality of that. Then from there, making what are called "medicine objects"—medicine in the vocabulary of indigenous people—it being a much broader spectrum than what we think of in medicine in Western culture. Medicine objects could be a medicine shield—a rattle or a particular object. I started working with those, and with different forms of jewelry. I would go to maybe a powwow or to a fair of some sort, or to the local Mountain Makins Festival, and have a booth, and do a little selling. I did make a little bit of money on the side doing that. And it was a creative outlet that I really needed.

Cece is a quilt-maker who started sewing early.

I always sewed ever since I can practically remember, starting with Barbie doll clothes, by hand, as a kid. Took Home Ec, and learned how to operate a sewing machine, and I have been sewing ever since. I became fascinated with the quilts in the area, and quilting itself, and then in '82, I made my first quilt. I bought an old, tattered quilt, and I used it for the filling of another quilt. I just made a top and a bottom and quilted right over it, and that was a simple rail fence [pattern] quilt, but I have been making quilts ever since. I picked up, at one of these auctions, an old quilting frame, in 1981 or so. This was one of those ones [with] four [narrow] boards [to make the quilt sides], with holes all down the middle [of them], and the ladies would put nails in the corners to hold them together [at the size they wanted]. They put the whole quilt on the frame, and then they would hang it from the ceiling from some hooks with ropes, and they would lower it down to quilt around it. Then, to get it up out of the way, they would raise the ropes and then tie the quilt frame back up. This was an old quilt frame. I believe it was made out of poplar wood. I still have it as of today and I've used it to make many quilts.

Marketing was an issue for most of the creators, like Yvonne selling her porcelinas.

I would sell those doll-like figures at fairs and exhibits. And then, more Angora products. Some of my paintings I sold, not too much. You have to be a real outgoing person. You have to go meet people, and show what you've got. And, if you don't do that vigorously, people will never know what you've got, or don't believe in what you've got. So, I was a bit in that spot! Yes, [that was mostly before the Internet]. But, when you do the Internet, you have to be a very good PR person. I had a website for a long time, but I didn't do any work to make people know about it. You have to just work at that, and I just didn't want to do that at all, so it's still a marketing problem.

Robyn and Sherri both traveled on the festival circuit, to towns in Southern Appalachia, where a day or an entire weekend is set aside to celebrate local culture with music, food, and crafts. The festival season started in the spring. "Actually, it went right up until Christmas. I'd do some indoor shows," said Sherri. Travel time and expense, and childcare made selling their arts and crafts difficult, particularly during the growing season.

Got kinda busy the past few years and started doing a show in Abingdon, Virginia, that was sixteen days long. That was when harvest was. Every year, at the end of July, I was doing a show, so

I was gone for about eighteen days—prime time! So for a couple years I didn't have a garden, [since] I used to come home every day, and I'd bring the vegetables to my friends, and say, "Please take this!" I didn't have time to cook 'cause I'd drive two hours each way. Then I started staying up there, 'cause the gas went so high that it was cheaper to stay up there for the whole time. *(Robyn)*

While the visual arts and the crafts afforded a mode of self-expression for these homesteaders, they found other creative outlets as well:

Poetry.

I have written poetry since I was, maybe twenty. The poetry reflects what I'm going through at the time, or observations I have about the human condition, or aging, or relationships, or some of the beautiful things that I've learned about horses. Several years ago, I decided to have someone typeset the poetry in a beautiful way on paper, and then I framed 'em. Much to my shock and surprise and joy, I've had people pay me for my words! And I totally feel so honored at that. Again, the joy of reproductions is you can keep on selling it for your whole lifetime. *(Tata)*

Theater.

I was involved with the Rogersville Theatre for many years, and was on the executive board, and would help direct musicals and musical reviews, and actually got the Clinch [School] Faculty Singers to come over and sing for it. I was in a play, *Steel Magnolias*. I just was involved with that for quite a while. At Cherokee

[High School], with Mary Lynn Lipe, we did a lot of musicals. And, if I wasn't doing musicals, I was doin' [directing] the winter comedies [for example, *Pygmalion*], which were also fun. *(Linda)*

Music.

I'm a classically trained singer. I like all kinds of music. I was inspired by Barbra Streisand and Joni Mitchell, Linda Ronstadt. I like it that I can sing something and cheer people up at a funeral, or add a note of seriousness and beauty at a wedding, or sing something funny. But even if I never get another chance to sing for another person, I sing for me almost every day, and it uplifts me, keeps my instrument remembering, and satisfies me, elevates me. I think the vibration within my own body is stimulating my energy flow. *(Tata)*

And various other creative outlets as well. We were building our house. That was certainly creative, both in the design sense and in the actual building of it. *(Beth)*

To me, it's outside, with the horses....It's what I just love to do. I taught [riding] for several years and I've been involved with several different therapeutic riding centers. *(Trudie)*

I think a lot of my creativity went into organizing—especially, with the [Friends of the] Clinch and Powell Rivers. I improved my public speaking, I improved my writing. At one time, I was writing four newsletters at once. I wrote [our group's] newsletter, most of the articles, and edited it for ten years. Writing, I've always enjoyed that. I really like to work with stone. I made a retaining wall, and made it curve around from a high [level] to a low. I like picking different colors of rock, and just finding the right size; it's like a great big jigsaw puzzle to me. So that's creativity to me; I really enjoy that a lot. *(Nancy)*

The rewards can be monetary, but there are also intangibles.

I probably did a little bit of everything during my lifetime, 'cause I love crafts. I never got rich off anything. I'm probably one of those that does a little bit of everything but master of none. I liked to decorate, and when I was younger I would sew, would make curtains, and things like that. I just like to decorate, I just like to play! *(Sandra)*

I enjoy being creative. And people loving what I do makes what I do way better! *(Robyn)*

Finally, there is the creativity that has no name—the creativity of living one's life.

I think I was all about making sure we had enough food, so my arts and crafts seemed to be in cooking, bread-making, and putting food by. *(Dianna)*

I realized how many of my friends here in this valley are artists, so I decided to, tried to, make things that I did, artistic. Whether it's the kids' Halloween costumes that I made, or how I decorate my house, or especially food. I love to cook—and I really try to put a lot of creativity into the way the food's presented. *(Nancy)*

I don't remember doing a lot of arts and crafts. I remember being creative figuring out what to fix for dinner with meager supplies, or being creative with children, and entertaining children—what we could do for fun. But I'm not an artistic person; I don't make things. I don't know how [the creative urge] was fulfilled. I guess just by being creative in my lifestyle. *(Carolyn)*

Creative endeavors can mean money for one's family, or even a treat for oneself, but there is no coinage to measure the intrinsic value of making something beautiful. From daily activities like planting flowers among the vegetables or sewing colorful patches on clothes, to the artistic endeavors of woodcarving, jewelry making, and painting, the women's creativity increased the pleasure and meaning in their lives. And, in the moments of creating, they could truly go with the flow, letting cares drift away in a mountain breeze.

Chapter Fifteen

"Ladies' Meetings" and Other Essential Gatherings

Not long after their arrival, the newcomers, many with the long-haired "hippie" look, started encountering one another when moving in nearby, working off the farm, visiting a school, or shopping. They started gathering for the achievement of common goals or projects, for the exchange of practical advice, for moral support, and for fun.

> I didn't know anybody when we came but [the group] grew, gradually, and it turned out to be a whole lot of people that had come from other places to this area. It is interesting. I have never hung out with local people. But, I have hung out a lot with all of these people who came from the outside and settled down here, and somehow, there was a very beautiful thing going on among the people, some sort of mind-set. Everybody wanted a simple life, and valued real things, what we called real then—like growing your own food, and doing work with your own hands—simple. But still, everybody had read plenty of books and had education. *(Yvonne Apol)*

> I don't think that we could have come here, buying the land, and I don't think that we would have wanted to stay, if it hadn't been for the wonderful people that we found here. Because, within a year, within a month of our getting here, our good neighbors Bruce and Yvonne [Griffith] showed up, and they ended up buying property right next door to us, and then, within another year, Wayne and Eileen Rudiger also bought property adjoining us. So, we had one little holler that had wonderful people in it. *(Beth)*

The back-to-the-landers' immediate need for affordable food led to the formation not only of food co-ops, but of lasting friendships. Chapter Seven described early attempts to obtain whole grains and beans. For a while, both ends of the long valley met at Clinch School to collaborate on an order for bulk foods, and a truck delivered the order there. Then, in 1990, the families in the eastern end of Clinch Valley established the Little Pumpkin Valley Food Cooperative.

> It was originally located just in a little house in Pumpkin Valley, and then it moved out to Highway 70 to an old school building that's a fire station. It's still there, and whenever we order, that's where the truck comes, from Atlanta. Brings us our food; and we all unload it, and we divide it up, and it's just been a great opportunity for a lot of people around here. *(Anne)*

Ron and Elaine Highsmith led the effort to form the cooperative and made the house available. The old school was the former two-classroom Lonesome Pine School. (The Clinch Valley Fire Department used one classroom for gear, and added a garage for the trucks.)

Meanwhile, women in the western end of the valley formed a buying club, whose members drove to a pick-up point on Highway 25 E. All the families in this book took part in one or the other, volunteering their time to unload the truck, organize the orders for each family, collect payments, submit group orders, and manage the accounts.

> It is just an excellent co-op. I've been in it for over twenty-five years. Even all the years that I was on food stamps, I could always get that good food, and I didn't have to drive far to get it. And, different times, they would also incorporate some local produce. (Anne)

> It was most of the imports—the non-natives—who got together and started a food co-op, which was really a buying club, and so we got a lot of our food that way. We would get together and order, and then get together when the food came in, and break it all down, and then people would come in and pick up their food. So, it was a good arrangement. It was good for our getting food, and it was also good as a social event and getting to know people. (Beth)

Another common interest that brought these families together was their desire to conserve and protect the beautiful, biologically diverse watershed of the Clinch and Powell Rivers. The group engaged in many activities and campaigns. "I remember helpin' clean up Sweet Creek," said Linda.

> I belonged to the Friends of the Clinch and Powell Rivers. We did a lot of things to protect the Clinch River, and that was a good social occasion as well. I think we did help. My friend Judy Moore and I in particular, did a lot of education programs. We

wrote a script and got slides for a program that we gave to every civic group that we could find, and church groups, too. And got articles in the newspaper. We just did a whole lot of stuff. We kept an ash landfill out of Hancock County. *(Nancy)*

We did clean-ups and education, and that was good experience for me because it was all stuff I hadn't done before. I had to talk in front of people, which I didn't like doing much. We worked with the Tennessee Valley Authority on a lot of issues, and other water groups. We went to conferences and things like that. We wrote a newspaper [special edition] that told about the river. We put together grants, I went to grant-writing workshops. We joined other groups that were involved with the environment, like the Coalition for Jobs and the Environment. *(Judy)*

For some, another goal was support of the public schools, for their own children and for the community.

I even liked PTA meetings. The school had problems and they [Hawkins County School Board] were gonna close it, so I got involved very early. And, I went there partly just to socialize, and that was fun. *(Nancy)*

Mutual support was the purpose of the informal "Ladies' Meetings."

We met a lot of people that came to the region for similar reasons, because we all wanted to live simply, and be in nature, and support ourselves. When my two older daughters were younger, we got together with our women friends, and we actually called it the "Ladies' Meetings!" *(Vicki)*

I think we would get together about once a month or somethin'—the Ladies' Meetings. I betcha we'd have sometimes twenty women, and all the kids runnin' around. So, that's how we would get by. [We'd] get to see each other probably once a month. That was a big highlight, a strong bond with everybody. *(Janet)*

Even before my kids were born, I went to some of [the Ladies' Meetings], and those were just great. I thought of it as a free-for-all, because the ladies would be sitting in their long hippie skirts all spread out, and the kids would be just running from one mother to another and falling into their laps, or wanting to be nursed, or pushing the baby out so they could get some attention. Then they'd be running around the yard. And we'd be eatin' all kinds of nutritious snacks, and have a potluck, and learn about how to garden, and talk to each other, and give each other moral support. *(Nancy)*

Some of us lived more than an hour away from each other, but pretty much along Clinch Valley. We'd meet at one person's house or another. Everybody'd bring a potluck [dish]. The ladies would socialize with each other, and the kids could go and play all around in the creeks, or the barns, and they would have a grand time. So the socialization for the kids, and for us, because a lot of the time you're just workin' and workin' seven days a week. *(Cece)*

Just to come together, to feel that kinship, because we were all pretty isolated and we really needed to come together and talk about our lives, and our children, and how we would handle some things, how we would handle our poverty. Because most of us didn't come from poverty. And how we would handle kids if we had problems, how we would handle problems in our marriage. Survival. We did not have family here so that really, really filled that void, that we would come together as family. *(Carolyn)*

Without the Ladies' Meetings I think I would have lost it.... We would share a meal, and share stories, and really bonded in a sisterhood, because we were all away from our families of origin. So we created our own family and our own support system. Our kids, then, came to grow up with a lot of cousins, so to speak. That was so wonderful. I see that as having been my saving grace, and I think the saving grace of many of us during those times. *(Micki)*

Other gatherings centered on music. Robyn remembered, "Sometimes getting together with friends, playing games, or listening to music, or playing music, or somebody was like having a drum circle."

I was somewhat musical, and I had a big, beautiful accordion. We made our own music, and of course my husband wasn't a great singer, but he knew all kind of verses to all kind of songs. I did belong to a church group and was soon doing the music for the church, and playing piano, and playing pieces, and getting other to do solos. *(Alma)*

We had music evenings. Our neighbors all played instruments. We would just have a big open-house, and they would come with their instruments. We got to know a few of them, and they would always come and play. We met a lot of people that way. We sorta saw ourselves as just offering what we had to the community. So, that was what we had—we had the house. *(Pat)*

Get-togethers were frequent and inclusive.

We would have gatherings. That's what we did for fun. We would all get together. We still do! But we made our own entertainment, and people would play music. *(Carolyn)*

Just big social gatherings of people, adults and kids, everybody. Everybody would bring food, and then you'd just visit. *(Judy)*

Oh, we had such fun! There was always somebody having a party. So we would get together and we would all bring a potluck dish to it. There would be some music, and some of the old-timers would come with some moonshine and we just had a really good time. There were lots of little kids so everybody was playing. Yeah, it was big fun. *(Joanne)*

It was a fun time. It really, truly was 'cause you created your own fun within your own community. Not just friends who'd moved in, but the old-timers too. *(Lee)*

Some get-togethers centered on informal sports, like volleyball.

We had regular volleyball games Sunday afternoon or Saturday afternoon. When the weather was nice, we had wonderful volleyball games, first at Gary and Nancy's. And everybody would come, and we'd play, and bring food, and hang out. Then in subsequent years we had volleyball at different places. In the winter, we used the gym at Clinch School; we had volleyball games there. *(Beth)*

Or swimming.

There was a couple of years where every summer, every Tuesday, we would go to a pond and all the mothers would come with their kids and bring food watermelons and cantaloupes and things to eat. There was this beautiful pond at Steve Harrison's and he didn't live there, but we were allowed to go there and we would go every [Tuesday] afternoon and swim. Sometimes we'd take the kids to the river. *(Judy)*

Many gathered together at each end of the valley to celebrate holidays, especially Thanksgiving, a holiday Carolyn remembers as quite big. "We would invite a lot of people and it would be at different places every year."

Thanksgiving, we all brought—and still do bring—pot-luck [dishes]. We'd gather in a circle, and we'd give thanks and do a big OM [chant], and everybody would share what they were grateful for. *(Vicki)*

I think we went to Lee's most of the time for Thanksgiving, and she would usually have a turkey that had been raised on her farm, sometimes a wild turkey. I also remember having rabbit at her house, because she raised rabbits. *(Beth)*

Lee decided that that very first Thanksgiving she "would have a celebration that couldn't be beat, even though it was just with new people that were here, which were not that many then."

> Over the years, so many like-kinds, the transplants, were moving in. They didn't have family the way local people did, and so everybody came for Thanksgiving here. To be honest, it just warms my heart. People came with what they grew, or what they killed, killing a turkey that was in the woods, or bringin' a squirrel. Just the best Thanksgiving, and every year, every year, it was just so wonderful to have everybody giving thanks for us all living here and for all this wonderful food that we all grew. *(Lee)*

Easter brought families together.

> We would have wonderful Easter celebrations, and we'd have egg hunts for the kids, and we'd have a big circle out in the yard, everybody sitting in a circle together, and some people playing guitar, and some of us singing, and the kids running around and playing, and having so much fun together. It was really, really joyous. *(Micki)*

Beth says that she doesn't know when Lee started doing Easter, but that it's "kind of a tradition now." Karen adds, "The Easter egg hunt was always fun. Then Lee'd always find chocolate eggs and stuff later, months after."

Group celebrations brought joy and a sense of belonging that was felt by those who stayed in Clinch Valley and those who had to move away. Joanne and Cece came back for celebrations before they were able to move back.

Cece said, "When I was living in Georgia I would come back up here for Easter and Thanksgiving and times like that, because *this* was my family."

The Fourth of July could include unexpected excitement.

> One of the ones that immediately pops into mind was a Fourth of July that we had on the mountain at Sarah Aaron's. We all piled into the car and up we went. She lived up on top of Clinch Mountain. We had all pooled some resources and got a little bit of fireworks. We'd all get dressed up in our little hippie clothes, and I had on a gauze skirt. It was just fun that everybody would be just into it—the pot luck, and a little fireworks and a lotta drinkin' and home-brew and stuff. So we're up there on top at her place. It was just gettin' dark and it's time to get the fireworks out. So the fireworks are shooting, and we're being very responsible and all sitting in a row with fireworks going away from this group and everything. This one firework came, went out and then did a complete circle and came back and landed in my skirt and set me on fire! That was fun because I immediately started taking off my clothes, and instead of everybody being concerned, they all started clapping! But no harm done. I actually had a pair of underpants on that day, so that was a good thing. *(Lee)*

There were celebrations of life events—for example, a party to congratulate Carolyn, a mother of three, on her graduation from nursing school. Or a celebration of a marriage.

> My sister got married at our place, her and Don. It was just on our farm, and it was very simple. I can't even remember who married them. We just had, like all our parties—a potluck.

Everybody brings something. We didn't have decorations, or anything like that. I'm pretty sure I baked a cake, but everything else was just friends come, bring food. I think they were married right there in front of the house, and then we just had a yard party. *(Cece)*

We had a great big ol' hippie wedding, I mean big. We had the bonfire. We had the pot-luck. I think Patty might have made the cake. And Carolyn went and snipped roses off people's hedges to put on the cake and made a little tiara for me to wear at my wedding! Gary had a friend [who] had become a judge in Sevier County, and he invited him to come over and officiate at our wedding. He brought his guitar and his girlfriend, who had the long hippie hair also. So they fit right in, even though he's a judge. He did the service, and our dogs came and stood with us, because they wanted to. We did the Apache wedding prayer. Nobody remembers any of that; they all remember the party. We had a case of champagne, and at the time we had this deck that just made all the mothers cringe because it had no railing around it. But somehow we kept all the kids from falling off of it. And people said it was swaying a little bit with all the people on it—oh, my gosh! We had a keg, and so when it came time to go home, some people didn't. They just lay down by the fire. *(Nancy)*

Or impending childbirth.

I remember one time I was living on Green Road and I was pregnant—and Lee said, "I made a cake. Let's just get together. Come on over." So I go over. I had seen in town this rocking chair I wanted so bad. I get over there, and I saw that chair and was so disappointed 'cause I had wanted that rocking chair for myself 'cause I was having a baby. Then people kept showing up, more people. It ended up it was my baby shower! And Lee had bought the chair for me! Yeah, I was so jealous over that chair, and then—she had got it for me! *(Karen)*

Or memorializing those who left the community and our Earth.

Later on [after the '80s] we did of course have friends who died— Dana [Hathaway], and we had a memorial for her at her home, and people just talked about their memories of Dana. And Ray Carr passed away. We had a memorial at his home. And Norman [Radin], we had a memorial for Norman. *(Carolyn)*

It would always be a funeral of their choice, and people like us usually made it clear how they wanted to be buried, or what kind of service that they wanted. Generally, they would be buried on their own land if they owned it, and friends gathering at their house and celebrating their life. A good friend of ours, his casket was made by another really good friend, so that was particularly meaningful. *(Dianna)*

When our friend Norman passed away, just the most beautiful memorial to him, and all the friends show up with food, and everybody stood up, and talked about Norman, and laughed and cried. And that's very different, a different way of doing things. *(Lee)*

We've gathered, and talked about the person, what we admired and appreciated about the person. Told stories, maybe had some music. Maybe a potluck. I remember we spread Ray's ashes. The telling of the stories, and what we learned from those people, and how much we benefitted from them, were a big part of that. *(Vicki)*

Celebrations enlarged the back-to-the-land community.

That was a neat way to meet people, by having celebrations, because people would meet new people that we'd bring in, and so the group would get larger. You would meet people with similar ideas about life and how they wanted to live their life. *(Carolyn)*

The gatherings—large or small, just hanging out or purposeful—served to unite the whole community.

It was a great blessing to have these other friends around. We saw each other regularly—these gatherings where you were really together with your "family" somehow. That was an amazing thing of living here. Very unusual, I think. I still feel that, actually, the people that we know now for twenty years or something [forty, actually]—they feel like cousins, sisters, definitely. *(Yvonne)*

Oh, yes! Those [gatherings] were wonderful, and some of our favorite, favorite times. It was always a joyous time to be together, and come together in community in that way, and celebrate occasions, and celebrate one another, I think, our triumphs. And also [to] bond together to support one another when things weren't working out so well. There was a lot of that, thank goodness, a lot of support, when there were times of hardship. *(Micki)*

All the gatherings eased the transition to rural living. They provided moral support, technical knowledge, tools for living successfully in a new place and culture, a feeling of unity, and often, joy. In short, they were essential.

Chapter Sixteen

Feeling the Spirit

In group holiday celebrations such as Thanksgiving and Easter, the religious, spiritual and secular melded together. Those gatherings and the "Ladies Meetings" helped meet the human need for fellowship. Of course spiritual practices center on individuals' exploration of themselves and the ethics of their relationships to others. Morality is at the center of religion also, as it centers on the teachings of a historical figure and ceremonies and places of worship.

Among the back-to-the-landers, religious and spiritual practices ranged from church attendance to solitary contemplation, especially in a natural setting. Regardless, these women, from various traditions and backgrounds, appeared to share a common set of values.

Some of the women attended church regularly. One is Lauren, who belongs to the Seventh Day Adventist Church, which observes the sabbath on Saturday.

> Church is a very big part of my life. Generally speaking, I go to church twice a week, at least on Saturday. We have a pastor that has two churches. So he has prayer meetings at one of his churches on Wednesday and one on Tuesday; so we're the Tuesday people. And then on Saturday [I also go].

The Church of Jesus Christ of Latter Day Saints, is just right for her, Sandra explains.

> I've just always loved my family. As a child, even on my Italian side up North—my father just had a sister, and it wasn't a very big family—but holidays, if we were up there, they were together. If something happened—at the time we were Catholics—at communion or something like that, everybody was there. In the South, my grandfather had a farm, and two of his brothers were right there with their families within five miles of each other, and so get-togethers were really big. You're talking lots of people. I just grew up that way, and I just had such a love for that, those people. That's how I wanted my family to be. And then I'm Mormon, and Mormons are family-oriented, so—[There is a Mormon Church] in Rogersville. We go every Sunday, and up until [my husband] Wayne got sick, he was what people would call a pastor. We call 'em Branch Presidents—because we're a little branch off of Kingsport's church—equivalent to pastor. That's why he could marry [our granddaughter] out here when he did. But, we attend all the time, have lots of good friends.

Newcomers to the South were unaccustomed to Southern church norms, such as proper attire, or certain practices.

> I guess when my children were young, quite young, I wanted to give them the same opportunities that I had as a child, to have a church if they wanted that. At least have that introduction. So I pretty much, on my own, just attended several churches in the area. Coming from Ohio, it was not unusual to wear pants or slacks to church. So that's what I had on when I visited one

Baptist church in Rogersville, and I immediately knew that I was going to stand out in that crowd, because no other woman had on pants. So, I felt a little uncomfortable there. I went to another church, which was also a Baptist church, and it was their policy to have an altar call [to publicly commit one's life to Christ] or several altar calls. They literally all turned around and looked at me, thinking perhaps that that's what I came for, to be saved that day, but I didn't. I was just visiting the churches to see where I would be comfortable. *(Dianna)*

The reactions to a woman preacher were disconcerting.

We visited the church [in Clinch Valley] with the pot-bellied stove. We attended that church for about five years, and it was a very small congregation. They changed preachers about every two years, and one year the preacher that came in was a woman, an ordained Methodist minister, and while [my husband] Bill and I thought she was fabulous—she had a great message and good life examples to follow—it was so unacceptable that our congregation went from about ten to about four. They never co-operated with her as far as singing or looking at her or anything. So, unfortunately, she had to move on because it was very, very difficult for her to minister to people who were just not ready to have a woman in the pulpit. *(Dianna)*

As were some forms of religious expression.

I did grow up in a Baptist church. It was a Southern Baptist church, even though it was in the North, and they didn't get all crazy and carry on and whoop and holler and things like that. It was a little more subdued. *(Linda)*

Dianna and a few other mothers traveled twenty miles to a large church for their children's benefit. "It takes a half an hour. It's a big commitment," she pointed out.

> Finally we got to a Methodist church in Rogersville where we were comfortable, and there were children my children's age, and activities for them, so I felt like that was a good fit for our family. So we go to church on Sunday. We go across the mountain. *(Dianna)*

> I did do the Methodist thing when the children were little, because I did want them to have training, and when they got old enough, "You can decide what you want to do, kids." *(Linda)*

> We did go to church for a while. My oldest daughter wanted to go when she was younger because all her friends went. So we started attending the Methodist Church. But then after the fourth child came we moved further away from the church and we just didn't go any more. *(Judy)*

> Views varied on taking children to a place of worship. I don't practice my religion and haven't since it was forced on me and never instilled it in my daughter because I want her to choose her own thing. 'Cause it just was not that important to me. *(Robyn)*

All the women recognized that church attendance is part of community life.

> When we were first here, everybody wanted us to go to their church, which is very nice. I mean it's wanting us in their tribe,

or whatever it is. Anyway, I ended up trying to analyze it because I didn't want to offend them, but yet I felt they were coming on a little pushy. [I felt] a little bit of like, That's not what I want; and, sort of, Leave me alone. But that's not a particularly nice way of saying it. So I've learned to say to them that my church is this beautiful Earth, and being outside—it's very spiritual here. If I have some issue that I'm trying to work out, I go to the top of the mountain, and talk up there, or think up there, and try to work things out, and honestly, it works. It really does. So, I think that there is a tremendous spirit within, or I guess you call it energy—spirit, whatever it is that you call it—from the Earth, and I draw a tremendous spirituality from that. Strength, I guess. (*Lee*)

As in Lee's case, personal beliefs were not always a good fit with organized religion.

Alicia and Pat had left the Dominican Order and their service as nurses. Church attendance in their new home required a thirty-mile trip one way, including ten miles down a gravel road.

When I came here, I was sort of disenchanted by my church. And, it was so far to go every Sunday, and I couldn't afford any extra [expense], and I thought this was extra, going to church. So I quit going to church, and I still don't go. But I think Nature—and I still believe in some kind of a god, not the same kind of a god that I was grown up with—but, Nature, and the generosity of my friends and neighbors—I think that has helped me to grow spiritually. The whole idea of ecology was one of the reasons why I wanted to come here. So that is part of my spiritual being, trying to conserve water, and trying to conserve whatever. It makes me feel like I'm doing something for future generations. Even though I don't have children of my own, I think of my friends' children, my nieces' and nephews' children, and, what is their life gonna be like. *(Alicia)*

When Alicia and Pat stopped going to church, the church came to them (and their dog).

Well we didn't go to church. We tried that; it didn't last long. But we did get to be good friends with some priests, who excused the fact that we weren't going to church. One of them, he was a pastor in Gate City [Virginia], and I think he always hoped that we'd return or something. But, he used to come and help us with the house. He had volunteers, and they painted our house one year. This other priest, who liked to climb the mountain, would come here as his base. He brought in other priests who would join him, look at the maps. And then they would go right up the mountain here, so that somebody would know they got back. So, everybody came here. Oh, no, [none said a mass]—well, Father Glock, a couple of times. Then I think he realized that we were just going for communion, but we weren't probably doin' all the rest of it. Like going to church, or anything. He brought these teenagers—Catholic volunteers. They would sit and have mass in the living room. One time he was standing there giving out communion, and all the people walked by him to get their communion, and here comes the dog! The dog follows the line of people. It looked so funny! So, he just stopped saying mass when he was here, but he still came with the volunteers. He encouraged us. On the bottom of a Christmas letter, he said, "I hope you come back to the Church." But the other priests didn't care, and any other priests that we got to know, they just came as friends, and that was it. No criticism, for sure. *(Pat)*

Pat explains how her spirituality has evolved from the time of living in the large, urban convent with many nurses, to the four-person convents in the coal fields of Kentucky and Tennessee, to her current homestead.

We were never that religious as Catholics, as nuns. We fulfilled our obligations [such as attending mass on holy days], but, ah, they had been kind of getting pretty free anyway, before we even left the convent. We had some inspiring books, though, that we did read at night, books on the environment, usually. I think that's where the spirituality is, probably more like Native American philosophies. I don't believe in organized churches very much. I had enough of that. *(Pat)*

Similar thoughts were expressed by other women.

Sometimes I pray, and mostly just try to connect with nature. I love water. I have a creek here, and [had] a creek on my other farm. I love to go out and lie on my trampoline and read, and just look at the sky. I just mostly like quiet time and like to be with my animals. *(Anne)*

I guess being around really good people makes everything better. [To satisfy my spiritual needs] mostly I think or [read] a good book; or just being outside in the woods on a walk; or just appreciating where, what we have, and just appreciating whatcha got. I have such a connection with woods and mountains. So I have a magnetism to this place, not just this place, but being outside, too. *(Robyn)*

Well, for a long time I pretty much felt like I was in a spiritual desert here, because it's a pretty fundamental Baptist Christian area here, and I came from a Catholic background. Neither lifestyle, neither religious spiritual life, appealed to me personally. So I think I fulfilled that need for a spiritual life by being out in the woods and finding my peace and my solace in nature. Still do. I think a lot of us do. *(Carolyn)*

I feel the Earth is my church. I don't need to go in a building to find God. I don't need to have another person tell me how to worship God. The questions I have about "What is God?" may never be answered, because there's so many ways to experience it, think about it, or revere it. I judge no one in their method. So I don't wanna be judged that my way is inadequate or somehow less than. I give thanks on a daily basis for, "I woke up and I have another day to live." I sincerely count my blessings every day, and I'm very optimistic, just generally speaking. If you go through life accepting all the things that happen ... [whatever] your spiritual understanding of whether it's God's plan, the Universe's plan, your plan, your friends' plans—all these things are subject to many events beyond our control. So, rather than reacting wildly, I take a deep breath, try and process it, find the positive aspect, and if appropriate, share the silver lining with other people, or not. I try not to cram my stuff down someone else's throat. I try to let them be their own version of spirituality and religion that they're comfortable with, and I try to, every day, acknowledge all the good things that have come my way. *(Tata)*

Meditation was the most common spiritual practice.

Clinch Mountain Girls

I guess, any spiritual need I have I just take care of it within myself. Really. I don't see any other way. I think you could say I do [meditate]...I put a blanket down on the floor up at my office and just lie there maybe fifteen minutes or so. I've found while I'm just trying to relax and take deep breaths, that I can just think about things, and a lotta times solutions come to me. I don't consciously think, I'm going to think about this, while I'm lying there. I'll put some music on or something, and, I find that very relaxing and it kinda clears my mind. *(Trudie)*

For me spiritually, especially now, during these trying hard times, the best thing I can do is to lie on my bed, and close my eyes, and visualize myself in my holler or on the property or places that I think are beautiful, and I really do feel a connection and a closeness to a spirit. But, I just cannot totally let go of my [Baptist] roots, though, and my upbringing. It's just a hard thing for me to do. *(Linda)*

For many, being outdoors was key.

The outhouse had windows in it and overlooked the creek. I was just sittin' out there one night and it was a full moon, and I could swear I could see Indian spirits out there. We found a lot of arrowheads on our property, 'cause it was three mountains coming together, and it was kinda hidden away back there. There was an Indian settlement there at one time, you could tell. It just was a very spiritual place to be. Probably the most spiritual place I've been. *(Sherri)*

I cultivated a very strong and powerful relationship with the river, with the Clinch River. That's where I would go, to pray, to explore my spirituality. My spirituality is very much grounded and rooted in the natural world, bringing heaven to earth, so to speak. When I was able to steal some time away, alone, I would typically go down to the river to meditate. The river still is one of my greatest teachers, and continues to teach me how to flow, how to allow myself to continue to move around obstacles, or flow over or through rather than becoming stuck or stagnated. Many, many, many things I was taught by the river and by the rest of the natural kingdom. *(Micki)*

Or practicing yoga.

Basically, I think it was the yoga that kept me, mostly, centered and going. Well, you get into a totally meditative state, right? You're busy for an hour! On your own! And, going through a discipline with a beginning and an end, and it's controlled breathing, so you enter a meditative state. *(Yvonne)*

Some included traditions used by Native Americans.

We used to have a meditation group a long time ago. We also used to meet once a month at different people's places and had a drum circle. We would drum, and we would sing, but we would take turns sharing our spiritual beliefs and philosophies, and we did some, maybe, Native American rituals. It was very nice. We would "smudge"—use sage and sweet grass and cedar—the area and everyone that came. I guess the Native Americans believe that there are components in those herbs that maybe help cleanse negativity. You have the herbs in a [river mussel] shell, and when you light them, as it's burning, the smoke does its thing. *(Vicki)*

Micki's spiritual journey and interest in natural healing led her to an Iroquois medicine woman.

That was through what is called a Medicine Wheel Gathering. I started going to some of those that were sponsored by what is known as the Bear Tribe. I had read some books that kind of led me in that direction. It just so happened that the Bear Tribe was having a Medicine Wheel Gathering right outside of Cincinnati, which made it convenient because the kids and I could drive up there, and I could leave them with my mom for the weekend while I went to the gathering, which was a camping sort of situation. That was wonderful. That was the first time that I was able to spend like a night away from the kids, from my responsibilities, and delve into something that was of great interest to me, personally. I went probably three years, and from there I met some other people then that I would continue a relationship with, such as [a certain] medicine woman.

For several, meditation meant mindfulness.

I can walk out to the barn and that's all that I'm thinkin' about, or I try to just only be thinking about what I'm doing out there. Any time I'm working with [the horses], my focus has to be totally on them, because, two things: I can cause them a lot of angst if I'm not clear, and, I can end up gettin' hurt if I'm not payin' attention. So that'll take your mind off a lot of such trivial things I feel that you can just get in your life. It's like having too much stuff in your house! *(Trudie)*

You could be meditating if you want, while you're peeling potatoes or doing anything else. But you're accomplishing something, getting something done. [By praying] you can't help people, you can't feed the poor. You wish [for] the poor—"God, please take away all other people's diseases." Well, go out there and help people that are sick! Don't just sit there and pray for stuff, do something! That's where I'm at, I'm a doer! *(Cece)*

Some took their ideas of spirituality from other traditions.

I don't feel like I need to worship anything. I think worshipping anything is misguided. I don't worship money, I don't worship the air, I don't worship the Earth. I just wanna co-exist, and I think all the whole thing is connected. And, I don't see God as any humanistic type creature who tells people what to do or listens in. My spiritual belief is that my religion is kindness. I'm kinda with the Dali Lama. Kindness, and The Four Agreements. If you stick with those you can't lose. *(Cece)*

Cece explains two of The Four Agreements taught by Don Miguel Ruiz, modern-day teacher of spiritual enlightenment.

One of them is, Be impeccable with your word. Another one is, Don't take anything personally. If somebody says something about you, then—it's up to you. You're responsible for your own emotions, not other people. No one can make *make* you feel a certain way. You can choose how you react to what they say! I'm not perfect, I mess up sometimes. But basically, if you're kind to everyone all the time, even if you don't like them, and you're kind to yourself, you got it made. You don't need anything else.

You get these spiritual feelings, or at least I do, and it's usually if I'm with a group, especially if we're singing. And also outdoors—that is my church, and I feel united with the world, outside. I did study Zen Buddhism on my own for a little while. Of course, I lived in a Muslim culture, too [in Iran with U.S. Peace Corps, 1968–1970]. But to me all the world religions, including Buddhism, all emphasize kindness to other people, and to all living things in the world—of course Buddhists are stronger on that point. So all the [living] things of the world mean a lot to me, and it really straightens out my mind if I go outside, if I breathe deeply. I think it's a good remedy for anybody, really. Just get outside! *(Nancy)*

In a community that stretched over thirty miles along the Clinch Valley, these back-to-the-landers somehow found like-minded friends. Fellowship with people with similar spiritual beliefs was one of the things that drew them together.

I feel sometimes very spiritual when I think of the people that are here with me that have moved here, why we all gathered in one valley, and having such common interests. I don't know why I've been blessed like that, but I think it's truly unique and sometimes I don't appreciate the uniqueness of it until other people [elsewhere] remind me. They're intrigued by it, when I've come to think it's the normal. *(Dianna)*

I don't know how it happened. Maybe it was just meant to be in the first place, that these ladies all ended up in this area, and they somehow got connected with each other, and found each other. *(Linda)*

I just feel privileged to have been led here, when I don't feel like I knew God. I feel God was leading me here, nonetheless. To be led here to have this setting that we did, to raise children, and the many people that He has used on my behalf. I'm grateful for each knowing of that person, and for each insight that every one has given me. *(Lauren)*

A good deal of my kindred spirits are here. I would say it's a value system that we have in common and very strong spiritual beliefs, although not particularly, necessarily, religious beliefs. And a bond of values, and doing the right thing, taking care of each other, sharing a common dignity with everybody. Nobody's below us or above us. We have a tribe, and have formed these really strong bonds because of the commonalities that we have—of family values, of raising our children the same way with the same ethics and methods. *(Cece)*

Some might look for distinctions between religious and spiritual feelings, or between gratitude and blessings, or prayer and meditation, friendship and fellowship, customs and individual practices, or morality and ethics. The group did not focus on definitions and differences. Instead, they formed an organic whole, a sisterhood, centering on family and nature, and engendering feelings of empathy, gratitude, and joy.

Chapter Seventeen

Family Matters—Holidays, Health, and Emergencies

Whether a family is two people living in a household or a couple with six children, it *is* the family that *matters*, not the straightness of plowed rows, number of quarts of beans canned, or office politics at a job in town. Adequate sustenance underlies all needs, but regardless of the size or makeup of the household, a great deal of a woman's time, then and now, is consumed by caring for and easing the lives of others. Those important family responsibilities include making celebrations merry, striving to keep everyone healthy, and educating children by word and deed. Education, in school and out, forms the basis of the following chapter. Here I present small celebrations and fun activities, as well as family health—the world of well-being. (The women also had to deal with some rather hair-raising accidents.)

Large gatherings ensured the cohesiveness of the community and provided a joyous outlet. In the small family group, celebrations were just as important. Health and happiness go hand-in-hand, and the right amount of time spent with each other engenders both. On some holidays families celebrated at home, for example, Lauren and her six children.

At Christmas time, I said, "Children, if you can cut a tree down in the woods, and bring it in, you can do it." We'd go to the same man year after year, Tiki Rogers, and [ask to cut down one of his cedars]. He'd point to the back of his property, and he'd say, "Cut the whole hill down if you want to!" We'd try to find the fullest one, which was not always easy. There was always several of us, and we'd take time to pick one out. Then we would string popcorn and we would make scallops, little scallops, all the way around the tree, all the way up it. It made the prettiest tree—whether cedar or not! And presents—I'm not a super, big, go-out-and-buy-a-lot-of-stuff person, and the gifts had to be ones given to us, or homemade. That was pretty much the set deal. We didn't go out and buy a lot of stuff! *(Lauren)*

Yvonne's family observed Hanukkah.

We did Hanukkah, because Bill is Jewish, and so he introduced that, first to [our daughter] Tasnima and later to [our son] Sabino, and it suited me just fine because it kept me out of the whole Christmas thing and that whole, like, commercial stuff. When we did Hanukkah—a tiny little present for eight days, a present a day—it could be just a tiny little thing. Aw, that was wonderful! And then we burnt the candles, and Bill sang his blessing. That was really nice.

Some celebrated with friends nearby.

We had these two friends over in Norton, Virginia, that we had been nuns with. Anybody that we were nuns with, it was like family. Some of 'em are still nuns, and some of 'em aren't. So, they would invite us, and we'd go over there one time, and then they'd come over here the next time. Then they started having a little group, and we'd go with that group for Christmas and Easter. *(Pat)*

For some, winter meant travel with the children, in one case to Illinois.

[My husband] Bert's family was from Chicago, so in the winter months when the farm [in Tennessee] was pretty dormant, covered with snow, there really wasn't much to do. We could get one of our friends, friend-family members, to come and make sure the horse had some feed and break the ice in the water in the trough if they needed to, and feed the dogs and the cats. One winter we went [to Chicago] and they had a hundred inches of snow! I really did not care for Chicago in the winter, but it was the only time that we would have to go visit. We did go [South] one winter [when] his parents got a place in Florida. It was before my youngest was born. The girls were maybe three and five. We had to rent a car because the pickup truck, we couldn't get all our stuff, and the kids, in the front of it. [It] was much better than going and visiting them in Chicago! *(Cece)*

In other cases, the travelers came to them.

Oh, gosh, we really used to celebrate Thanksgiving here! His family, a lot of 'em would come from Connecticut and middle Tennessee, and my folks would come, and my sister and her husband. The ones that came from some distance would stay overnight. You would walk downstairs, and there would be kids sleepin' all over the floor. That's why we built the bunkhouse out there was to take some of the overflow, give people a place to stay that wasn't underfoot so much. *(Trudie)*

Birthdays required celebration, of course.

When the kids were younger, they always had a party, because their birthday was the same day, and we'd always have all our friends come, and have a party on the creek. *(Janet)*

My middle son's birthday's in January, so to get somebody [school friends from town] to come across the mountain then, sometimes didn't seem like a very good birthday party. So sometimes I would have a birthday in Rogersville at the Pizza Hut or something like that. But most of the time it was cake at home and family, our immediate family. *(Dianna)*

Lauren made a natural, er, wholesome birthday cake.

And birthdays, everybody had a cake, mother-style. Now they think back at the birthday cakes I made them that were so devoid of sugar, and this-and-that-and-the-other, and all of us just heave a collective sigh, and wonder how we got by—yeah, honey and whole wheat, stick-to-your-ribs. A little bit chewy! *(Lauren)*

Besides holidays, well-being requires some down-time, doesn't it? Answering a question about that, Micki said, "There wasn't a lot of time for entertainment, to be honest. We were so exhausted!" And Lee quipped: "Entertainment? You're kidding, right? I don't know, it seemed like life was our entertainment!"

As far as, "Oh, I need somewhere to go," I think most of us live out here because we don't need somewhere to go. *(Robyn)*

Of course families played games together, read, and even watched TV—maybe while Mom sewed a shirt or patched blue jeans. That is, *if* they even had one, *if* it worked, *if* there were stations broadcasting shows they could receive, and *if* they could afford an antenna and rig it up on roof or hilltop. (Recall Buddy scratching his butt on the antenna in Chapter Ten.)

If we had time to do something like watch a TV show—we didn't have a TV for the first several years, and then we had an old television, and the only station we got was PBS. We did watch *Masterpiece Theater*. That was kind of our big deal. *(Micki)*

Once a week we watched *Dr. Who* [on PBS], but for the rest, you couldn't get TV here. *(Yvonne)*

We had a TV—well, we had two TVs. One had sound and the other had a picture. So the TV with the picture was on top of the one with the sound. And the TV with the picture had to be turned on an hour or two ahead of time because it took a long time for it to come on. [My husband] Rick and [our daughter] Sarah liked to watch *Jeopardy*, so they would turn it on about five, and then the show would come on at seven. *(Carolyn)*

Music was always important. "Sometimes we would go to little bluegrass festivals with the kids," Janet said.

We listened to a lot of music, so we had the radio going or we had the music that we had brought with us, mostly Sixties and

Seventies folk and rock. I was probably introduced to reggae in the late Seventies, early Eighties, and I loved it! We did a lot of dancing, just dancing around the house, having fun, puttin' music on and dancing, like while I was cooking. When my brother moved down he was a good guitarist, and so he would come over, and he would play and I'd sing. *(Micki)*

Idyllic pastimes were part of the country life, but so were mishaps. To make matters worse, most of these homes were at least a half-hour's drive to the hospital.

Well, one time Alyson was riding [her horse] Diamond, and I was out in the field with her, 'cause I would not let her ride unattended, but a bee stung Diamond in the eye, and she bucked. And bucked Alyson right into barbed wire! So, that was a rush trip to the hospital, and many, many stitches later. I didn't think she would ever ride her after that, but, she did. *(Linda)*

When [my daughter] Monica was two, she'd stand back on the kitchen chair, and she'd rock back and forth and back and forth until the chair went over! Then she'd get up and do it again. Well, one time she tried it in this youth chair, which is significantly taller. Well, she went over in that, and when she went over, she nearly bit completely through her tongue. There was black and blue underneath, and it was connected out on the edges, but there was this huge gaping hole in her tongue! And blood all over the place! So I'm in the kitchen with her, in our little place up the hollow, by myself, and I'm saying, "Oh, my God. Cold water, I need to get cold water. I need to stop this bleeding!" I'm trying to hold her up to the sink, and I start feeling faint, and I get my back to the counter, and I'm sliding down. I got down on the floor before I totally keeled over. Well, I called the doctor. We had a phone, a landline. I called the doctor, and he said, "There's nothing—" I said, "Should I bring her in? She's gonna need stitches." He said, "We can't. We don't stitch tongues. It'll heal up by itself." After it stopped bleeding—and she knew she had this hole in her tongue—she would go around, and stick out her tongue, and this big opening—for the first day or so [would] open up. It was like—oh-h-h! It was awful! *(Cece)*

But if you had no phone and no transportation—

One time [my son] Joseph put his foot in hot, boiling water that I—that I had been canning with. And he was a toddler. That's when we lived on the hill. So I put his foot in cold water for a while. He and I and [my little daughter] Rachel were the only ones home. We had to walk down the hill to some neighbors. We didn't have a telephone. The Heltons up in Helton Hollow called [our friend] Oliver, and he came and took us to the emergency room. Joseph was okay. *(Carolyn)*

Even with a phone, first aid may still be needed before the harried trip to the hospital.

If a need arose, we would go get medical attention. Like, [my son] Jared had a barbwire stuck in him one time [in his abdomen], and I pulled it out, and of course he had to get a tetanus shot. [My daughter] Molly rode her bike off the bridge one time and of course she went to the hospital. *(Vicki)*

I worried a lot because I knew if there was a serious accident, it was going to be my own first aid that would be possibly the difference between living or not. We had some chainsaw accidents, and fortunately they weren't to the point of bleeding out. We were able—it was my husband—to get him to the hospital and get that taken care of. I was glad [I was a nurse] but that gave me a responsibility that I didn't really want. I felt like that it was definitely my job to make sure that not only [my family's] injuries were taken care of and their illnesses were properly cared for, I also felt a responsibility to my neighbors. Many of my them would call me for advice. I did the best that I could but I doubted myself a lot of times. *(Dianna)*

One time we definitely used the hospital because [my daughter] April got knocked down and bitten by a Great Dane, the neighbors' dog, and [it] tore out her teeth, and [she was] terribly scarred. So it was racing to the Rogersville emergency room! So we did use it for that, but then [later] she had to go and have plastic surgery and all sorts of stuff, but that day the Rogersville hospital seemed to do the trick.

You remember me telling you about the "Ambulance" [white Plymouth station wagon in Chapter Eleven]? Anyway, stretched her out, and oh, gosh, it was pretty sad because she was like four years old, something like that, and she kept wanting to pass out, and just bleeding like you wouldn't believe, and her face is all tore up, and you know her mouth—her teeth are gone, and I just thought to myself, This can't be! "Please, April," I kept saying, "please hang in there. Please don't be gone on me." *(Lee)*

[Author note: April had good care and surgery, and today, thankfully, she has no visible scars.]

Clinch Mountain Girls

Not only was ambulance travel time a problem, but also the expense was an obstacle.

> My husband got the produce for the school system in Hawkins County. He would go to the farmers' market in the early morning, twice a week, and he'd pick up [the orders]. We homeschooled our children, and he would often let my two oldest sons go with him, Timothy and Aaron, and they'd help him with whatever—figuring out what went where. On this particular day, he had just delivered to the school in Surgoinsville and they were starting to pull out. Well, a couple of things went wrong. First of all, my son, sitting by the window, Aaron, did not buckle up. Second of all, he did not shut the door completely. And, third of all, he was peeling one of those oranges from the farmer's market. He was havin' a hard time getting the peel off—and it came off with a flourish! His elbow hit the door, and it flew open; he kind of tipped over and went out the door. Well, my other son was looking in another direction, and he turned to his right, and his brother was no longer there, and the door was open! He said to my husband, "Aaron's gone!" My husband stopped, and he said it was the longest thirty seconds of his life. He went clear around the back of the truck, which was perhaps the size of half a "semi." He came around to the other side, where he found my son, who was kneeling, and holding his elbow. He looked at his daddy, and said, "Daddy, I believe you just ran over my arm!" And he had! He ran over his arm! I think his forearm was good. It was his elbow that was in such bad shape. But anyway, he took him to the hospital in Rogersville. After they had bandaged him up, [my husband] called me, and he told me a big lie. He says, "Well, I've run over Aaron—but he's okay." So, I got there, and

he hurriedly got Aaron in the car, and explained to me that we have to go to another hospital, and it's *not* okay. *(Lauren)*

Lauren explains that the hospital wanted to send Aaron by ambulance to Laughlin Hospital in Morristown, but they couldn't afford it because, "We didn't have insurance."

So, anyway, it was interesting! He had surgery the following morning. They pulled a lot of pieces of bone out of his elbow, and sewed him back up, and we were on our way. Aaron got away with murder for six weeks. All my children had chores, all of them had to work. One day I was lookin' out the window and he had that arm—that bad arm that was gettin' him out of everything—he was holding a hatchet with that arm and swinging it for all it was worth! On a piece of wood on a chopping block. I knocked on the window, and I said, "Come here!" He came in and I handed him a broom, and that was the end of that. And to this day, he is a hard worker, and very productive. *(Lauren)*

A project could suddenly become dangerous for these independent, determined homesteaders. Trudie and Steve bought some glass for large windows they were putting into an addition they had built, so they made a plan for how to unload it.

The worst—knock wood—accident, I guess, that happened here, we had bought a big crate. I think it had at least ten huge panes of glass. They were like maybe four feet by five feet, they were really big, and they were all on this large crate in the back of our pickup truck. We were gonna like try to slide the crate off, just the two of us. Why we didn't do it when somebody was here to help us, I don't know. But, anyway, it's coming! We had put up some rails to slide the crate off, and it tips, because it gets to a certain point on the truck where it tipped the crate over. It's coming down on top of Steve, and he's got his hand up like this [bent back from the wrist]. Luckily, there's a wheelbarrow there, which gave him some place to kinda crouch down under before all that glass could come down on top of him. But what it did, it took his hand and bent it so far back, that when we finally got him out of there, I mean, it swelled up! It was just huge! While he's squished under there, he says, "Get the handyman jack out of the truck!" [to prop up the crate so he can crawl out from under it.] And those things are heavy! [That sized jack weighs thirty pounds.] It was in the front seat of the truck, and I grabbed it with this [left] hand, and I'm pulling it. There was cloth [upholstery] on the door, and I got caught in the cloth, and so I'm holding the whole thing up with one arm, and I'm tugging and tugging [with the other hand to free it]. I finally pulled it and got it out. By the time I got the handyman jack over there, I think he had crawled out under the wheelbarrow. But, it pulled so many muscles across my shoulder and back, that for days I couldn't take a deep breath. And his hand was just horribly swollen. We were both incapacitated, we were both in pain, and we were not getting along! That was a close one right there, that was—to me—That was pretty scary! And those things can happen just like that! [Snaps her fingers] You think you've got a plan. *(Trudie)*

Prevention was the only insurance most could afford. Living far from medical care necessitated skillful first aid, as well as home remedies.

> I took my children to the doctor. We did some herbal remedies. Rachel had her tonsils out at one point. But we didn't have a lot of health issues when the kids were young. But I did take them to a doctor if I felt they needed to go. We kept up with their vaccinations, that sort of thing. Probably our life style [kept them healthy], because you know, we were tough. And we ate well. We didn't eat—we couldn't afford—like sugary things, or go to a fast-food place, or anything like that. We ate really well. *(Carolyn)*

At that time, some feared vaccinations due to a doctor's claim that more research proved untrue.

> I did have them vaccinated, and I remember I chose not to have all the vaccinations. But I remember that being some of the most difficult times for me, was sitting there and signing the paper, the release. That was really difficult—to make the choice about vaccinations. *(Micki)*

The mothers usually treated ailments at home, and some medicines came from the land where they lived, not the pharmacy.

> When they got sick, when it wasn't like an accident requiring stitches or something, I treated 'em with the herbs and the tinctures and things that I had learned. They were by-and-large, effective. I can't even remember whether any of my kids ever had antibiotics. I'm thinking, probably not. After they started school we dealt with pinworms and we dealt with head lice. Up until then, they hadn't [had those]. Gosh, I remember, for the lice, mixing tea tree oil [melaleuca] in their shampoo. I also learned a bit about the herbs from the neighbor, Ruth. She

taught me about catnip, for instance, [for] when a child is teething, or colicky, and how to make the tea. *(Micki)*

If the children got sick, I gave them barley green and organic frozen cherries. [Barley green] is just a powder, made from barley grass, and it gives them extra nutrition. Sometimes I would have to take them to a doctor, and then it may have been a few times that they took antibiotics or something. Pretty much just let them sleep; that's the best way to get them well. And, just try to give them fruit and things like that, that had enzymes in it; that could just help them, help their insides. *(Anne)*

Besides home remedies, families kept a positive attitude and bravely withstood illnesses or injuries. The school gave rewards for being well—that is, for perfect attendance.

It sounds crazy but my kids didn't get sick. I mean, they really, truly didn't. They took pride, you know, in getting—what did they get, a dollar at Clinch School if they didn't miss a day? We did have a couple of sort of messed-up accident kind of things. I remember Kurt one time fell out of the barn [while hanging tobacco] and scraped his leg pretty darn bad. A lot of home remedies went on here. I just, just did what we could. *(Lee)*

I would hug and kiss 'em and look at their boo-boos and everything, but it was basically, "All right, get over it." *(Nancy)*

If it was a cold, or flu, or something like that, I'd say, "Drink peppermint tea, vitamin C, lots of water, and you'll be all right." I really believe the body is a magnificent healing machine, and if we take care of it, for the most part we can be healthy. If we need to go to the doctor's, we do. I did get cancer. Well, it was just *carcinoma in situ*, on my cervix. And that was before Molly was born, and I told the doctors at UT Hospital that I would like to try to heal it myself, and they got very angry with me. They told me I was gonna die. But I did research, and I did what I could—some really strange things, some cleanses—and looked at my thought processes and my body connection, and went back to some other hospital a year and a half later, and it was gone. Years later it came back, and I had a little laser surgery, but I felt like I had the tools to take care of myself, so I wasn't as concerned about it. *(Vicki)*

[With illnesses] we just—just, made it. You had to feed the animals, and when you fed the animals, you came back and went to bed. What did people do, when they didn't have a car? When they didn't have a—whatever? You just toughed it out. *(Alicia)*

These few sketches of the families "in sickness and in health" illustrate how the homesteaders coped. Fortunately, they all survived the illnesses and accidents that occurred back then. Whether the families had children or not, all had to plan ahead, and keep a positive attitude.

All repeatedly stated the importance of a healthy lifestyle. And did they have good food? You bet! And did they get plenty of exercise? Are you kidding? How about sleep? No traffic noise, dark night skies, and the feeling of safety led to a peaceful night's rest. Plenty of family time and small celebrations rounded out their well-being.

Chapter Eighteen

Teach Your Children Well

On the north side of Clinch Mountain, schools scattered among the hills and valleys ranged from a couple of classrooms to somewhat larger consolidated secondary schools in the 1970s and 1980s. High schools of a thousand or more students were located on the south side of Clinch Mountain in Hawkins and Grainger Counties. All the schools reflected the norms and life goals of local people, the value placed on education, and the lack of equitable distribution of resources in county and state school systems.

Of the eighteen mothers in the group, only two of them had finished raising their children prior to arrival in the valley. All were enthusiastic about their children growing up in the country learning about the natural world and appreciating a simple life. Some had decided already to homeschool their children. Almost half tried homeschooling for a time, with varied experiences.

> We started our own preschool. I had a station wagon so I became the "bus driver." Carolyn would [teach on] Mondays, Patty would do Wednesdays, and I'd do Fridays. Once I'd dropped off [the kids], I could go work on my canning or whatever I wanted

to, uninterrupted. Each of us had parts of two days a week that we would have free of our kids. [On the day] we would do the school thing, we'd plan projects, we'd go to the library, [we'd] use eggshells for planters and have 'em plant seeds—all kinds of different stuff. Carolyn was a former teacher. I was the daughter of a teacher. It worked out really well. *(Cece)*

They learned from a young age. We would take them to the field with us, because also, where are they gonna go? They were homeschooled, so it was a part of their education, really. So, for example, Zack was our eldest, and as soon as he was old enough, we gave him a small plot of "maters" that were his responsibility to take care of. He would care for them, and then he would pick them and go to the flea market with us. So he learned like, for instance, mathematics. He would be responsible for learning how to make change. He would be given a dollar bill or maybe a five dollar bill, and would have to calculate the change. There was a real marriage between their schooling, their education, and just our day-to-day lives and working on the farm. [They were] learning how to speak and communicate with other individuals who were not a part of their typical scene. Because the people we hung out with were, by-and-large, people of what we considered to be our "tribe," they were "other." Our sons had long hair. They were used to seeing other boys with long hair, because those were most of the kids they hung out with. We'd go to the flea market, and I thought it was really important for them to have the experience of interacting with people that were not from their typical social group; they could learn that diversity of different cultures, because we really were a particular culture. So they learned how to be comfortable in speaking to others, and adults in particular. That was certainly part of their education as well. *(Micki)*

I tried to homeschool, and my daughter was of the opinion that I didn't know anything, so she didn't want to learn from me. And that was fine with me, although, poor thing, she had a really rough time in school here—really rough. Eventually we sent her to high school for a few years to a private school in Knoxville. Our son, yes, I homeschooled him, but I did realize he needed socialization. So he started to go to school, but his level was, like, w-a-a-ay somewhere else. In fact, I think he was in second grade, and they did a vocabulary test with him, and he blew the top off the test, through twelfth grade! His vocabulary was richer than what they could provide for him in their textbooks, even. So, what we finally decided, he went to school part-time, and then they had him read, go read stories to the second graders, or something. They didn't know what to do with him. So, he also went to a private school, in Morristown I think, from third grade on. It was very nice—they worked with us, with this part-time idea, going to school part-time. That suited him, and, well, I loved it. He learned very well from me. It was a pleasure. It was very organic. You take him in the woods, and we go and collect mushrooms, and we look it up in dictionaries, and we make pictures. We'd talk, and before you know it, the kid has learned an enormous amount. And so, yeah, both of them did very well in school. *(Yvonne)*

Although Vicki had to return to teaching to support her family, she was able to homeschool her first two girls, including when the family went tree-planting in the winters. The oldest daughter later wrote a letter of appreciation of the way she was taught, as Vicki remembers.

Well, she entitled the letter "Freedom." And I think they *were* free from a lot of influence from the media, especially the older girls, because we didn't have TV. I think with the home-schooling they were allowed to learn at their own pace. They had a variety of experiences even though, looking from the outside, it may have not looked like that. They also were part of a community of people that cared about one another. And Nature was available to 'em. I think my daughter also mentioned in that letter, that she felt like she had the freedom to think for herself. (*Vicki*)

Several mothers had to give up homeschooling, like Anne, who said, "When I started workin', they had to all get into public school." Divorce could put an end to homeschooling and bring complex changes for the children as they transitioned into public school.

They were homeschooled up until the time that their father and I were divorced. Joe insisted—the kids' homeschooling was my responsibility, and because our joint arrangement was six months with each parent—that the kids would go to public school because he didn't want the responsibility of taking on the schooling. Now, in terms of regrets with that? It was most difficult on Zack to go into school as a freshman, having not, "people" [kin] here. Kids around here—it's a very small community, the schools are small—and they become very cliquish, and it's already a little bit of a point against you if you are considered sort of a foreigner, which we were, and our children were, despite the fact that we had been here for so long, and we were accepted. Still, [our] children were not from the local clan. But then, he also was the new kid coming in, so nobody knew him.

And that's hard when you're fifteen. For Seth going into sixth grade, it wasn't as difficult. He did struggle with that some, to be sure, and there was this jostling for position 'cause he came in and then the other boys of his age [had] a little bit—you know, 'cause all the girls go to the new kid—of an issue there. But he was a terrific athlete, so that helped him to kind of find his place. Luke went into second grade. It was a difficult transition for him. The divorce was difficult on all three of the kids as much as we tried to make it as easy as possible. But he eventually did fine. I was able to hand-pick their teachers, and when I went into the school system, I told them, "These are the things that I must have if my kids are going to come to school. I must have control over *these things*," and so that helped. I would not have changed homeschooling them. But there were some difficulties that came as a result of having made that transition. Academically, they were totally up to snuff. (*Micki*)

Cece wanted to homeschool, but things didn't turn out that way.

Because I was very unhappy with the Hancock County schools and the prospects for my kids' education, I wanted to homeschool my kids. My husband did not want me to homeschool the kids. He wanted the kids to, quote, "Be like everybody else's kids and go to school." So, I said, "If you want that, then you're going to have to find a job where there's some better schools." That's what led us away from here. When I came here I was just pregnant for the first time, and I was not thinking about schools at that point! School was a long, long ways away! The county that we moved into did not have very good schools. My only option was to homeschool at that time, and since that wasn't acceptable to my husband, we ended up leaving this lovely place. For a while.

Lauren was homeschooling her six children while baking bread, cooking from scratch, washing diapers and clothes, line-drying them, stoking the wood stove, finishing her GED, and going to nursing school. Then she was forced to choose another option.

> My kids were not always homeschooled, because I almost died. I was in the hospital for twelve days. A friend came to me and said, "Sign right here"—not, "Do you—[want to—]" I signed my kids into the Seventh Day Adventist School in Greeneville, Tennessee. So, from then on, we had this incredible hour-plus commute, one way. Didn't have the money for it, didn't have the resources for it, but I had a bunch of smart kids that they felt were valuable and somehow the money always came through. And, they had all kinds of opportunities.

Like Cece, a number of parents were concerned with the quality of education in the public schools. A little about local schools: Clinch School, due to its isolation north of Clinch Mountain from the rest of Hawkins County, is the smallest K–12 school in the state. That school, and Washburn School in northern Grainger County, are the exceptions to the usual pattern of small rural elementary schools feeding the large consolidated high schools located in towns. Clinch School is described by a teacher, a back-to-the-lander, who started teaching there in 1989.

> I think it averages, usually around one hundred forty to one hundred fifty students in grades K–12. I think for the most part, they felt that was an advantage. They were getting a lot of

individual attention, and they thought it was a definite advantage that such a wide age-range of kids were in one building together. I suppose it made it feel a little bit more like a family, because you were aware of kids growing up over the years. We're on the north side of Clinch Mountain, in Clinch Valley, and we are definitely isolated from the rest of the county. There have been various times when the county has wanted to shut down the school, so there has been a lot of local involvement when they threatened to close down the school. Those were times when parents really came out and said, "Hey, we want this school!" But, for the most part, when we weren't under those kind of threats, there was less activity. There were years when we had good parent involvement. We had PTA—but it was always a small group of people, and not the majority of the parents. Sometimes it was more of the newcomers than it was the locals. Not always. *(Beth)*

Here's a newcomer parent's perception.

They went to Clinch School, which was just this sweet school at the time. The kids [of all ages] traveled on the [same] buses, and they were kind; the older kids even knew the younger kids, and would tease them. I remember going in there one day, and one of the high school kids was teasing my six- or seven-year-old daughter about her silly laugh. You know, just fun things. When [my older daughter] was in the third grade, there was this wonderful teacher, and she got the whole school together and did a play called *Alice in Wonderland*. She involved all of the grade school children in the cast. The high school girls, I think, did all the make-up and made the scenery. The high school boys did all the lighting and electronics for this. If you wanted to be the caterpillar—I think she had seven caterpillars! She had a whole row of singing flowers. Nobody was left out. It was just this wonderful program. I thought the school was so neat 'cause the kids were so gentle with each other. *(Joanne)*

The goals of both children and parents led to some tough decisions as the children reached their teens.

When they got older, they wanted to go to a larger school over in Rogersville, so that was difficult. It was difficult for teenagers because of the socialization they desired. That meant I either took them to school or when they got old enough to drive, they drove that distance to school in Rogersville. *(Dianna)*

The reason we moved them into town [Rogersville schools], is because [at Clinch School] they have the same teacher for math from the eighth grade into the twelfth grade, and for all other subjects also. So if they had a bad teacher, they were stuck with him for five years in [eighth grade and] high school. The class sizes were small, and those kind of things were good, but they didn't have advanced classes at the time my kids went to high school. They didn't have teachers willing to go an extra mile—now some, they did. They can't prepare as well for goin' on to college and things like that as they can in bigger [schools]. *(Judy)*

Carolyn's family moved several times, so her kids attended the tiny Kyles Ford School (Hancock County), then the K-12 Clinch School (Hawkins County), then larger Hawkins County schools in Rogersville.

If I saw Sarah coming back up the hill in the morning I knew that the bus didn't show up, and she would be so disappointed because she loved school. Sarah and [her younger sister] Rachel went to Kyles Ford School, just a little school on the river. It was wonderful, lot of attention paid to all the children. Corinne Bowlin, Pat Nicholson—those were the two teachers [for grades one through five]. We loved it; the kids loved school at Kyles Ford.

Then we moved, so the kids had to attend Clinch School, and by that time Joseph was also in school. That was, I think, a difficult change for them. But they did well in school; they all did very well.

Then we had to switch again when we moved to Rogersville [for a short time]. By that time I had gone to nursing school and was working in Rogersville, so it was much more convenient for the kids to go to school there. For Joseph that was fine. He was still in elementary school, and he did really well with the transition. They were all up on everything, they weren't behind. *(Carolyn)*

The teenagers who left a small, rural school experienced challenges in a huge high school in a town twenty or more miles away, but most appreciated more social opportunities.

For Rachel and Sarah [Cherokee High School] was a difficult change. The school was much bigger and the children at Clinch came from a much different background, I think—there was more poverty so you weren't judged by what you were wearing. But when they went to Rogersville it was much more about, "Oh, you come from over the mountain." They were called "Clinchmanites." But they did okay; they adjusted well. Their education was, I would say, satisfactory. Wouldn't say it was exceptional. *(Carolyn)*

[My daughter] went to Cherokee, and it was okay. But she didn't gee and haw with the people here as much as she does somewhere else, because a lot of the kids her age don't aspire to do a whole lot, to put it bluntly. *(Robyn)*

Linda, a teacher as well as a parent, began her career at the tiny Rock Hill Elementary School, and then taught at the eleven hundred-student consolidated Cherokee High School in Rogersville, where her daughters attended. Linda discussed the breadth of activities needed to supplement her daughters' education in a school system with a stringent budget.

[Raising kids here was] best of both worlds, I think. You felt like they were safe. You felt like it was a pretty wholesome environment. But on the other hand, sometimes I felt like, Oh my gosh, am I giving them enough enrichment?

Nature and creeks and crawdads are all fun, but there has to be other things too. It was just difficult keeping the kids involved in dance, or whatever they wanted to do at the moment, here. But for the most part, I think it was pretty great.

Yeah, [we felt we had to take them to museums and on trips]. That's the only way they were gonna get there. The schools might have occasionally taken trips, but not nearly enough. Again, you don't want to use the standard of what these children are exposed to, as the standard as to what you expose yours to. You gotta be a little careful there, I think. We saw to it our kids got to do a lot of diversified things.

Lauren, raised in an educated family who lived abroad, regretted dropping out of school, and was glad her children went to a Seventh Day Adventist school with more opportunities.

> I learned to be a mom here. I did what all other mothers did, took care of their children. I read a lot of books. I wanted to do it right and of course I did it all wrong, lots of times, and wish I could go back and change this, and change that. But, that was my devotion, to bring up my children. I wanted them to know the Bible, and they're all pretty well-versed. And, I wanted them to have opportunities. I saw some of the things that I missed because of the decisions I made, and it was very important to me that they had every chance available to them to have a well-rounded life. Just about all of them have been to other countries on mission trips. Martha went to Austria last year, but she also went on multiple mission trips to Guatemala, to Dominican Republic, different places. [She] helped when the Camp Creek Community [in nearby Greene County] had the tornados, and people were killed there.

The parents encouraged sports and experience of the natural world. Several families participated in league soccer teams. "We did a lot of fun things with the local kids here, had soccer teams, and always went to the basketball games," Lee said. Basketball was popular, especially in the small schools across Clinch Mountain that did not have football teams.

> We always had a place to play basketball. We had a hoop out here on our property, but the church is across the street. The road was the court and the church parking lot was also sort of part of it. There's almost no traffic, and if they couldn't be

smart enough to get out of the road, then I wouldn't let 'em to ever start it. [The children] put the hoop there—I felt a little weird about the church bein' there and everything—but they did it. Rick [Novkov] gave it to us. It was set in concrete; it was really a good one. They did it all. They got the neighbor, and they went with [him and] the tractor and brought it down [from Rick's], and dug the hole and so I just let 'em do it. I didn't want to stand in the way, and the church didn't care. They're alright with it. Lots and lots of basketball [at the kids' schools] for years and years, including four years with my daughter in college in Virginia. That was a great source of pride, and a little bit of excitement, for someone that doesn't have much excitement in their life. That would be me. *(Anne)*

We played hacky sack. [My husband] Jerome and [our son] Jared played basketball. [The children] hiked on the farm and played—they had games of imagination. And did not have any technology! *(Vicki)*

All the mothers mentioned their children's exploration and enjoyment of the outdoors.

As a little girl, April's next door neighbor, her playmate, was Liz. And Liz and April were just—I mean, they were sisters. So Liz lived here a lot and to my pleasure also. Those two were absolutely a joy. A lot of running around in the summertime like just little wild animals, just exploring. Had ponies, the two of them, and just absolutely adorable, chasing chickens and seeing it all, and having pets like you wouldn't believe! Knowing the farm, knowing what was going on. *(Lee)*

Clinch Mountain Girls

They spent a lot of time outside. One time we lived in a house, the big log house on Mountain Valley [Road], and the whole hillside was covered in those rambling roses, *Florabunda*, and daisies. It was just covered with them! One day Rick had somebody come and bush-hog that hill [using a rotary mower pulled by a tractor], and it broke Rachel's heart. She cried and cried. I just thought, Wow, I had no idea it would affect her that way! She was so enthralled with all those beautiful flowers out there she didn't see them as any problem. *(Carolyn)*

The kids splashed in creeks, ponds, and the Clinch River.

Most of our friends had children around the same age, so when they came over, fun was playing in the creek, and finding crawdads and periwinkles, and building up dams in the creek, and going to the pond, and riding their bicycle off the dock into the pond, and playing in the treehouse—so it was just great! *(Dianna)*

We loved the river, [would] go down there in the summer all the time, and swim, and play in the river. It was wonderful. Sarah would go dig up grubs in the grass and go down and fish in the creek. She'd take Joseph and Rachel down there, and they'd just play in the creek, and she'd fish. *(Carolyn)*

On Sabbath, we'd go to Bays Mountain often. We had a year-long pass. It's a nature park, in Kingsport, Tennessee, on top of Bays Mountain. The only place that has fresh-water jellyfish. *(Lauren)*

My focus was on raising my family, raising 'em healthy, and giving 'em additional education that they weren't going to get in school. We went on walks around here, and we'd pick wildflowers, and we'd talk about, "This type of a—" and, "See this nut; this came from this tree." I took 'em to the university of life, all along with their regular schooling. *(Cece)*

A few homesteaders had small boats and enjoyed going out on nearby lakes, like Linda and her family. Janet said, "We had a little aluminum fishing boat. We'd pile everything on there; we'd go out to the islands and camp." The parents were glad of the learning taking place outdoors—although often ignorant of the details as their children roamed fields and woods.

When I moved to Gainesville, Florida, people were scared to let their kids play outside. I mean, what kind of life is that? But [here] she could have wandered through the woods for hours and hours, which she *did*, and it doesn't matter, everybody's okay, and she was happy. *(Robyn)*

My kids, I still think it was good raising 'em here because it was so healthy, and they learned about the outdoors. And I'm still finding out places that—"Yeah, we went up there, Mom. We climbed up [to] the top of that tree." They [tell you] they did that—and, they did that one thing that just makes your heart stop. It made them resilient and in a lot of ways they conquered new projects pretty easily. *(Nancy)*

The young absorbed the community norms of the back-to-the-landers.

We had very good friends that made up for any of the other shortcomings. They saw how—not just my mom does it that way, but Judy does it that way, Carolyn does it that way, and lots of our other friends—so that's the way you should be in this world. They learned from the role model adults that we surrounded ourselves with, and I'm really proud of that. *(Nancy)*

The mothers reflect on the principles by which they raised their children. First, as Lee said, "You learned how to do without and to do with what you had." And Dianna stated, "I think they appreciate having something when they know what it's like to be without."

The whole time they were growin' up they didn't have anything fancy, or usually, brand new. They don't have to have everything, that society tells you you need to be happy. I feel like they got that out of the way that they were raised. *(Janet)*

Janet includes the values of work and perseverance. "They see that you just gotta keep pushin' on, and don't give up."

I think that actually it was a better thing for them to be here because it did give them a sense of where things come from. You work very hard to get what you want. They each grew their own tobacco field. When they said, "We really want to buy a car, Mom"—well, John and I really could not provide a car. So, you grow a field of tobacco, and you get a nice cash sum, and you go out and buy yourself a car! They took care of their car. John showed them how to. *(Lee)*

Lauren taught teamwork.

My [six] kids all knew to work. Some of the chores went around just a meal. The kids all learned to make different parts of it.

And, following the meal, one kid would wash dishes, one kid would rinse dishes, one kid would clear and wipe, one kid would clean the bathroom, one would sweep the floor. And, the guy that cooked, he was free.

Mothers also emphasized their relationship to the wider world. Being, quote, hippies, as we were, I think we wanted to be a part of making the world be a better place. Part of that was some social activism, and being aware of social issues. I remember taking Erin and Annie, one of them on the front of me, and one on the back of me, and demonstrating against Phipps Bend Nuclear Power Plant. Then later, when Erin was older, we demonstrated at Oak Ridge, the nuclear [National Security] Complex, [so] that they would know that there are things that we can do to make a difference. *(Vicki)*

Whether sons and daughters moved away or stayed, their values remain with them.

[One son] is still here. We built him a house on the "lower forty" [acres] and he's still here. He's not about to grow tobacco or anything like that but he loves it here. I don't think that he would ever go anywhere else. [The other son] has wonderful stories about here. I think it has given him an amazing work ethic and appreciation, and I hope that he passes that on to his kids. *(Lee)*

[My children] have told me that they have gotten a lot out of being raised here, and not having a lot, not being raised to thinking they're entitled. I think that's a wonderful gift that they received, that they appreciate everything that they have, and what goes into earning materially. And spiritually they're all in different directions. I want them to choose their own path, and I try to be a hands-off mom. I don't think [being raised here] hurt them particularly, but any way you raise your children, I'm sure there are things that could have been better. So—you could ask them! *(Carolyn)*

Of the sixteen women who raised their forty-seven children here, there are many success stories that are not part of this book. These grown children are in the trades, business, education, communications, law, and health. Among them are five teachers and two professors; three physical therapists and one orthopedic surgeon, two lawyers, a radio personality, a hair stylist, a social worker, a mason, a fireman, a welder, a postal worker, a video producer, and a small farmer. A few work in sales and a couple have tech jobs. Thirty have offspring of their own. This chapter is still being written by the grown children themselves.

Chapter Nineteen

Meeting the Neighbors

The focus of this book has been on the strong women whose mutual support was vital, but the technical skills and generous assistance from local people have been threads throughout the stories. In the next chapter you will encounter the rocks in the road and see how the path was smoothed out. But what was the local reaction when the greenhorns began streaming in from all over the country?

When the back-to-the-landers arrived, the people living in the remote Clinch Valley were curious about them and were often eager to share their knowledge with the newcomers. The homesteaders were happy to learn more about the Appalachian culture in general as well as the specifics of farming in the area. Many of the newcomers had come with preconceived ideas about the local people.

> I am so embarrassed to admit this, but I'm going to. Being raised in a middle class home in Cincinnati, Ohio, I watched *The Beverly Hillbillies*—and thinking that people with accents that sounded like *The Beverly Hillbillies*—there was something about the accent that made them not as intelligent. But, you know, I was proved wrong over and over again, and I know now, that wisdom and intelligence

has nothing to do with, a lot of times, what we think intelligence means. It's not a nice thing to have those ideas, and I guess we all learn ideas, and we have to un-learn 'em as we get wiser.

They knew how to farm, and they knew how to can, and they knew how to live off the land. And then, I work with people that have southern accents, that are well-educated, smart people, and it was just a ridiculous thing to think. *(Vicki)*

I did have an idea that they would actually be much simpler than what they were. I didn't even know if there was any TV over here, and a lot of people had TV. We did not, but a lot of people had televisions, and nice cars, and jobs that they traveled to go to, hours or more, when I thought everybody just stayed home and farmed.

Some people had a lot more education than I expected them to have and chose to live here. Some illiterate—by never *having* to learn to read or write—were extremely smart about life, and machines, and many, many things. You could just tell in conversation, they were very smart people but just not educated. Those were the people I learned the most from probably. *(Dianna)*

I had gotten into the folk music scene in Ann Arbor [Michigan], so I was very excited about the Appalachian culture, and I probably romanticized it quite a bit. But, you know, after a while, really, working [as a nutritionist] with people in the health clinics, and trying to find out what they ate, and then trying to advise them on what to eat, was a real wake-up call about reality and peoples' beliefs. *(Nancy)*

The newcomers needed to discard old ideas and open their eyes, ears, and minds.

I think people around here are pretty set in their ways, so we just kinda wanted to not make a lotta waves, and kinda go with the flow, and learn how to live in this area. And, we did! I always appreciated that they were country people. I never thought that they were below me or anything, or that much different than me. Of course I was young, and they accepted us, and they took us right in as good people. *(Janet)*

First, however, there were some interesting encounters.

We had decided to go check out this stream that was close by. There was a waterfall on this stream, and it was beautiful. [My husband] Jerome and I decided to skinny-dip, and we were new to Washburn. We didn't think anybody could see us, but after a little while, a police [sheriff's] car drove up the road. We hurried and got our clothes on, and got back in our car, and drove a little ways to the little house we were livin' in.

The [deputy drove up] and got out and said, "Somebody's been skinny-dippin' in the creek up the road." And we said, "Oh-h-h, yuh?" He said, "They better not do it again."

We said, "O-o-kay!"

I guess the lady across the road had seen us. *(Vicki)*

When we first moved here into that little house, we hadn't been there maybe like a couple weeks or something, and we came home and there's a truck parked out front, and there's a man on our front porch, and he's doing something with the light bulb up top. This is interesting! And he just acted like he had every right in the world to be there, and he said he was hooking up an electric fence charger to keep his cows on the pasture that was next to our piece. He found us to be very curious, and we found him to be kinda curious. But he turned out to be such a nifty person, his whole family. They would bring us literally carloads of vegetables from their garden when we first moved there. And they would make it seem like we were doing them a favor. They'd say, "It would really help us out if you would take this"—the cabbages, and corn, and beans, and everything else. I'm quite sure they thought we were going to starve to death or something. They just turned out to be wonderful people. *(Trudie)*

I think I was hanging up clothes or something, and I looked off to the hillside not far from the house, all wooded and brush and everything, and there was a plume of smoke coming out of the bushes! This person was smoking a cigarette. They didn't realize that the smoke was giving them away. I realized that people, the mountain men, would crawl around in the mountains up there, and watch us. Sometimes it was like the old moonshiners looking for places to set up their moonshine stills. There was one on our property when we first bought it, which was quickly removed, but you could still smell it, you could see the place where it had been. When they heard [the land] was being sold they had to move their still. So they moved it across the road [to] the hollow on the other side. We could see their fire and their lights over there when they were up there cooking their mash for their moonshine. We did buy some local moonshine and tried it. *(Cece)*

The back-to-the-landers checked out the local people.

[A neighbor] got stuck, so he had to go get help, and it was Ruth and Albert [Burton] come over with the tractor to get him unstuck. Well, what was so cute, I'll never, never forget, is they looked like somebody—now here it is, almost the nineties, we're talking '87 there—and they looked like something out of the Thirties or Forties! I mean, she had like the kerchief on, and the dress with the apron, and they were both adorable! He had overalls on, but I think it was her more than him. But anyway, they looked like if somebody was casting for a movie, for the Thirties or Forties, they probably would've gotten it.

I hadn't really met anybody, and so I didn't know [what local people were like], but they were nice, and that's what I was caring about. They were nice, and they treated us very nice. *(Sandra)*

I remember one day looking at a property. The day before that, we were up staying [in New York City], walking a dog in Central Park, and the next day we were on Pumpkin Valley Road, and there's [wild] turkeys all over the place, running around. It was a big change, but everybody's friendly, and then some people did have us visit quite often, and learn how to make banana pudding, and to see how big a spread they put out on the table. *(Karen)*

There is one family that I got to know, a real typical big ol' Tennessean family, and with a sort of matriarch, Pearl. She was really fantastic! She was wonderful. But the whole family—they were good people, but, like the guys were all spitting tobacco juice, the women had these hair-dresser hair-dos, and then the whole thing with church, also—you know, I felt too alien from that. *(Yvonne)*

One time we were going to Kingsport to trade our car in. We were just hoping it'd make it up there. We'd already done the deal, we just had to deliver the car. And it had got a flat tire. So we pulled over on [Route] 11W, but we didn't have a jack. About that time, this truck, this old beat-up truck pulls in behind us, and this man got out. This guy was rough-lookin'! And, I was like, "Oh, boy!" He had probably several days of beard growth, and a ball cap, and greasy hair kinda stickin' out from under it, and raggedy-looking clothes, and didn't appear all that clean. He was so rough-looking you'd have trouble trying to guess his real age. Anyway, he got out and he walked over, and said, "You need some help?" And we said, "We're gonna change a tire and we don't have a jack." He whipped out a jack; hell, he changed the tire, wouldn't take anything for his trouble. Later I said, "Well, there's judging a book by its cover, you know?" *(Trudie)*

And the old-timers checked out the newcomers.

When we first moved here, Jerome wanted me to set up a bank account in Bean Station. They would not talk to Jerome, because he had long hair. But it was okay for a female to have long hair, so I went in to talk to 'em. *(Vicki)*

When we came to Tennessee, and we moved up there, up the hollow, we kinda thought that there was really nobody else around, and some of the ladies that came from California, particularly Vivien, who was originally from Italy, would go and garden topless. Well, oh my gosh! Did that cause a lot of ruffle among the natives, let's say, "Here's all these foreigners come in, and they go around naked!" *(Cece)*

This neighbor that lives above us, we thought we would use his water, because that's what the students [former tenants] had done. But he didn't want a full-time family using his water. And I think he thought we were drug sellers, anyway, because everybody that visited us was from different places. And we were the first outsiders they'd ever had in here. They knew everybody else from birth. We were the first ones. We did get to know them finally, but he wouldn't let us use the water. *(Pat)*

Jerome and [his brother] Joe played on a basketball team, in the Washburn School, and I would take the kids to go watch, and we would have a good time watching, but I would breast feed my kids right there in the school, and not think anything of it. That's the school I work at now, so it's kind of an interesting thought and memory. The counselor at my school says she remembers when she was young, that her parents would ask if they wanted to "go see the hippies." Then they would drive down the road and see the hippies. She said, "Then we saw these little naked kids, and they had long hair, and they turned around." And then, [her folks declared], "Oh, they're boys!" But those weren't my kids. They were Joe's [my brother-in-law's]. But it was just funny that she shared that with me. *(Vicki)*

When we moved into the valley, the local people that lived there learned a lot about us, and we were sort of really interesting to them, as they were to us. I never felt like it was any animosity on either side at all, ever. *(Carolyn)*

At first the newcomers faced a language gap.

> When I first started working at Bean Station School the teachers would have to sit at a table in front, where the kids would come and find out what class they went to, and the dialect was so much different to me that I had to have an interpreter. It was like a different language. *(Vicki)*

Linda, whose parents and grandparents were from Clinch Valley, but who was raised in Ohio, found it difficult to understand her students at first.

> There was this little girl [who] said, "Ah-loht-a dahm, ah-loht-a-dahm!" she sounded like a bird crowing. I couldn't figure out what she was saying! Finally, I asked this other teacher [to listen]. The teacher told me right away, "She lost her dime." I said, "Oh, okay. Well, we can fix that."
>
> Somebody'd say, "Well, that's a right smart—" and it didn't mean that it was intelligent, or that it showed knowledge. "Right smart" meant "quite a bit"—so that was a phrase. "Carton-a-dope," which was Coca Colas. "Light bread," which was white bread. "Sweet milk," which is regular milk—buttermilk is sour milk. Aunt Sarah always said, "pawn my honor," and I never could figure out what "pawn my honor" was—well, "*upon* my honor." I guess that's what Southern ladies said back then, I don't know.
>
> At school, the kids would talk about "grading" tobacco. And I thought they were saying "grating," like you would grate cheese. And I thought, That must be a heck of a job, to take those big [six-foot stalks]—I'm dumb. I thought they were grating tobacco! [They were sorting it by leaf size.] And I never did understand what they meant when it "came in case." [It became limp; in

humid weather dried tobacco is limp enough to pull off the stalk and grade.] They would ask *me* to slow down. I *have* slowed down over the years. I even have a Southern accent. But at first I was, "Ka-*kah*, ka-ka-*kah*, ka." You know how those Northerners are! They can get goin' sometimes! *(Linda)*

Misunderstandings caused community amusement, as Dianna found out.

Being [originally] from West Virginia, there was a lot of the dialect that I did understand, and I quickly found out that there was a lot that I *didn't* understand. [During the process of] buying our house, our place, in 1979, Jim and Berthie lived there. Jim had lived there all his life—his great-great-grandfather built the house—and Jim had never left it. Didn't learn to drive, and he didn't marry until he was seventy-three years old. So, when we would come down, between 1979 and when we permanently moved here in 1983, we would of course visit our house. We'd have a nice visit with them, and she'd prepare a meal oftentimes, and then when we'd go to leave, they would walk us out to our car, and they'd say, "Well, just stay *with* us." Well, we'd always make excuses for not being able to stay with them, and my husband and I talked about it, and we said, "You know, that's really rude of us. So the next time they ask us to stay with them, maybe we better say 'yes,'" even though we didn't really want to. So sure enough, the next time we came down—we had by now two kids and a Great Dane with us—and we had everybody packed up in the van, they walked us out to the car, and they said, "Well, just stay *with* us." Bill and I looked at one another, and we thought, Well I guess we will. So we said, "Well, okay." So we all got out of the van, and went back into their house, and they were very nice and hospitable about it. Jim, he brought down a potty chair from the barn, so I wouldn't have to go to the outhouse 'cause I was pregnant and put it in one of the bedrooms for me. So, the next time that we came down, I guess the whole valley had heard about that, and our host family that we *usually* stayed with, said to me, "Dianna, if they ask you to stay with them, they don't mean that!" It was just a cultural statement that they would make to say, "We were glad to have you," or "Come back sometime," but they really didn't mean us to stay and we didn't know that, so we did.

Linda, for one, reflected and adjusted. "I honestly did not understand the way the people spoke. Finally, then, I had to say [to myself], No, it's you that needs to make a change, not them."

Despite the awkwardness of some encounters, misunderstandings, and differences in speech, customs, and age, the young newcomers and the older local citizens began to interact.

> We had a neighbor here, Dolly, and she taught us how to find greens, so we made poke salad [with pokeweed]. Our neighbors were awfully good to us. Our neighbor next door would invite us for Sunday dinners. *(Alicia)*

> We would walk down to the end of the road. A little store was there, and they would be playing rook at night around the wood stove. A lot of card games and stuff like that in the winter. They were all friendly. *(Karen)*

> We had the barn built for the goats. And, oh, God, that was a neighborhood thing. First of all, somebody came and cut down

big cedar trees for the uprights. A neighbor came with his tractor [with a front bucket], and he dug the hole. We had people that gave us old windows for the stalls—every goat had a stall with a little window on it. We were the youngest people here, when we moved here. We were an oddity. People were willing to help us. We gave them lots of laughs—funny, didn't know how to do anything! *(Alicia)*

[Our neighbor] Lon [Shortt] was on our property all the time. If we were puttin' in the garden, if we were puttin' in tobacco, bringin' logs off the side of the hill, the whole building-of-the-house project, Lon was just there kind of fascinated that we were there doing that! I don't know how many outsiders he'd met before. He probably gave us some advice about different things, but he was more there just as an observer, just fascinated by the fact that we wanted to be there. *(Beth)*

As interest and mutual respect developed, some old-timers virtually adopted the newcomers.

We had help from our neighbors, and we did respect their knowledge—that they had lived here all their lives, and they were living on almost nothing. From tobacco they got so little; some of 'em like eight hundred dollars a year. They would raise a family on that. But it'd just be because they were able to utilize everything. They [cut] wood for the fire, they raised animals for food, and they just knew how to pinch a penny. They certainly didn't waste anything. So we really respected that culture that had developed here. And, lucky that we found a place that took us in, because had they not, it would have been hard because we were so different. *(Pat)*

I would take the stroller up, with a kid in the stroller, and a kid walking beside me and I could tie a jug of milk onto the bottom of that, so we could bring it home from the neighbors when we would visit them, Ruth and Luther Harville. I was nineteen when I moved here, and they became my sorta surrogate grandparents. They taught us a lot, just about everything, when I just didn't know anything about hardly anything. We were real greenhorns. So I learned really at the feet of the mountain folk, and the wonderful people who were so open to embracing us, and teaching us. *(Micki)*

Our closest neighbor was Lon Shortt, and he became my best friend. He was like in his seventies at the time, and I was twenty-something, and we hung out a lot together. I had a lot of experiences with Lon and animals. Lon showed me how to do tobacco, to plant *any*thing in the garden. It seemed everybody that moved here had an older person take 'em under their wing 'cause their own kids didn't wanna stay on the farm. Lon's son couldn't wait to move to town and work in town. So he'd show me all the stuff he woulda shown his own kids. So actually Lon acted sorta like my father, and we would go to First Monday Market. He was like eighty and I was twenty-four, so we looked sorta like the odd couple, and everybody would look at us. He didn't like to drive so I would drive his truck all the time. Of course all the other groups of people [newcomers] had their own person. *(Karen)*

While Lon Shortt was absorbed in Karen's and Beth's families' activities, they also admired his wife Anna Rae's friendliness and know-how.

I was fascinated with Anna Rae. She had a well about five or ten feet off of her back porch. She had no running water in the house and yet, her house was spotless. You know the phrase, "You could eat off the floor"—well, you *could* eat off the floor, literally, because, she did everything on the floor. She was this tall, skinny woman, but very strong. She had this old-time well. But [there] wasn't a bucket; [there] was this long tube, and it had like a valve on the bottom. You would dump it down to the bottom of the well. It would fill up with water, and when you pulled it up, the bottom of the tube would close up, and she would pull that up. It was heavy by the time it got all the way up to the top of the well, and she would have to dump it, then, into a couple of buckets that she had waiting there. And then she would carry these buckets into her kitchen for washing dishes. She'd heat the water on her wood cook stove in the kitchen, and then pour the water into this metal pan....She crouched down on the floor, got down on her haunches, and she would wash the dishes that way. She grew shelly beans, and she would do her bean shelling in that on-your-haunches position on the floor, and I'm just thinking, Wow, I couldn't do that and I'm forty years younger than you! *(Beth)*

When you got to know local people well enough, they might even pull a prank on you.

The first time I saw tobacco I thought it was leaf lettuce. It was my first year teaching here, and my Aunt Sarah Hurd, I would come with her after school to count her cows. That's something she did every day. I can remember seeing the tobacco growing and askin' her, "What do they do with all that leaf lettuce?

'Cause you can't freeze it." So she says, "Well, rech [reach] down thar and git ye a bite." So I took a bite, and it was "backer" [tobacco]. Horrible! *(Linda)*

I did home health nursing for a long time, which is probably when I really learned a lot about my neighbors, the people who were born and raised here. Learned about how to put food up and how to be resourceful, and all the folklore and rich, rich stories that I learned from my patients in their homes, because fortunately, I was able to visit them within a twenty-mile radius of where I lived. I really learned a lot from them. And they just loved me, and trusted me, and shared a lot with me. I think I was very fortunate to get to know 'em that intimately, through nursing. I remember going to a house one day and they didn't think I'd ever seen a hog killed before, but I had as a child. My grandmother—we went there every Sunday—in the fall they would kill a hog [for her], and it would be a big celebration for all the family. Anyhow, they had this hog, hanging, and they had already scalded it to remove all the hair, and they told me that they would then cure it and put it in sawdust, which they showed me the pit where they would put [it] in sawdust. But I never saw that process carried through. They also told me they would have a present for me when I returned that evening. I was visiting them twice a day. It was dark when I got back to their place, and when I pulled up I saw something on the porch. What they had done was cut off the head and put a candle underneath it, and had the head for me on the porch. So that was my gift! I told them I just couldn't take such a fine gift! *(Dianna)*

There was mutual aid between the newbies and the old-timers.

I liked my neighbors. I did things with them. Of course I was at the hospital every day so I knew a lot of patients from the Sneedville area and their families, and I enjoyed meeting them and learning about them, learning about their connections, working with the staff at the hospital. I know I was always a "foreigner" and they didn't always understand what I was saying, but I think that over the years they learned to respect my care and my concerns for them. Then, some of them came and helped on [building] the house! *(Joanne)*

One year John broke his leg and the whole neighborhood showed up when it was time to start cuttin' tobacco 'cause there's a lot to it. It's labor intensive when you have a lot. It was the most beautiful sight to see, to see all these people. I didn't know they were coming. They found out that I was gonna be cutting tobacco that day and they all showed up. It made me just proud to be part of this community. *(Lee)*

[Nursing here?] I took blood pressure, and I inserted a couple of catheters, and that's about it. I didn't come here as a nurse. But they knew I *was* a nurse, so— *(Alicia)*

Nelly Lawson, I remember Miss Nelly. She was an old lady, a maiden lady, lived with her mother. She had to go to the doctor in Knoxville, and she didn't know how she was going to get there, 'cause she'd never left Hancock County, ever in her entire life. I think she'd been to Rogersville a couple times, but mostly just into Sneedville, and not very often then. [Rogersville's population was four thousand and Sneedville half that.] I remember she made a dress. She worked all week on that dress, and she called [my husband] Dale every day to make sure the truck was going to run. She was real worried about ridin' in the truck. I went to pick her up. She had her little hat on, and her little gloves. She looked like she was going to church. I took her down to Knoxville to the doctor, and she just thought it was amazing that I knew how to drive. [She wore her] brand new dress that she made with her Singer sewing machine. She was so cute. Everything about it amazed her. I was just amazed at her amazement. It was quite an enjoyable trip for me, very enjoyable. *(Sherri)*

There are many more examples of neighborliness—for example, help with horses, as Cece describes.

[My husband] Bert had never worked a horse. He had had a riding horse when he was younger, but he knew nothing about how to put a harness on, or how to hook up a sled or a plow or anything—learned that from the locals—and what equipment we needed to work a horse.

Or with building projects.

We were gonna do something—propping up the front porch. We would do things like that. Start doin' 'em, just the two of us, and then somebody would come along and say, "Well, that isn't quite how ya—let me show ya a better way."
And then they'd often just help us do the rest of the project. *(Pat)*

Or farming.

[My husband Jerome] learned farming by doing it, but he learned from other people as well, because people in this area have been tomato farming for a long time. He's a pretty friendly guy, and got to know people, and really became a very good farmer. *(Vicki)*

[Joe learned] by working alongside [local farmers] in their backer fields. That's how we learned about that—which is about the best way to learn anything. Joe and Jerome both would hire themselves out to help hang backer. They were sought after as backer hangers because they were very tall, and strong. They were both at the time fully vegetarian, and I remember a lot of people commenting, "How can you be so strong when you don't eat meat?" Joe learned by doing [tobacco] with the neighbors, and then I learned from Joe. *(Micki)*

Or raising children.

I was raised in the suburbs. There wasn't a lot of dirt! So when my kids would crawl around on the floor, and as little crawlers they would be picking out the specks of dirt and little pieces of stuff, and puttin' 'em in their mouth, 'cause that's what they do, when I would move to [say], "Oh, get that—take that outta your mouth!" Ruthie Harville would say, "Oh, honey, you just let them go now. Doncha know every child needs a certain amount of dirt to grow up healthy?" Turns out to be true, but I didn't know that. But I trusted her. I mean that was something I'd never heard, never been told, but I really trusted her. So I was like, Okay. And I'm really glad I listened to her. *(Micki)*

The learning could be mutual.

Bobbie Soloman had to be like in her sixties or early seventies when we came here, and I was of course in my twenties. She showed me how to milk a cow, and she showed me garden things and all that. Then I ended up showing her how to put things in beds rather than in rows, things like spinach, 'cause she didn't know about that and she just loved it that there were things she was learning, too. So it was definitely a give-and-take. I love one of the expressions, that people like Herb Ferrell said: "Well, I don't mean to tell you what to do—" And John and I would go like, "Tell us, tell us!" But very humble people, and I really appreciated that. They were willing to hear what we had to say. We knew a few things that maybe would be new and different and would work a way of doing things. *(Lee)*

Any activity could be an opportunity for socializing.

A lot of times when we weren't getting our own goat milk, we would get cow's milk from Willard and Ina [Jones], and butter. It wasn't just knock on the door and get your milk and pay 'em your money and walk out. Every time you went to get milk, you were invited into the house, and you sat down, and you talked about what was going on in your life, and they told you what was going in their life. They were just very friendly people, so it was much more of a relationship than just buying milk. Not like going to the store is today. *(Beth)*

Somebody came from Watauga Library District, and asked us if we wanted to be a part of the mobile library system, and so, we had a back room, and we put up shelves. Somebody made us shelves. The mobile library would come once a month, and we'd get books that people would like. *(Alicia)*

So, the neighbors would come, and they would look through the books, and stay a while, and then take some books out. We liked doin' that; that was fun. *(Pat)*

Appalachian culture included a graciousness.

One time the Presleys invited us down to the river for a cookout, and they caught a big turtle and we ate parts of the turtle and everything. Just really fun times! *(Nancy)*

What I learned the most during the Home Health Nursing, was the welcoming, to make people feel that they wanted you to come into their home. After they trusted you, they wanted you to come in, they wanted you to feel welcome, they wanted to feed you, they wanted you to stay the night if you would. They just made you feel welcome, and that was different for me. I always felt like I had to be prepared for company—not that spontaneous welcoming. *(Dianna)*

The old-timers were kind and tolerant of the enthusiastic but naive homesteaders, patiently offering explanations, working with them, and giving philosophical as well as practical advice. At the same time, the lives of local people were changing. Their children were moving away, and the newcomers helped to fill that gap. Some of the newcomers had even bought land that formerly belonged to their local mentors' families. As several of the local families took the newcomers under their wings, it became an opportunity for them to pass on their knowledge about rural life, while their own children might be choosing to leave it all behind.

> It was so interesting to move here, such a completely different culture. The people that we met who have lived here for generations, the local people, were wonderful, and reached out to us, and taught us things, and taught us their superstitions and their beliefs. And really helped with gardening, telling us how to garden, when to plant, where, when to harvest. We learned a lot from local people. They were wonderful. The local people were really the most wonderful thing coming here! *(Carolyn)*

Chapter Twenty

Learning to Get Along

Inevitably, even during the "honeymoon period" of enthusiasm and learning, there were culture clashes. Newcomers expected some differences, but while some customs were intriguing, others caused discomfort or dismay.

> The first time we went to vote, [our neighbor] says, "Now election's comin' up. We got our election money. Vote so-and-so for sheriff." Well, we say okay, we'll go along with the locals and do what the locals do. We go down to the courthouse. They have you fill out an absentee ballot, in their presence, while they're watching you. Then they would hand you your twenty dollars. I was in shock, money for votes! I mean, it amazed me that that was still going on in the late 1970s, early Eighties. But it was! (*Cece*)

> Guns were another thing. We never had any experience with guns, but they are part of life here, so, we just accepted that. No! [I didn't have a gun.] I was afraid I'd shoot myself. But other people get a gun and learn to shoot. Just don't like the idea of it, so, no. But, we always had neighbors right close that

had 'em. And we wouldn't hesitate to ask 'em to bring their gun over if we needed it. Mostly it was just to kill something like a rattle-snake. But, you think, We're so far from "the law," they would never get here. Well, if you had a problem, you'd call a neighbor, and they all had guns, but I never had to. I never had any trouble. *(Pat)*

"The law" was thirty minutes away—if you had a phone to call them. People definitely took the law into their own hands. Definitely did. *(Cece)*

In the local community, church played a central role and defined an individual's identity. Several homesteaders reported being invited to attend one of the small Baptist or Methodist churches.

When we came here and interacted with locals, the first thing almost, after someone asks you your name, and who you might be kin to, they want to know, "Well, what church do you go to?" Or, they'd invite you to come to their church. So, I was invited to come to Friendship Baptist Church, which is just down the road from where we are. Never went, and after awhile if you don't show up, and you've been invited several times, people just get the idea that that's not your thing, and so they kind of leave it be. *(Beth)*

Most of the newcomer families were not church-going, and their first exposure to local religious services was, in many cases, a funeral.

I guess the very first funeral I ever went to when I first came down here was for Willard Jones. I was raised an Episcopalian, and funerals are very private. That religion is sort of very quiet and very private. Willard was a Baptist, and there was this wonderful little Richardson Creek Church right down the road from where we all live. Willard was a friend of ours, and he was an older man and he had passed away, and so we thought, We'll just head on down there to this funeral. When we got to the church we saw that there weren't very many seats except up where the pulpit was. We thought, Well, we'll go find a seat there. There we are sitting, and the preacher gets up, and we'd never seen or heard anything quite like this, with the pounding, and the saving, and the "You're gonna go to hell if"—And after each of these amazing statements, this group that we were sitting with would all stand up to their feet and yell out, "Amen!" So there John and I were, not wanting to be any different, so up we went "Amen," and we sat back down again and, back up we went again, "Amen." So that was the first funeral we went to that was an eye opener—they definitely do things differently here. *(Lee)*

The first funeral we went to was of a man who helped us put up tobacco when we first came. When he passed away, Bill felt we should attend the funeral. Being that I was born in West Virginia, I was not surprised by the service, but my husband was a New Englander, brought up in the Episcopalian Church, and so he was very concerned about the service. There was a church packed full of people that knew this man. There were three preachers, so they sorta did tag-preaching, and they were loud, and got down on the floor, and pounded their fists on the floor, and sweated and kind of huffed—something my husband had never seen. So he thought that perhaps one of them was even having a heart attack! And he thought that perhaps I should go check on him, me being a nurse! But, anyhow, that was our first experience of a funeral here. *(Dianna)*

Beth recalls that funeral experience as painful.

I did go to Willard's funeral. I kind of sat near the back. Of course he was a wonderful man, so it wasn't just the local people that showed up; it was most of our friends, I think. At the time, we were also friends with Willard and Ina because we got our milk from them. So, when he died we were all very sad. I'd never been to their church, and probably a lot of my other friends had never been to their church, and so we were quickly recognized as outsiders. Even though we were all there because we loved Willard and to support Ina, his wife, I came out of that church service not feeling welcomed at all because, um, well, it was pretty "out there" that, You shouldn't be here—you people who do not come to church on a regular basis, and probably do not believe in God or Jesus. If we weren't willing to accept their religious beliefs, what were we doing there? There were enough of us outsiders, that the first person speaking was speaking directly to us, saying, "What are you doing here?"—intruding on their, their respectful service. We were just trying to be respectful of the person.

The women encountered funeral customs new to them, as when Karen went to the funeral of her friend and mentor, Lon.

I actually hadn't been to many funerals and only one memorial service for a friend in grade school. So going to a Baptist funeral was a lot livelier. A local man did the funeral. Lon's niece, who really I didn't think liked him, was the person that was the wailer and cried and screamed and everything at the funeral. I just felt sort of uncomfortable 'cause I wasn't used to it. I mean they were used to it, but I wasn't.

I was told that the woman [at another funeral] was a professional mourner. She wasn't related but she did a lot of crying. I don't know whether that sorta helped people have permission to grieve—what the theory was behind that. *(Dianna)*

The Southern Baptists and Methodists were concerned about their new neighbors' welfare, including in the afterlife, and perhaps about the perceived integrity of their community.

Their neighborly interest clashed with the more private view of religion and spirituality held by many of the homesteaders as described in Chapter Sixteen. In many cases, those different idea presented a gulf between newcomers and old-timers never to be bridged, but eventually overlooked.

My neighbors [Lon and Anna Rae] were different. They didn't proselytize or try and get me involved in their church, other than a quick invitation, but they were very welcoming people. You know, I was in their home; I would very often go and sit on their front porch, and we'd just "shoot the shit"—just talk about our lives. They were very, very sweet people. *(Beth)*

I think I questioned their religious beliefs a lot, but I've also learned that that is not for me to question. So, that was not a problem for me. *(Carolyn)*

Consumption of alcohol was forbidden in the teaching of the small rural churches, and this presented a dichotomy.

Almost every church here is a Missionary Baptist Church. It seems like there's one on every corner, every intersection, every anywhere. And they're real Bible pounders, a whole lot of 'em. But—they're also moonshiners. *(Cece)*

My husband, he was social with the neighbors. There were other people from the North that lived on his farm, and it bein' a big farm, there was a lot of work, just clearing and and stuff. With the music, [local] people would come and hang out, but I noticed right away, they were so into drinking. And really, you just immediately see this real problem with the people and their drinking. I mean—it's why you see such a strong Baptist tradition here. It's like, you're either a drinker, or you go to church. You're one or the other. So, I think a lot of women, they go to church, and they raise their children in the church to try to avert the alcoholism and the entire lifestyle that goes with it. *(Anne)*

Of course alcoholism can be a societal problem anywhere, but the prohibition on alcohol was alien to most of the newcomers. However, the significant factor for non-church-goers was that much of the social life of the community centered on churches, which held services two or more times a week, including tight-knit Bible study groups. Some observances brought people together around a covered dish dinner. Invitations to join the parishioners gradually faded away.

Besides religious differences, there was another unsettling situation. The women's liberation movement had not yet come to the valley.

Here's one thing that I did not expect—the attitude [toward], and perception of, women. I really can't say I had much of a concept of people who lived down here until I came here, but, the only thing that struck me as strange was the way the culture here had a thing about men not looking at women, for instance, when they spoke. So we'd be in conversation and if Joe and I were both there, and having conversation with one of the local men, the local man would look at Joe and address Joe even if he was answering my question. So that was really strange to me because, sure, where I came from in Cincinnati, it's not that women had equal rights, but it was a lot more advanced than it was down here. *(Micki)*

I would just be friendly, but particularly after I became a widow, I just really had to try to keep to myself and try to stay away from men. They will make assumptions, maybe, [about] a woman living alone. *(Anne)*

I had lived in Iran, so I took things a little bit differently than some. A lot of men, I did not look directly in the eyes, and I [knew] right away, that country men here really were brought up to be shy of women, and I knew they weren't supposed to be in a room alone with a woman or alone in a house. I kinda respected those customs because of living in Iran, and it wasn't so hard on me that I think it was on other people, because of that. I kind of looked at it from the anthropological point of view, and that made me able to take a step back and go, Oh, those are their customs here. *(Nancy)*

Another difference was the varying views on the use of chemicals in farming, as most of the homesteaders tried to live up to organic growing standards.

Absolutely, definitely, [I grow] only organic. I see the neighbors spray things along the creeks and in the fields, and it freaks me out a lot. But you know, that's such a way of life for so many people, not just people around here, but so many people. "In order to get something to grow, we have to spray everything. Or if there's a weed." *(Robyn)*

A dispute could develop over a property right-of-way.

I bought a piece a property [that] in the past everyone else had reached by through the neighbor's land, which was flat, back to the house. After a year or so of going through the neighbor's land, the neighbor said, "Hey, you need to build your own driveway." And I was not prepared financially for a ten thousand dollar extra make-your-own-road-on-the-side-of-the-mountain-and-scare-yourself-to-death-every-day! I felt because we were outsiders, they were doing that to us. *(Tata)*

Despite her hurt feelings, the cost, and advice to sue, Tata and her partner made a decision.

There's no etiquette that says, "Move to the new place and sue the people that have been livin' there for two hundred years." It just doesn't work. Get over yourself! We got a driveway. We didn't alienate the neighbors. And because we did what was the right thing, the neighbors respected us to their best ability, and said, "We're glad you made your own road. If you ever have a big piece of equipment, or you need to bring something in through our road, we will still let you use it."

Local attitudes about education varied. In an area of agricultural lifestyles and traditions, families wanted their children to be educated—up to a point—and some feared that their educated children would move away.

> I did get hired in 1989 to work at Clinch [School] and I worked there for twenty-five years! As I got to know people, that gave me a lot of insight as far as the lives of my students, and what their family life was like. I had some real bright students, and I had some students that didn't have it goin' on. It was really hard. Growing up, I remember our parents say over and over again, that what they wanted was for their children to have a better life than they had—better education than they had. What surprised me at Clinch—what I was hearing instead was, "Well, my eighth grade education was good enough for me, it should be good enough for"—their son or daughter! So, expectations to do really well in school were not reinforced at home, except for in a few individual cases. For the most part, I think that we were always confronting the fact that the parents didn't find education to be all that important. *(Beth)*

Thoughtful attitudes eased the newcomers into their new lives. Later, as the women mellowed with age, their outlooks evolved.

> Some people wanted to come in here and change the local people; they wanted things their way. Some people weren't accepted because they tried to come in here—like a bull!—and we just came in and wanted to fit in and just get along with people. You know, just look at 'em as equals. Don't look at 'em as just dumb hillbillies or something. Really! They're smart! *(Janet)*

I guess most of [the old-timers] I met were always really nice and helpful. Most of the people I met that were local had never maybe even been further than Morristown, maybe just Rogersville and Sneedville. Because of that, it's hard to have an open mind. But that happens all over the world. Yeah, absolutely [my travel helped a lot]. And just growing up around certain people—your parents and extended generations—just seeing how different people act. And learning how to *be*, I guess. *(Robyn)*

I can remember when I first moved here, and people would say to me, "Now, don't you go down into the lower end of Poor Valley, they'll shoot ya down there." But, you know, I would [teach] those kids at school, and I'd put 'em in my car to take 'em home after ball games. That's back when ya did stuff like that. Most of the time, the parents were very appreciative that I brought 'em home. I would look around and think, Why am I doin' this? There's all kinds of vehicles here.

But they were always good to me, and waved to me, and were friendly. I think the whole idea is, if you show that you care about them and their children, they're gonna be good to ya. I think that's the bottom line. *(Linda)*

When I first joined the Head Start [mothers] up at the school, the people that had kids my [kids'] age were not nice. They weren't real welcoming, and they didn't become my friends. I learned how to get along with them, but they weren't my friends. [I've lived here] close to thirty years and it's beautiful here. I love it. This area is very conservative and we're liberals, so that's a big difference. When I meet locals now, though, they do become my friends. And the teachers at the school, they were always really, really great, but different kinds of lifestyles than we had. *(Judy)*

As the back-to-the-landers adjusted to their rural life and culture, there was personal growth. Keeping an open mind is key.

> When in Rome, do as the Romans do. I learned a long time ago—and I was guilty of [not following] it myself somewhat—not to be critical of the culture, not to think that you're a step above, because you're educated, from the North, or something. I have seen a lot of people that have moved in from other places. I'm not talkin' about our hippie friends, not them. But, other people that are very critical. To come into a place, and to start bein' critical of the way people live, and how they eat, and what they dress [like], and what they believe, that's not gonna endear you to anyone. So, I think, just bein' open. You know, not everybody's like we are! *(Linda)*

A sense of humor helps.

> Well, I go for a walk almost every day, for half a mile down and half a mile back. I used to pick up paper, and whatevers, to keep the area looking nice. So apparently, this guy drinks—he drinks a lot—and he saw that I was picking up beer cans. So now, he puts the beer cans in plastic bags, so that when I go for a walk, I can pick them up. So I call this man my "benefactor." I love flowers. I always have that money for buying new plants from recycling beer cans, so I have to tell the lady at the recycling place, "I don't drink this much beer!—It's my benefactor." *(Alicia)*

Clinch Mountain Girls

Barriers can be broken.

> I have [massage] clients in all walks of life, of all education levels, all degrees of narrow-mindedness. I love it that massage therapy can cut through all those barriers. If you have a skill that you can help somebody feel better, even if they're against you politically, religiously, or whatever their trip is—guess what—they gotta like me a little bit because I helped them. *(Tata)*

No relationship is perfect, but effort and mutual respect can go a long way.

> When we came we were accepted in a way that surprised me, because we did look very different, and we were culturally very different—the way we dressed, our appearance, and the way we spoke—everything. But I was very happy with the way we weren't judged immediately, we were given a chance. They were interested in getting to know us, and very quickly I felt like we were taken under the wing of these folks. Partly what helped with that was that we came in very humbly. We knew we didn't know anything, and we weren't going to pretend that we knew. So when we came in, we were asking for help. "Could you help us learn how to do this? Could you teach us about that?"
>
> We were very interested in learning the ways of the folks here, the mountain people. We wanted to be self-sufficient, we wanted to learn how to do that. I think that what they really liked about that was that so many of their children had been moving away because they weren't able to find work here. So they moved off. They weren't valuing so much—or felt that they couldn't stay with—the ways of their parents. But here we were coming down, and 'bout the same age as their kids, or

grandchildren, and saying, "Please teach us. We value what you know."

I think that was like this perfect marriage; it benefitted both sides. *(Micki)*

During this time when many of the younger local generation were leaving for a life elsewhere, a considerable number of young strangers were moving in. The welcoming tolerance of local people helped them to overlook most of the mistakes of their new neighbors. On the other hand, the back-to-the-landers took note of cultural differences, adjusted their attitudes, and mostly appreciated the differences that kept life interesting. Challenges and prickly personalities became part of the many stories they now tell. The "hippie" philosophy of "going with the flow" and keeping relationships peaceful helped smooth the integration of newcomers with the local population. In addition, a youthful readiness for novel projects and ideas, and in many cases, a background of travel and education, helped the back-to-the-landers adapt to local culture. And then of course, "the girls" had each other.

* * *

Over the years new generations were born and raised. The transforming world economy, including the off-shoring of manufacturing jobs, brought cascading affects to the local job market and to educational requirements. Improved roads and educational opportunities led the young away. After health concerns and new laws demolished the major cash crop, tobacco, the subsistence farming way of life basically ended for the traditional farmers. These factors, plus satellite television, better long-distance telephone service, and then the Internet (also by satellite), affected the valley's relationship to the outside world and brought changes to the local culture. Clinch School remained open—with a new building as well. However, due to commuters shopping in town at new supermarkets and big box stores, every single country store and gas station in the valley closed.

Changes were unsettling for locals and newcomers alike.

It was already beginning to change for the locals [when we arrived]. Their tobacco was going out, and nothing was really there to replace it. The younger generation was already much different from the stories we heard about the older generations, about people getting together to help each other [in] whatever kind of house- or barn-raising. I taught at Clinch School for twenty-five years, so I had a long period of my life, where I was very much involved in the life and lifestyle of local people. And, it was—troubling. I think a lot of the good things that we think about have gone by the wayside. Nutrition is one thing that really upsets me. *(Beth)*

Nobody gardens anymore either. The guys work in factories, and the women also work in factories or in offices, and they buy frozen food and put it in the microwave. *(Yvonne)*

The old people stayed the same. But the younger generations had a lot of trouble. They didn't take up the lifestyle of their parents, because that was all work to them. Maybe they didn't want that lifestyle, and didn't value it as much. Then, the ones who left—they left! They got a job somewhere, and now they're fine. They come back and they visit. But this is the place they *visit*, this isn't the place where they were gonna try to make a life for themselves. *(Pat)*

The older people, I would say, they're less—not exactly less friendly—but they have to make a living, too. There might be the men who are still here farming, but the women are all gone out to work. You have to have money. There's no parties anymore. Nobody plays the instruments like they did years ago. The young kids have computers and whatever. *(Alicia)*

I guess the [multi-]generational welfare thing has made a lot of people not so good, is what the bottom line is. *(Robyn)*

A lot of the old-timers are gone, and that's sad. I miss a lot of them, I really do. They were very knowledgeable, and like if I had a problem with something growing they would help me with it. They'd say, "Well, try so and so and so." And I loved listening to their stories, their times being here. *(Sandra)*

The old-timers, a lot of them that knew all of the crafts that we were so enamored of when we moved here, have now died. It's kind of a different feel around here, definitely. And drugs have taken ahold, too. *(Nancy)*

I think the people in this area are really sincere, good people. I really, really do. I know we've got some people, some druggies, some meth-heads, we do. But we never hung around with those people to begin with. We don't get into their energy. So, they're here, but yet, they're not here. Does that make sense? *(Linda)*

Dianna does point out that although the old-timers are no longer with us, "Some of their children have now come back to live here." She also notes a change for the better.

On the roads there would be a lot of trash, and in the creeks, and it was disturbing to me that, as beautiful as it was, it wasn't respected. I hope it's not just that I've gotten used to it, but I think the consciousness has been raised as far as respecting the land that we live on. I see less trash, more of a consciousness about keeping our water clean, and using our water as recreation, as well as drinking water, and how it should be not polluted. So I think that's one thing that's improved that I was pretty disillusioned with when I first came.

Change is undeniable.

> I still appreciate the people that are here. I think a lot of the wisdom is being lost because the culture is changing so much here. The elders that farmed and planted corn on these hills, and worked with mules; and the women who did everything, worked on the hills, planting corn, fixing meals, hand-washing [clothes], having babies, all that—that's pretty much not happening so much anymore here because those elders have died. They've passed, and their children do not want that lifestyle. This is my take on it, anyway. There's still some that do, but they pretty much have found jobs in factories, or make their living a different way. And as far as my friends, my friends that I've "grown up with" here, we have changed also. *(Carolyn)*

Yes, the Clinch Mountain Girls went through more changes, of course, as their children became teenagers and young adults. Those are described in the next chapter, and some may surprise you.

Chapter Twenty-One

Back to School and Other Changes

In the Eighties and Nineties, jobs required increasing technical skills, and some were off-shored. More rural women worked outside the home, and tobacco was virtually eliminated from the local agrarian economy. Each new decade brought more and more technology, and consequent changes to the community.

The Clinch Mountain homesteaders faced personal challenges, and financial survival was chief among them. In some cases divorce forced entry into the job market. Would these suburban girls, now strong women, empowered by their hard-won skills, now abandon Clinch Mountain and each other? You know they didn't. Here's what happened.

A few of the women had to migrate elsewhere for a while. Rural Tennessee had relatively high unemployment, so a college-educated woman with little job experience and no family connections in the area, was usually destined for a low-paying service or clerical job. Over half of the mostly college-educated group decided to go back to school. Other changes included evolving family structure, and later, physical challenges as they aged.

Nursing was a choice for some who sought more education, for example, Lauren, who already had six children.

> Well, I went to school! Now I'm an LPN nurse. I work a lot. There were some math things that I had to take, 'cause I only went to the ninth grade. But once through that, I did pretty well! *(Lauren)*

> I think I was forty-seven when I went to nursing school because I wanted my kids to go to college, and I thought that I could help them more if I had an income. My husband was not well, and was not providing well for his family, and I knew I had to do that. Nursing seemed like something I would like—hands-on caring for people. I loved nursing school—that was sort of an extension from being a lay midwife. I thought, Well, I could get paid to take care of people. *(Carolyn)*

Carolyn returned to school again as she took up another healing profession.

> [After] fifteen to twenty [years] I knew I didn't want to do nursing any more, but I knew I had to do something else. I can't support myself with Social Security—so I thought that massage therapy would be something I would really like to do because it's hands-on care, and I like hands-on care, and working for myself.

With one child in school, and two at home, Dianna decided that she had to upgrade from Licensed Practical Nurse to Registered Nurse, and went back to school. She worked in several hospital positions, including administration and training. Meanwhile she took courses in reflexology and opened her own practice as well.

For others, teaching was an option.

We didn't have all that much land to do anything with. So, in order to survive we were definitely going to have to get jobs off the farm. So, I went back to school to get my Master's Degree in Education. That was a fifty-minute drive. I was still married at the time. Finished in eighty-seven, I think. My perception of what teaching would be like—summer vacations, and school's out at three, so I'll have the late afternoon and evening hours to do stuff at home—seemed like an ideal situation. Nobody wanted to hire me. Couldn't find a job until I got an offer outside of Atlanta, Georgia. So I moved [there] and taught school for a year. I was very fortunate, because I *did* get hired in 1989 to work at Clinch School. And I worked there for twenty-five years! *(Beth)*

I realized that being a stay-at-home mom didn't leave us with much savings. Also, I needed health insurance. I decided that teaching would be it, so I could garden in the summer. I went back to school [for two years] when I was fifty-six. I was a full-time student and commuted every day, an hour one way. Then taught for ten years. *(Nancy)*

After nine years of homesteading, Sherri and her husband divorced, and the next year she moved back to Indiana. While there, she went back to school, returning to Clinch Valley about six years later.

I first got my teaching degree a B.A.E., Bachelor of Art Education. I've taught at Grainger [County] High School for eleven years now. I went back [to school again] when I was fifty years old to get my Masters of Instructional Design and Technology. I teach online now [for] small, rural schools in middle Tennessee, five schools that have never had an art teacher, never! They got grants the same year our school got grants to get web-conferencing equipment. I'm just so thrilled to know that I can bring art to any kid anywhere in the world now in any rural school that can afford it.

Alicia traveled an hour and a half one-way to study art.

I went over to ETSU [East Tennessee State University] for art classes. I was sixty I think, when I went over there. I went for three or four years, twice a week.

Micki learned house construction by helping her husband build a new house. Five years later those skills came in handy.

[My] interest in building was really ignited by building the house over there. Then after Joe and I divorced, I took that a step forward to design and build the straw-bale house I live in now. I needed to figure out another way of making a living. My grandfather was a mason and a couple uncles and my dad. When I met the man who is my current partner, turns out he was a concrete finisher and taught me how to finish it. I stuccoed [my straw-bale] house with it. Concrete, then, became my livelihood for the next about a dozen years. My kids were in school by then—in the summer they would come on the concrete jobs with us. I have continued to learn along the way how to do things, to become even more self-sufficient. So I am living a much cushier life.

Then Micki sought more education, this time in college, earning Bachelor and Master Degrees.

After a few years of doing just straight concrete work I started going to school and doing the concrete work at the same time. I decided to pursue a degree in social work. I was forty-two. I did internship work with a large community service organization in Morristown with whom I'm still affiliated. Currently, my social work practice is some grant-writing and quality assurance for programs funded by the government. And then I have my own practice, because I've also pursued my interest in holistic health and healing of the mind, body, and spirit. I've studied many different modalities, and utilized those in a kind of hybridized form, seeing clients in my office in Morristown. I have a very sort of fluid and flexible schedule. That's always been my MO. I've worked for myself since I've become an adult, and that just works out better. *(Micki)*

Further learning can enhance one's knowledge and lead to personal growth.

I decided that I wanted to become a better yoga teacher. So I thought, If I learn this Feldenkrais Method [Awareness Through Movement program], my yoga will become richer. It did, and, eventually I didn't bother with yoga anymore. I thought Feldenkrais had more to offer. That was a four-year training. I went two times a year to San Diego, and two times a year to Bloomington, Indiana. I went away, on my own, which was really a nice, nurturing experience for me. *(Yvonne)*

More education pays off financially but may result in compromises in one's way of life, like farm upkeep that gets pushed aside.

I got my real estate license twenty years ago, and that helped tremendously. It is a trade-off, though. It definitely is. I could see things here at the farm that definitely had fallen by the wayside that you just didn't do anymore. *(Lee)*

Of the ten married women who became widowed or divorced, seven had children. For two of them, becoming single moms meant moving away from Clinch Valley for a long time—as well as more schooling.

First I went back to school in California and got my Midwifery Certificate. [Already an R.N.], I thought I was going to come back here to Sneedville to the Hancock County Hospital and do women's care. That was my plan and the agreement I had with the local physicians there. When I got back they had transferred all their OB/GYN care to Morristown, so the job was not available to me. I couldn't find work in Rogersville in this field, and I could've gone back to work at the hospital as a staff RN, but that just seemed wrong after all the work I had done, and putting my kids through that transition. So, I started interviewing for other jobs, and we went to South Carolina. Over the course of the next twenty-two years, then, I got my Bachelors Degree in Nursing and the Masters and then the Post Masters. And I kept trying to come back here. I kept applying, sending my resumé—You know, it seems like life is a struggle of trying to get all of these factors together: you want to be with your friends; you want to be at the location you feel the most comfortable; you want a job that's satisfying and pays well; you want your kids to do well. I couldn't seem to get those four components together. There was always one of them missing. When we went to South Carolina that was a good move as far as education went, for both me and the girls, and the job was really good. I just didn't have any friends. And, although I had a house I liked, I didn't like being in South Carolina. So, finally, finally, after twenty-two years we got to move back! *(Joanne)*

Karen, too, moved after a divorce, and "lived in exile" for twenty-five years. During that time she went back to school.

I moved away probably in eighty-seven, because Moriah was still in diapers when I went to Ohio. I drove up there all night, took the kids, dropped them off at my parents' house and interviewed, and I got the job [in a nursing home]. I worked there for several years, so my kids got to grow up around my parents in that community, and that was good. I became a nurse. To be an LPN [Licensed Practical Nurse] is a one-year course, and I did that at a vocational school. My first job was at a VA Hospital. Then I got married, and my husband wanted to transfer to Georgia, so we did that. In Georgia they pretty much expected you to do what an RN can do, and so that was sort of "heavy." As soon as I could transfer off the regular medical floor, I got a job in rehab and worked there for about ten years.

Nearing retirement age, and having divorced again, Karen was dissatisfied with the increased requirements and the decreased compensation at her job. She decided to return to Tennessee, so she put her house on the market.

I started showing my house, and the first person wanted to buy it. [My friend] Doyle came down [from Clinch Valley] and helped me move a lot of my things. I went to the closing. We went from there to my job. I quit. Then I went home, finished packing two vehicles up, and came back up here. [Away for] twenty-five years! It's hard to believe. But it gave me a chance to get a little ahead, and be able to buy this house.

Though not a single parent, Cece left the valley for a long while because of concern about the quality of her children's education. The family moved to the Atlanta suburbs.

I wanted to be home with my children when my children were home, so I started a day-care business, and I took care of teachers' children, only. That's the name of the business, "Teachers Only Daycare." So I had my summer vacations and my Christmas vacations and my Easter vacation.

Later, Cece worked at a small restaurant and caterer, at H&R Block, and as a picture framer, before she sought more education.

Eventually I went back to school, and at fifty years old began a career in IT [internet technology] after going back to school for two years. I kinda became a techie in my old age. My kids were very proud of me, that their mom, who knew nothing about computers, could become a computer professional! But, something resonates with me, with this place. It tore me up to have to leave and move away from here. I did it for my kids, and for my kids' education, 'cause I was totally committed to raise my kids the best I could, wherever I had to be. I feel satisfied that I stuck to those goals and I carried 'em out. Now I'm back reliving this life again but with a different viewpoint, more like the retirement angle. Instead of building a whole new life here, I'm kinda winding down my life here. *(Cece)*

While she did not move away entirely, Lee experienced a nomadic life for a few years while her husband John completed his Bachelor, Master, and Ph.D. Degrees at East Tennessee State University in Johnson City.

> I thought it was going to be just for two years—it's what he needed to [finish] just a regular [bachelor's] degree. So we did pack up stuff and go there. I sold all the animals that needed tending, but I did come back here on Wednesdays [from Johnson City] 'cause at that time I was [wood]carving in a big way. So I would come back on Wednesday, stay all day here that day and Thursday, do my carving, get my orders in place, and get them all shipped out. So that was nice, and then he'd come back here on the weekends.

Meanwhile, Lee's daughter April, proved to be exceptionally talented in gymnastics, leading to more changes.

> We found a coach that was down in Athens, Georgia, and she and I moved down to Athens. We were there for two years, and I worked for a potter down there. And that was wonderful. Had a great time, made a little money. Bought a little condo down there. It was such an interesting concept to go from this huge farm to owning everything inside the building and nothing outside.
>
> I was definitely a country girl. I can remember applying for jobs down there 'cause of course I had to have a job, and I'd never worked anywhere. So I brought my portfolio of all my [wood] carvings around with me. And of course everybody was going like, "Ah, no thank you, no thank you." It was sort of discouraging [also] 'cause they sure didn't want to know how to milk a cow! That was not what I was applying for.

Lee was hired by a potter, and then commuted from Athens.

> That's what I did for two years. And just absolutely loved it. I was gone about eight years total. Long time, but always coming back. I'd drive from Athens, Georgia every single weekend back up here to the farm, about a four-hour drive. I had to; I had to get recharged.

Alma had to move also, but initially not out of state. She and her husband Sid left Clinch Valley and resettled in the nearby small town of Rogersville, a half-hour away.

> [In] ninety-six, after he recovered from that cow accident, I said, "Sid, we really can't live here any longer." If you couldn't drive, there is no transportation. It's [over] a dozen miles to town, to get to anything. He did agree with it, and we moved to Rogersville.

Sid later died, and Alma eventually made the more drastic changes of giving up driving and moving to an apartment near her sons in Minneapolis in 2014. She explains the problem that exists for elderly rural residents.

> The small towns even like this one have had buses; there was a bus depot here. It is no longer. There was a cab here. There is no cab any longer. A railroad came through town. [The depot] is a museum now. *(Alma)*

Judy left in 2014, accompanying her husband to the state of Washington. One daughter already lived there. Later, two other daughters moved there as well. At the end of the interview she said, "You know, I'm going to leave here in two weeks and—" She sobbed for several minutes.

Vicki did not move but did resume her career. She explained, "I taught at Bean Station School from seventy-five to seventy-six, and then did no teaching until ninety-four."

> I'm a Special Ed teacher, so I work with students with disabilities, at a K–12 school, Washburn School. I started back there in ninety-four, when [my youngest child] Jared was probably about eight years old. At eight, he thought I'd abandoned him.

Others tried out one or more new ventures.

> I worked for a newspaper in Rogersville, for probably over two years. Then I worked delivering newspapers for another couple of years. Then I think I got into the tobacco for several years. Now, I'm a school bus driver, a job that's a good job for me. I can work in the morning, and I have my days. Work in the afternoon, I'm home again. *(Anne)*

> As years went by, we went to the bank to get loans to buy small houses that we felt that we could fix up and then move [into the market]. It was interesting 'cause when we went to the bank they wouldn't give us a loan because we had no credit, meaning we owned everything. We had to go get something that we didn't own in order to get a loan. *(Lee)*

> [In later years] I worked [off the farm] until I was eighty-one. That was a good experience. I worked for about thirteen years for the Mountain Empire Older Citizens Agency daycare. The last job I got was to be the RN at the daycare. It was close by, and I liked working with people with Alzheimer's, too. A lot of

times they remember what they love. Music really stays with ya a long time. Of course I love the old songs, so I used to find ways to play the old songs and get them to sing. *(Pat)*

After retiring from various secretarial and administrative jobs for public agencies, Trudie taught horseback riding to disabled children.

I met a lot of really fun people, had a good time with a lot of little kids, who are just great! It was very fulfilling to see them go from being really timid to ride to, "Are we gonna do this now? Let's do this!" Just see that whole turn-around and their confidence build—I really like that!

Later in life, artists often find more time to pursue their art. After her children were in school, Yvonne devoted more time to her porcelain figures. Then there was the hiatus while she immersed herself in learning the Feldenkrais Method [Awareness Through Movement].

I was very deeply involved in learning that method, and neglected my work in the studio. Stopped making [porcelain] figures for a good while, to practice that. Actually, right now I'm painting—I've started to paint! Since over a year, I'm doing that! That is actually the most important thing I want to do now, here. Not gardening. Bill is doing the gardening. Before, it was like this slogan, "back-to-the-land," meant a lot to me. But now I'm more like, "back-to-the-studio!"

Lee has returned to occasional woodcarving, especially chairs for her young granddaughters. Also, she is busy with the designing, building, and landscaping of tiny cabins for her latest project, "Lee's Sweet Retreat," a rustic bed-and-breakfast place on her picturesque farm.

Others had more time for creative pursuits.

> I did get involved in the theater—enjoyed that—but that was really when my kids were old enough to be by themselves. I did poetry, and entered my poetry in some poetry slams, which I won! *(Dianna)*

> I bought a Nikon [SLR] camera. I did start taking a lotta pictures—a lot!—and so, I tend to put many of them on Facebook but certainly enjoy that. In my free time I can do those planters, the hypertufa things. I don't have a website but I sell some online. Hypertufa is a mixture of Portland cement and pearlite and sphagnum moss to make it lighter. You mix it up like cement and pour it in a mold, or you can free-hand it. I usually make planters that look like heads, and then the plants should look like hair. The Collins House [another project], I bought from a friend of mine. It's an older house, farmhouse. I like to garden here. It's a lot of yard work, and I'm enjoying that, landscaping. *(Karen)*

Alicia's art classes inspired her. "I do watercolors. I am doing pottery, I have a kiln. I sell my stuff, when I sell it, at the Local Artists' Gallery in Rogersville." She also continues to make quilts.

The Local Artists' Gallery is a cooperative formed in 2005 when it had become clear to the women that the time, trouble, and expense of traveling to market their work did not always pay off, nor was Internet marketing a workable solution for most. Lee was a moving force behind the artists' cooperative's formation and functioning. Eight other women in this book, as well as other artist friends, helped with renovations and exhibited work there and several still do.

Of the original nine, seven are active artists today, such as Janet, who says, "I started to make my own lampwork beads, and that's now what I do. I combine the lampwork beads and the wirework jewelry. And I sell them." Janet makes the beads using a torch to melt colored glass.

Tata works with flowers as well as with photography and painting.

> Because I grow many, many, many dahlia flowers, it's gotten past being a hobby and become another way for me to make money by taking them to the farmers' market. I take a lot of pictures of them [and] make reproductions onto canvas so they can beautify other people's homes. It seems wrong for me to have all of these flowers and for me to hold on to all of them. To get to hand somebody some beauty is a joy. *(Tata)*

Tata makes music, too. A classically trained singer, she offers solos at events. "Music has been a very, very, very powerful force in my life. Some of the most unifying experiences I've had with other people is singing in a group. There's just a power in that!" she said. She practices singing every day—sometimes with surprise accompanists.

> Even if I never get another chance to sing for another person, I sing for me almost every day, and it uplifts me, keeps my instrument remembering and satisfies me, elevates me. I think the vibration within my own body is stimulating my energy flow. I go outside to practice, and the coyotes start singing with me. More than once I've started singing and then one-by-one they'll start howling with me. Then the ones across the road will start howling at the other ones. I just can't tell you how funny it was to start them singing! And howling! It was daytime, which shocked me, four o'clock in the afternoon! With certain provocation, they'll

just start! I just thought, Instead of "Dances with Wolves," it's "Sings with Coyotes." *(Tata)*

Besides schooling and new careers, daily life has changed. Paved roads, well-running vehicles, and labor-saving appliances have made life less challenging in many ways.

> My life's easier physically. I don't garden as much as I used to. I don't have four kids to feed, so I don't need to put up thirty quarts of tomatoes like I used to! And I always now have running water and electricity which is also easier. *(Judy)*

> We have some modern things—got my dishwasher hooked up. Oh, I'm so excited! *(Trudie)*

> Being warm enough in the winter time—I really like the propane [heat] now. *(Pat)*

> I have a bathroom! And my walls are insulated now. I have a washer and dryer. I don't make everything from scratch, although I do try to eat very healthy. I'm not married anymore, so that changes a lot. Physically, yes, it's absolutely easier. *(Vicki)*

They tried to balance physical abilities, their need for comfort, and their back-to-the-land ideals.

> You have money [so] you are able to have people that either help you, or you buy a piece of equipment so you are not doing things by hand. I find myself being older and not actually able to do the grunt work. A lot of things are already in place, too.

I'm not planting two hundred blueberry plants anymore. Now it's a matter of tending them. *(Lee)*

I hardly ever use the dryer. I put my clothes out on the line. In the wintertime, I hang 'em on the stairway. I use a rain barrel. I do that for ecology. I try not to use too much water. I wash clothes all together, once a week. I'm proud of that. *(Alicia)*

I do have a heat pump and air conditioner. I don't use the air conditioner much. I might use it if I clean the carpets and I need to pull out the moisture, but usually I don't. I do have a wood stove for a back-up, plus there's just no heat like a wood heat. So in the wintertime I fire up my wood stove and I just love still cooking on it. *(Sherri)*

With every change there are trade-offs, but sometimes there is just plain ol' satisfaction. Vicki declared, "I have nine grandchildren, so that's a big change. That's fun!"

I got twenty grandchildren and twenty-four great-grandchildren. And we just *started* with the great-grandkids! I know I'm gonna have a bunch of them! *(Sandra)*

I finally got on just a really beautiful farm, that I really love. *(Anne)*

When I first [lived here] I didn't have enough money to go even once a week to the store. Now, I go to Kingsport twice a week for my exercise, and for entertainment, meeting my friends in Kingsport. *(Alicia)*

I feel very privileged. We have doubled the size of our house. We're pretty warm; we no longer heat with wood. We have social media available; we have television if we want that; we have grass that used to be dirt. Many things that have changed for the better as far as making us comfortable. But we worked for it. It wasn't something we bought and was already there. *(Dianna)*

I've got everything I need, and more. [I'd] like to downsize, and give something to everybody that walks out my door! *(Robyn)*

Change happens in every life, including in one's health and abilities.

I keep telling [my husband] how old I am, how strong I am not, and how bad my back is, and how a lot of these things I am *not* doing. Like right now—he splits the firewood and I say, "You need to split a lot of it again for me, so I can easily carry it in the house and easily put it in the stove." *(Trudie)*

I did finally buy a tiller a couple years ago. I used to do two acres by hand, back when I could do that. It's just, hands hurt and wrists hurt. *(Robyn)*

Linda experienced a challenge that did not end well. While principal of the K-12 Clinch School she contracted breast cancer. Her strong will and spirit carried her through a double mastectomy and many treatments. She retired and, though often ill, enjoyed her life immensely—traveling, becoming a grandmother, and seeing her second daughter get married. She died, however, one year after being interviewed for this book.

As they aged, the women encountered problems that required their courage and adaptability.

I got one hip replacement after another and a knee replacement. But I always knew in my heart, even if I couldn't get repaired, I could always still be an artist and a good person in a wheelchair. It made me a better massage therapist, 'cause now I know exactly what it is to go through that. I have not wanted to get on a horse again, because of fear of an accident, but luckily for me, my love of horses is not contingent on sitting on their backs. I love training them from the ground, hanging out with them, and the rituals of their care have been in my life so long! We all decline in strength, something I accept. Getting older has its boohoos, but, we all know someone way worse off than ourselves, so why go down that path? Celebrate what you *do* have! *(Tata)*

They find ways to stay healthy.

I go to Senior Citizens [Center] twice a week in Kingsport and take Tai Chi. I was [also] doing line dancing. *(Alicia)*

We dance tango. We have been taking classes for a long time, and you find out that it's about the dance, and it's about the community. It's a mixture—that is the nice thing about it. You make quite close friends—dancing together, and learning together. So that is a healthy, nice, positive atmosphere. I like it. It's a creative thing, two people dancing together. *(Yvonne)*

The discussion of change led to some thoughtful conclusions. Change can be bitter-sweet.

Now that I'm not in the [school] community [my life] is more like it was thirty-some years ago. Because, now again my social life is my friends, who are not local people, and I can just forget—I *can't* forget—but I can close my eyes, I guess, to the fact that there are a lot of people out there that are dealing with abusive family situations, drug addiction, and poverty, and those things that I think are hurting the community. I cannot forget it, but it's not in my face every day, so, it's kind of like we don't deal with it. *(Beth)*

What needs occasional retuning? Attitude.

Change is good. It gets too stale when it gets the same, same, same. You gotta do something different. *(Robyn)*

On some levels [life]'s easier. Materially it's easier. But there's always something, isn't there? Spiritually always growing and changing and questioning. And still, that curiosity—you wanna learn more, develop. I'm a massage therapist now. I wanna learn more so I can be a better therapist. [Life]'s always changing. *(Carolyn)*

Everything that happens, it could be something bad, but opportunity can spring from it if you have your mind open to it. *(Cece)*

When things don't remain in harmony, or juicy, or interesting, or productive, I'm a person that moves on. You have to have more good in your life than not, or it's time to change things, shake things up, change partners, change locations, change your attitude, change what you study, change who you hang out with. I'm flexible, and I know that change is one of the strongest forces in the universe, and I accept that. *(Tata)*

Clinch Mountain Girls

What, hopefully, remains the same? Gratitude.

I think when we first moved to the Alum Well Community, I never even thought about anything we didn't have, because I guess I thought we had everything. I guess I still kinda feel that way. I think every night when I crawl into my nice warm bed and my house is secure, and all the chicks are in the nest, the dogs and cats and everybody fed and cared for—I think, God, I am so lucky, I am so lucky. *(Trudie)*

Chapter Twenty-Two

Looking Back, Looking Ahead

From the beginning, the lush folds of Clinch Mountain drew the women in and have held them ever since. Each one, after reviewing the changes in her life, reflected on her arrival in the countryside, the decision to stay, and the effect of the life she chose, on herself and on her children. Obtaining water and keeping it running in winter, raising enough food to last all year, chopping wood and tending the fire, and looking after animals while caring for babies would test anyone's will. What was the meaning and value of all their efforts?

Looking way back:

> These mountains have a magnetism for me. They're the oldest mountains in the world, the very oldest, the first-born. *(Cece)*

> I just love it here. There's an Indian folklore that Cherokees would come here, and that they considered it sacred because of the peacefulness, and—I don't know why—but I feel a specialness here so they mighta known something we didn't. *(Sandra)*

Once we got here, we knew we didn't wanna leave. There was just the feeling of the whole area. It kinda embraces you. The [local] people that are here—a lot of 'em are here because they wanna be, even though it's harder to live in the country. *(Janet)*

But being a newcomer is daunting. Vicki said, "Well, at first I felt a little isolated, because I didn't know anybody, and it was such a change." Alicia exclaimed, "When I first moved to Tennessee, and it was night, I said, 'My God, it's so dark!'" And Linda admitted, "The first couple of years I was a pretty miserable lady. I was lonesome, I was young. I didn't understand the way the people spoke."

Today, how do they see their young selves?

> [I was] maybe thirty-two. Until that point, and maybe even for quite some time after that, I honestly don't know if I had a brain in my head. Or don't feel that I really used it. *(Trudie)*

> We worked all the time. In those days we were young, healthy, and strong. *(Sherri)*

> We were bound and determined to make a living as farmers here. When I moved here at nineteen, I was still very much a kid. But that challenge was what really shaped my character, taught me a lot about myself and what I was capable of, and empowered me to a tremendous degree. That was really when I truly grew up. *(Micki)*

Their confidence increased.

We just did everything we wanted to do. And nobody bothered us. We fixed the front porch. We did that ourselves. We bought the wood, we cut the wood, and we filled that hole in! *(Pat)*

I embraced challenge. Like, yeah, I'm the pioneer woman—I'll ride my horse to the mailbox 'cause the snow's too deep. In the winter I started carrying a sled in the truck. I'd buy groceries, and I'd park my truck out at the highway, and put the groceries on the sled, and walk the half mile up the hill to the house carrying the groceries in a backpack and the sled. I just thought I was hot stuff 'cause I could do it. I wasn't cryin' about it. I was feeling empowered. *(Tata)*

I was there all by myself one day, and I heard a goat screamin' and I ran out, and this little goat, her name was Reggie, had tried to jump out, but when she did, a hind leg had caught in the wire. The wire had twisted [in a loop], and she's hangin' in this twisted wire, just like that, [head-down], all her weight's down. I'm there all by myself, and I'm thinking, Well, you gotta do something. She's caught right above a hind foot, and she's dangling. I said this to myself, and I still say it sometimes when I need it: "Just screw your head on and think." 'Cause what I would like to do is just run around going, "Oh-my-God, oh-my-God." By the woodshed there was a shovel, so I picked it up. I got the handle wedged in the wire, and managed, with the shovel, to flip the wire, so she fell free, and she dropped two or three feet, but all-in-all she was okay. Her foot didn't get cut off. She didn't die hanging upside down. I thought, Thank God, you actually used your brain. I was very proud of that, that I was able to think through what to me was a very scary problem. *(Trudie)*

There were some hard lessons, like deaths.

> I had to learn all about animals, and, as usual, you lose some as you're learning, which is not very fun, like losing the cow to staggerweed. *(Karen)*

But knowledge is power.

> I learned [things] from books and from doing them. And I feel like a stronger person due to having done that. *(Vicki)*

> I guess the biggest thing was running the chainsaw. And I never had actually mowed and "weed-eated," which is so easy it's ridiculous, but there was things like that that I hadn't done because I had rented places, and never had to. None of it's hard, and it's empowering, all of it is. Like cutting your own wood without having to call somebody and say, "Help me!" *(Robyn)*

Feeling independent frees you to experience new things.

> I found power in the challenges that were my harder than average life. I felt that if you like living out away from conveniences, it colors how you relate to all other aspects of living out in the country. I can't tell you how much I enjoyed hanging my clothes on the line buck naked. I mean that was just so cool! Because you had no neighbors and nothing but greenery around you, if you needed to run out and do this or do that—and it's a summer morning, it's eighty degrees at nine o'clock— *(Tata)*

But, for the women who had come of age during the exhilaration of the women's liberation movement, the reality of traditional roles in the country was revelatory.

> It was just the beginning of women's liberation, feminist activism, and I was pretty into that, and didn't think that I would necessarily fall into traditional roles. Living day-to-day, trying to act like self-sufficient farmers even though we really weren't, there were more tasks that Ray was physically able to do, that I wasn't able to do. So I think our physical limitations kind of set the plan for who would do what. So, I always milked the goats. He always drove the tractor—most of the time. We were together working, it was just that I don't have any knowledge of machines. Yeah, *I was out there* with the hoe! I didn't have kids. So, I think I had a little more freedom in that regard, because I wasn't tied down to, like, breast feeding or child-raising, so I was probably more hands-on than some people that had those duties. *(Beth)*

That common division of labor could be extra hard on a woman. Besides work in the tomato fields, Micki made meals from scratch, nursed the baby, and tended their sons (with no running water the first five years). She discusses how that affects a marriage.

> When all of your time and effort and energy is expended just trying to make it through all the responsibilities of the day, it doesn't leave a lot left, so I think our relationship suffered as a result of that, as I think many do. On the one hand we had common goals that we were working on together. On the other hand, we did not get any space from one another. So we spent

a lot of time together, but it was all as business partners or as parental partners. It was not time together that was spent as a couple. Our parents, our families, were far away, so it's not like we had someone who could keep the kids while we had a quiet dinner together. That never happened, never, ever, ever. That also can be hard on a relationship. *(Micki)*

Clearly, the peaceful life in the country has its stressors. For whatever reasons, almost half the marriages dissolved. Whether parents were divorced or not, the children were central in the lives of the families, two thirds of which raised young children while living in the valley.

Several mothers stated they felt their children benefited by being part of a cohesive community, being "part of the tribe." Vicki and others hoped that their children would continue the social activism they had modeled and realize, she said, "that there were things they could do to make a difference." Many stated that their grown children appreciate the natural world, and that they work hard but are less materialistic than the general society.

[I hope my kids got] a sense of well-being and that they love nature. I don't think any of my children really felt overwhelmingly poor or anything being raised because of me and my mentality. *(Anne)*

I hope they have gotten a strong sense of themselves. That was primarily what I was going after. That is a huge reason why I didn't want them to go straight into school at a young age, because I really wanted them to know who they are, what they think, what they believe—allow them the opportunity to really explore within themselves. *(Micki)*

> We felt good, the whole time we were here, calm, and safe. We just thought it was the best place to raise our kids 'cause this is a safe environment, and [because of] all our friends—we met so many good friends—and to give them a love of nature. *(Janet)*

> Both of [my children] grew up way away from the mainstream of society. Even though they went to public schools, still they had something very different here. I think that has shaped them the way they are. *(Yvonne)*

The mothers speculated on how their children's views of their upbringing evolved.

> I think overall, as they get older they appreciate where they grew up, but they didn't always appreciate it while they were growing up. When they got town friends, then they really wanted to stay in town a lot. *(Judy)*

> There are times, probably, in their lives, when they might have probably rather lived in a city, to have more access to more social networks. But, I think they really appreciate being here now. *(Vicki)*

> Well, they had fun, and they may not have known that at the time, but now they do an awful lot of laughing about it. *(Dianna)*

> They have all told me over and over again, that they would not have been raised anywhere else, that they were glad that they were raised where they were raised. They love bein' out in the middle of nowhere. They love bein' out in nature, and they're all still very much that way. *(Lauren)*

As for the women themselves, they all seemed to share these two opinions about the early days:

> We ate well. We ate all our natural, organic stuff. *(Alicia)*

> The best thing I've always thought about living here is, life was very simple. *(Yvonne)*

Nevertheless, the homesteading life entailed hardships and difficult adjustments.

> Being prepared for winter weather, not only staying warm, but keeping power going. We've never had a generator, so if we lost electricity, which used to happen with regularity, we always made sure we had many candles sitting around, and kerosene lamps. If you go to the grocery store for things you're not raisin' on your own, then you don't want to come home without it because it's not going to be an easy trip to go back and get it. *(Dianna)*

> Living meagerly, that's been somewhat challenging. Trying, sometimes, to stay on top of things that needed to be taken care of, like keeping the house warm in the wintertime. And getting [to] places if needed, if the road was icy. [My husband] really became a very good farmer. But, he used chemicals that would waft into the house sometimes when he was sprayin', but I guess in order to have a very successful crop, he felt like he had to. We had some differences on that. *(Vicki)*

> Mostly, I think, financial problems. Just bein' out in the country, and an inability to work, because you have small children, or

maybe you don't have a reliable vehicle. And bein' away from your family. And, not really havin' anyone to relate to, except a few, some people call it "transplants," other people from the North or the South. I like it here now, so it's hard to regret the past. Somehow the past brings you to the present! I was extremely fortunate that I found a really beautiful farm later, and it's just got the most deluxe pasture and fresh water. All the food that comes from that, that's extremely vital. Just try to keep your friends, people that are like you, and then you're all right. *(Anne)*

The cultural difference between life in the country and life in the city may seem obvious, but that contrast holds complexities. Carolyn, who later became a nurse, said, "If you make [a living], it's a choice, Do you want to stay home and be self-sufficient? Or make some money and buy some of the food that you would ordinarily be home working on? Either way you're working. But I did not want to be isolated like that."

"Isolated? No! This is the center of the world!" *(Alicia)*

You have to really be a go-getter—you really have to make your opportunities because there's not a lot of stimulus. It's not like living in a city where there's all kinds of activities, and classes, and places to eat. I guess I kind of have some regrets that I didn't have more of that in my life because I think I would have been a different person, if I'd challenged myself more, or if I'd had more of that kind of external stimulation.

Now that I'm not working, I've got some of Elaine's black walnut, and I've made some tables, and I do like making things. I designed my house. I liked doing that. That was cool. But, I don't know—Still doing gardens. I planted forty asparagus plants yesterday in one of my raised beds. I've got a few things comin' up in my kitchen bed outside the back door, greens comin' up. But, I'm still figurin' it out, still figuring out who I am, and what I'm gonna do with my life. Now I've already had these forty-some years here in this valley, but don't know how much more I've got, and I really don't know what I'm doin' with the rest of my life. It's kind of a big question. I don't know if I'll ever figure it out! *(Beth)*

I realize this is fantastic here. I don't know where is a more beautiful spot to live, than on this mountain. But, I'm just going to travel, and spend time in Amsterdam each year to sort of get that stimulation that a city [offers]. It's so art-oriented, and so cultural, and they put so much money, subsidies, in visual arts, and orchestra. It's really wonderful. It's like every choice made means another choice not made. I guess I waver a bit—in general, it's *fantastic* here! It is paradise. But, but I wish that on the other side of the ridge was—Amsterdam! *(Yvonne)*

I can look around, I'm seeing a panoramic view. I live out here all by myself, and I feel safe. I think it's been a wonderful, wonderful life. I love it! *(Janet)*

Had they changed in response to their lives here?

I haven't completely slowed down, but it's helped. I think I probably take life less seriously. I think having so many physical things happen, you have to get a grip; you just can't let every little thing bother you. *(Nancy)*

We found we really had to depend on one another, and also that we had to depend on our neighbors. It's a humbling experience when you come here by choice, you didn't grow up here knowing the natural resources, and your family wasn't from here. *(Dianna)*

I don't feel like it changed me that much. It seems natural. I've been here so many years, this seems normal. *(Janet)*

The aging women ponder more recent accidents and illnesses.

When Pat broke her leg, I just happened to have the truck where she was, and, I helped to transfer her. I got a chair and she sat in one chair, and moved her to another chair, and she got in the back of the truck, and I drove her to the hospital. *(Alicia)*

[My husband] Wayne has asthma. Real severe asthma. There's been many a time I would have to get him in that truck. He was barely breathing, having an asthma attack, and I'd have to get him to the emergency room so they could give him some oxygen and get him back breathing. Many, many a time did I worry that I wasn't going to make it. He could hardly breathe. It was very, very scary. And that's the bad part of livin' out here, is him with his asthma.

This last time, that was hard, because he had that heart attack. Two ambulances got stuck trying to get to us. It was not just snow, it was ice on top of the snow. So they couldn't get to us, and finally they got a four-wheeler, and a nurse practitioner in here. His heart was beating so fast, they were trying to get it under control, and they finally had to shock him with the paddles. They finally got him on a stretcher. Then they had to get him on a second four-wheeler, and they got him and the nurse to the helicopter [on the Clinch School grounds]. Then they came back and got me.

It was rough that night. That was a fear thing but once he got his asthma under control, now it makes me a little nervous only when it snows. *(Sandra)*

So, you might wonder, was moving to the Clinch Mountain area the *right* move?

I think that some of the things written in the last twenty years about environmental concerns really made me feel I'd made the right choice to move out in the country. I knew it for my own health and peace of mind as I watched more and more intense energy in cities. When things happen in a city so many more people are crashing into each other. Sometimes I like viewing that crash from a distance and not having to be in it. *(Tata)*

We wanted to move here, and [our Catholic Order] said, "No, you better come back to New York." And we said, "We can't!" That was it! We said, "We don't want to be better than the poor. We want to be among the poor." And we were! *(Alicia)*

We've lived in paradise all these years. This is paradise, as far as I'm concerned! You could offer me places—and other places, I wouldn't want 'em! I'm right where I wanna be. *(Linda)*

I think that for a long time I really wanted to move back to California because those days living there in the community were so idyllic and utopian, they really were. But, when I went back to visit, the last time I went, I loved being there but I was so glad I didn't live there anymore. I was homesick to come back to Tennessee because I feel like it's my home. *(Carolyn)*

It was always there in my mind, trying to get to the farm. You know when you've gotten where you wanted to go, I think. Maybe it doesn't last—can't last—but you got there. And you did it, and you don't have any regrets. I'd say that it was probably a dream of a lifetime, that I could live in the country, on a farm, with animals—with all the animals I want, and nobody to tell me it's too many animals. And, in a friendly place, and I liked it. I don't know how it's gonna end. Nobody knows that. *(Pat)*

We really knew, as soon as we saw the community, that it was our home. We both independently felt that, didn't voice it to one another for a while because it was kind of a scary thought of being moved—big transition from hot running water to no running water. So, it was definitely life-changing, but it's never been anything that we would have given up or changed at all. We wouldn't have moved anywhere else. *(Dianna)*

It fulfilled a dream. It made me have new dreams I didn't know. *(Tata)*

More of the twenty-four sum up their feelings about their homesteading experience. "It's been just full of imagination and creativity and innovation. I wouldn't change my experiences for anything. It was a very rich and romantic life," said Sherri. And Robyn declared, "I would do it **again, with** or without somebody, I would definitely do it again. I don't know what I would do different—probably build a smaller house." And Vicki said, "I think it's been a rich life. I feel really blessed by my friends and my family, and this lifestyle. I don't think I would change anything. I love this place, and I love my friends. It's like we've got roots here, now."

Three women, Cece, Karen, and Joanne, who were forced by circumstances to move away for more than two decades, express their intense feelings about that.

> I feel incredibly blessed to have been a part of this culture, to learn about the ways of doing things here. And [to] tend to the Earth itself. I'm glad to be back. I'm glad to be part of this place because my heart has always been here. That's why I came back so much, and that's why, thirty years later, I came back here to live a good part of the time. *(Cece)*

> Telling a lot of the stories that we went through is entertaining to a lot of people. Where I used to work in Georgia they didn't believe any of my stories. Now that I'm back here and they *see*, they *know*; they see my pictures on Facebook, and see the people I was talking about. Yeah, they really exist! Oh, yeah, it was a good idea to homestead. And it was a good, good idea to come back, and I'm happy I did. Sometimes I feel like I've never been away, but of course I was. Missed a lot, but I still do enjoy my friends. *(Karen)*

> I loved Tennessee. I *do* love Tennessee. It seems like my spiritual home. When I had to leave it was like grieving the loss of a family member. I wasn't expecting that. I just grieved so much, and I was really glad to get back. On looking back on things,

I'm glad I did things the way I did. I love my friends, love Tennessee, love this community. I'm glad to be retired though. I didn't, coming back, like the job I had here. It was okay but it wasn't as satisfying. So now I think all of the components of my life are balanced! *(Joanne)*

The friendship of what some termed "the tribe" was vital to all the women. The group gave its members the freedom to express their authentic selves and the security of lasting relationships.

I think my experience here has enriched my life, truly. It's so many things to laugh about, cry about. I think that, in all honesty, the family exists here, not just my immediate family, but our core of friends is my family, and we take care of one another. So, all in all, it's accomplished my need for being real. Not feeling the pressures of having to have certain name-brand furniture, certain name-brand clothes—not working to live, but maybe living to live, or living to work. My priorities have changed [with] the love that I feel for this community, and my friends, and my family. And, my children all moved away, and then they've all come back. *(Dianna)*

I just feel privileged to have been led here, when I don't feel like I knew God. I feel He was leading me here, nonetheless. To be led here to have this setting that we did, to raise children. And the many people—you, Patty, Carolyn, the Haverlands [Micki and Vicki]—that God has used on my behalf. I'm grateful for each knowing of that person, and for each insight that each one has given me. Just thankful, thankful to be here. *(Lauren)*

The best part of all this life is the group of people that lives here, the "import people," that have come from very different backgrounds, and yet, having something in common, some thread in everybody's life that connects us. That is the most amazing thing, really, about living here I think. *(Yvonne)*

I'm just really glad we all had each other. 'Cause even if we didn't quite fit into the local mode, aren't we lucky? We do have the best of both worlds! *(Linda)*

The homesteaders philosophize about living in the present, as in a slogan of the Seventies, "Be here now." (After the title of the book by spiritual teacher, Ram Das.)

Sometimes I think that it was hard for my children, that it could have been easier, maybe, but I get rid of that thought real quickly because I don't believe in regrets. There's nothing you can do, but be in the present. And that's what I try to do, be in the present. *(Carolyn)*

You live sort of in these stories and [it's] such fun telling them when we all get together. We laugh and tell stories about the past and all that, and that is great fun, but it's not good to be living in the past. It's really a good thing to "be here now" and to really recognize what's going on right now. There's still stories to be told, I mean *today*. This way of life will continue on if that's what you choose. People should just keep on goin', keep doing, find something, find something to do today. *(Lee)*

Looking back, Alicia says, "I've had a great life. I've had a very satisfying life." Then, she looks ahead, and adds words of hope and advice.

Good luck to anybody else who wants to do something like this. I'm hoping that people will. I'm hoping that more people get concerned about what we're doing to the Earth, and consumerism, and waste. Waste! God, we waste so much stuff! That's why I have the chickens, basically. I feed them all our [kitchen] waste. If I don't eat it, they will. I get an egg back. We've got to learn that the Earth cannot support millions and millions and millions of people. That's one reason why I don't want to disturb the Earth. If I can put compost back into the earth and just dig a hole and get another set of something I can eat, that's better. I think, if people really want to live here, they'll develop what they need—they'll do it some way or other. And the world is different. Maybe they'll learn from the computer. Who knows? *(Alicia)*

I think that our farming and our whole way of living filtered down into our kids and hopefully our grandkids. *(Cece)*

The back-to-the-land movement was a movement to be able to grow your own food, own your own property. That kind of died down, and now it seems like it's kind of buildin' back up again. I think it might be the people that had wanted to do it, all these years, they still wanna do it, and some of 'em are still comin' back to this area, to try it again. It seems like there's a little bit of a movement with younger people, too, with havin' good food. We were kind of pioneers in that, eating vegetarian and organic foods. Now that's kinda comin' back with our kids' generation. They were raised that way, and they know it's right, and I think that's part of the movement. *(Janet)*

If you have kids you want them to be an asset to the country. And then you want them to make their children even more so, if we're gonna keep this all going. I just believe it's good having kids and everything, but those kids should know how absolutely wonderful it is to be here, and they should pass that on to *their* kids. *(Lee)*

When these homesteaders moved "back to the land," into East Tennessee, they were not in retreat, but were moving forward, demonstrating a possible life—one of simplicity, with flourishing gardens and healthy children. Their desire was to preserve land, not take resources, to treasure the land and water instead of clothes, cars, and furniture. Valuing harmony, they learned from their local neighbors, and shared their tools, vehicles, labor, produce, and stories.

The Clinch Mountain girls-turned-women and their families faced the challenges of providing their own heat, water, and food. The women tended gardens and livestock; preserved food and managed waste; and raised their children far from their extended families. Since the young idealists did not inherit their land or any equipment, they needed income, and over half the women worked off the farm at least part-time (while worrying about their vehicle running). The women accomplished their tasks with intelligence, hard work, and humor. They expressed simple but profound philosophies embodying a love of nature and a generosity of spirit.

Through all the years, these women formed a cohesive group, teaching each other practical skills, lending a hand for childcare, and providing moral support. Now they all have computers and well-maintained cars, but they still spread manure on their gardens, perhaps raise chickens or other animals, buy organic food when available, and compost and recycle. They work for causes they believe in and do not hide their thoughts, nor do they thrust them on others. Their earnest wish is that their efforts show one possible way for healing people and our Earth.

As I write this on New Year's Day, the men in their houses are settling in for an afternoon of football and/or napping. The women are chopping, stirring, and baking for the annual "Ladies' Gathering" on New Year's Day, where they will feast into the evening, drink wine, swap clothes and books, laugh over tales of the past, and express their support for each other in their current projects or concerns.

They will celebrate the new year, each other, and the fact that, for all these years, the Clinch Mountain Girls—over some bumpy roads, up hills and down—have journeyed together.

Afterword

When the Clinch Mountain "girls" met for wine and gab (and still do), they invariably told tales from their own lives—about killing a rat with a skillet, rounding up runaway piglets, or going to bed with boots on. Then came gasps, laughter, and the declaration, "Someone oughta write this stuff down!"

I am that someone, having written here about this group of women who moved with their families to the Appalachian foothills in eastern Tennessee in the Seventies as idealistic back-to-the-landers. Clinch Mountain, at the western edge of the Southern Appalachians, is part of a group of ridges that stretches from Georgia to Pennsylvania. Clinch Mountain itself runs for one hundred fifty miles from near Knoxville, Tennessee, northeast into Virginia. Most of the women interviewed for this project lived on the northern, less-populated, isolated side of Clinch Mountain in the watershed of the Clinch River in three of the Tennessee counties north of Clinch Mountain—Hancock, and parts of Hawkins and Grainger Counties. Two lived on the mountain's southern slope in Poor Valley. North of the mountain the only two incorporated towns—in Grainger and Hancock—each had populations under 2,500 people. The Hawkins County portion had no town center, a few tiny population clusters, and several small stores and churches scattered along paved and unpaved roads. Its closed Lonesome Pine School had been converted into the first Clinch Valley Volunteer Fire Department.

The Eidson Post Office was then housed in a tiny cement block building with an outhouse in the back. Clinch School in Eidson was, and remains, the smallest K-12 school in the state.

Other physical details may be found in the introduction and throughout this book, but the main idea here is that a bunch of young, naive idealists decided to settle here because the land was affordable and the people were interestingly traditional—and welcoming. Looking back, we all seem a bit stunned by the decision to stick it out through the cold winters and the immense amount of work.

Thinking that the stories, anecdotes, hair-raising tales, and thoughtful reflections were worthy of being recorded and as an admirer of Studs Terkel, I decided to combine oral history and writing. Many oral histories by and about Appalachian people already exist, most notably the *Foxfire* series. However, I felt these women's stories came from a different perspective: that of twentieth-century moderns trying to fit into an older style of life and a different culture. I have an advantage as the participant observer—a firm grasp of what the women faced.

I composed my questions based on my knowledge of survey research from my studies in sociology, and on interviewing skills grounded in my work in nutrition counseling as a public health professional. I also profited from my study of methodological literature from the Oral History Association. Studying other languages and anthropology and living abroad enhanced both my sensitivity and objectivity toward other cultures and people. Writing and editing three newsletters over twelve years, including feature articles, gave me confidence in my nonfiction writing ability.

I recorded interviews with twenty-three of my friends and fellow back-to-the-landers. Then they insisted on interviewing me. Each session lasted one to two hours, based on the same list of questions. I decided to limit the scope of the project by not including the families of the women—that is, partners, husbands, or children—nor did I interview descendants of the original settlers of the valley. Three quarters of the narrators arrived in the 1970s, the rest in the 1980s. All the recordings with their transcriptions, are permanently stored and available to the public in the Appalachian Archives at the Center for Appalachian Studies at East Tennessee State University in Johnson City, Tennessee.

My intent is to leave a record of the women's lives, to write something fun to read, and I hope it tears down some of the hurtful misconceptions about hippies and hillbillies. Lastly, I feel that as we look again at the twentieth century we should include some of the social movements that have helped shape this nation's modern history. This story may also give some people hope for the future, and one possible way to move toward a more joyful, peaceful world that does not gobble up the Earth's resources while defiling the land, air, and water.

Biographies of the Clinch Mountain Girls

Raised in The Bronx, **Alicia Salzman** is one of the **"Goat Ladies,"** with fellow former Catholic Sister, **Pat**. Arriving in 1976, she raised many animals and gardens. She makes and sells pottery, paintings, and quilts; and shares, with Pat, a historic farmhouse.

Alma Hester Smith, energetic retiree, grew up in Kansas and Nebraska, taught school in Minnesota, and raised two sons there. Widowed, she came to Clinch Valley in 1981 with her second husband Sidney Smith, where they actively farmed. Sidney died, and she lives in an assisted living facility near her sons in Minneapolis. She also has three stepdaughters.

Anne Norris, from Philadelphia, was educated in private schools, including in California where she worked as a horse trainer. Anne arrived in Tennessee in 1977 as a young bride, but was soon widowed. She remarried, divorced, and raised three children. She still farms with her younger son and has seven grandchildren.

Beth Wallace, of northeastern Ohio, graduated from Arizona State University, interned at an organic farm in California, and arrived in Clinch Valley in 1976 with ex-husband Ray Carr (now deceased). Beth retired from Clinch School after twenty-five years, then cared for her mother until her death at age ninety-six. Beth gardens and attends concerts with her longtime partner Gil Johnson.

Raised and college-educated in Cincinnatti, **Carolyn Schrand Novkov** traveled in Europe, then lived at the Harmony Hill commune in California with **Judy** and **Cece**. She arrived in the Clinch Valley in 1977 with husband Rick (now deceased), two daughters, and a baby boy. Carolyn was a lay midwife, a nurse, and a massage therapist. She now lives in a creekside cottage in Surgoinsville and has two grandchildren.

Cecelia "Cece" Hall Lakin, raised in Detroit, attended university, but soon left for California, where she lived with **Judy** and **Carolyn** at Harmony Hill. She and husband Bert Lakin arrived in Clinch Valley in 1977 and worked in market gardening, but moved in 1984 with their three daughters to Atlanta. Cece visited her "Clinch family" often, and returned in 2013. Now married to Fred George, she has four grandchildren.

Raised in West Virginia till age of eight, then in suburban Ohio, **Dianna Beckwith Young** also lived in Germany and Key West before marrying Bill Young. In 1979 they bought Clinch Mountain land and moved there in 1983. Dianna, a Registered Nurse, worked in home health and hospitals. She now works part-time as a nursing instructor, and has a reflexology practice. She has three children and eight grandchildren.

Janet Weller Hechmer, originally from Independence, Missouri, visited San Francisco, and in 1973, she and husband Jesse Hechmer came to Clinch Valley, and lived in a tepee, an abandoned Victorian resort, and a log cabin, before building their dream house on the Clinch River, although soon, sadly, Jesse died. Janet has continued to live there, still makes jewelry, and enjoys the river view with her partner, Phil. She has two children and three grandchildren.

Joanne Diffley Irvin, raised on the Mojave Desert, arrived in 1974 with a husband who soon left. Joanne worked as a nurse while building a log cabin for herself and two daughters. She earned a Midwifery Certificate, but left with them in 1985 to find a job. After twenty years in South Carolina, and earning degrees in nursing, Joanne returned as a Family Nurse Practitioner. Now retired, she restored and lives in a solar-powered Victorian house. She has four grandchildren.

Judy Stocko Moore grew up in rural northern Ohio. She lived at the Harmony Hill commune in California with **Carolyn** and **Cece** before arriving in Clinch Valley with husband Wesley in 1984. Judy raised huge gardens and earned money by cleaning houses and eldercare. She moved to Bellingham, Washington in 2014 near three of her four daughters. She has five grandchildren and two great-grandchildren and visits her Clinch Mountain "family" every year.

Raised in a small town on Long Island, New York, **Karen Dykstra Berg** studied art before arriving in Clinch Valley in 1974. A divorce forced her to move with her three children in 1986. She became an LPN, and worked in Ohio and Georgia. Karen returned in 2011, and lives with her partner Doyle on a farm with numerous animals. She has three children and five grandchildren.

Lauren Fritz Friere, daughter of a foreign aid professional, was raised in India, Sri Lanka, Kenya, and Virginia. In the late Sixties, she dropped out of high school and attended the school of life. In 1978 she crossed Clinch Mountain with her husband Joseph Friere, and they raised six children. While homeschooling her kids, she earned a GED, an LPN certification, and recently retired from nursing. Lauren has six children and nine grandchildren.

Lee von Gal Hoellman is from Brewster, New York. After college in southwestern Virginia, she moved to Rogersville in 1972. Two years later she bought Clinch Mountain land where she and her husband John ran a self-sufficient farm. She started an art gallery in Rogersville and created Lee's Sweet Retreat, a rustic bed-and-breakfast with tiny houses and a school bus. She has three children and seven grandchildren.

Linda Anderson Long was raised and educated in Ohio. Arriving in 1972, she started her teaching career. She assisted in high school musicals and plays and in community theater, and loved to garden and cook. She was principal of Clinch School for several years before she retired in 2014. Sadly, she died two years later of cancer. She is survived by her husband Ron, two daughters and two grandchildren.

In 1976, at age nineteen, **Michelle "Micki" Mercurio** married Joe Haverland, and they followed his brother Jerome and wife **Vicki** into tomato farming along the Clinch River. Later, Micki attended college and grad school for social work. She is currently a social worker, and a Holistic Practitioner and Spirit Life Coach. Micki lives on a hill overlooking the Clinch River, growing a big garden and enjoying her three sons and four grandchildren.

Nancy Withington Bell, a native of New Hampshire, arrived in Tennessee in 1976 and bought a farm while supporting herself as a public health nutritionist. In 1978 she moved over Clinch Mountain after marrying her husband Gary, and together they farmed and raised a boy and a girl. Nancy, a life-long environmentalist, later became a Biology teacher.

Raised in Minneapolis, **Pat Grimes** left for nursing school with the Catholic Dominican Order in New York City. She served as an RN in that city, in Cincinnatti and Columbus, Ohio, and in Kentucky and Tennessee. She quit that vocation to fulfill a life-long dream of having a farm, raised goats, and made renowned cheeses. She and former Dominican Sister, **Alicia,** known as the "Goat Ladies," moved to Hancock County in 1976, and live there still.

Robyn Persky Willman, raised in suburban North Palm Beach, Florida, worked her way through college cooking in restaurants. After travel out West and to Bali, she arrived in Clinch Valley with a trade, jewelry making. Mostly as a single parent, she grew gardens, cut wood, and raised her daughter while making and selling jewelry and wind chimes. Robyn recently sold her homestead, and moved to the Asheville, N.C. area. She has one daughter.

When **Sandra Filetti Riner** arrived with her husband Wayne, she already had grown children, but raised sheep, goats, and angora rabbits, and spun wool. Originally from the Bronx, she spent her teen years in Georgia, and helped on her relatives' farms. In Tennessee, Sandra worked part-time in eldercare. Now she tends goats, chickens, and a garden. Sandra has four children, twenty grandchildren, and twenty-six great-grandchildren.

Sherri Hudson grew up in a small Indiana town and attended a university art school. She and ex-husband Dale arrived in Tennessee in 1983. Besides painting, she developed crafts from her many farm products, exhibiting at Dollywood and at the Museum of Appalachia. After a divorce and a few years in Indiana, she returned to teach art at local schools. After retiring, Sherri created online courses for rural students and now devotes her time to painting, bee-keeping, and gardening.

Mildred Andres, known as **Tata,** grew up as an "army brat" raised in Austria, Germany, Kansas, Virginia, and Louisiana. Arriving in 1989 with ex-partner Denny, she established a therapeutic massage practice, while raising a large garden and horses. Tata is a classically trained vocalist, and a painter and photographer who still practices all those arts while raising beautiful, rare breeds of chickens with her partner Bobby on their mountain farm.

Trudie Markt Hurlbutt, an Oklahoman, was raised in small-town Pryor and in Tulsa, where she attended university. When Trudie and her husband Stephen arrived in 1976, she had experience with horses, he on his family's farm, and they shortly established a homestead. Trudie worked as a secretary, executive assistant, and helper for Stephen, a surveyor. They still farm now and raise horses just outside Rogersville.

Raised in Cincinnatti, **Vicki Sweet Haverland** arrived in 1975 with a degree in Special Education and newly wed to Jerome. They settled down on a farm on the Clinch River where she still lives. Jerome's brother Joe and wife **Micki** moved nearby. While raising four children, she raised tomatoes with Jerome and went tree-planting in the winter. She returned to teaching and now manages a special education program. She is divorced and has ten grandchildren.

Yvonne Apol is a native of Amsterdam where she attended art school. She lived in India for two years and in London, where she met her husband Bill Kornrich. She moved to Tennessee in 1977 and plunged into homesteading. A prolific artist, working in painting, mosaics, sculptures, porcellinas (doll-like figures), jewelry, and metal, she and Bill live on a ridge overlooking the Clinch River. They have two children and three grandchildren.

Acknowledgments

The Clinch Mountain Girls, now strong women, showed faith in this project immediately and did not hesitate to let me record them, to use the recordings as I deemed appropriate, and to cheer me onward. Thank you so much, ladies:

Alicia Salzman, Alma Smith, Anne Norris, Beth Wallace, Carolyn Novkov, Cecelia Lakin, Dianna Young, Janet Hechmer, Joanne Irvin, Judy Moore, Karen Berg, Lauren Freire, Lee Hoellman, Linda Long (sadly, now deceased), Micki Mercurio, Mildred "Tata" Andres, Pat Grimes, Robyn Willman, Sandra Riner, Sherri Hudson, Trudie Hurlbut, Vicki Haverland, and Yvonne Apol.

I am so grateful to friends and family for all their help and care. From the beginning, Tina Schwartz's valuable advice on content and concepts, in addition to her copy editing, kept me going. I came to count on Randall Wells for his wit, wisdom, and practical and literary advice. To have material to piece this book together, I needed transcriptions of the recordings; Roberta "Bobbi" Smith volunteered to do at least a quarter of them, saving me many hours of work. Carolyn Novkov first urged me to record oral histories, and encouraged me throughout, as did Joanne Irvin, who gave advice, helped me with a new computer, suggested an editor/coach, and provided promotion ideas. I'm grateful for Linda Dobkins' technical advice, tutelage, kindness, and encouragement at a crucial moment; and for Guerry McConnell's wise counsel. I appreciate the knowledge I gained from the members and speakers at the Lost State Writers' Guild meetings.

Thanks also goes to Jen Bingham at the Archives of Appalachia for showing interest in this project from the start, and having faith that I would finish all those transcripts and create a book.

I am so grateful for my daughter Marissa Rose Bell's help with copy editing, website and other media design, marketing and media advice, and for her steadfast cheering. My brother Richard Withington Jr. read my first attempt as I emailed him chapters, and never flagged in his enthusiasm. I also appreciate that my first Clinch Mountian sister, Lee Hoellman, prodded me when I needed it. To my brother Robert Withington and my son Adam Bell—thank you for your interest, encouragement, and affection. I am so grateful to my husband Gary Bell who never expressed doubt about the value of the project or the time it took.

Lastly, I am delighted with Tata Andres' charming art for the cover. Thank you. I hope I have not neglected to mention anyone, for I have enjoyed the love and trust of so many strong women of our valleys and am so grateful for our community.

About the Author

Nancy Bell studied anthropology at Bates College and the University of Michigan. She holds three degrees—a B.A. in Sociology, an M.A. in Middle East Studies, and an M.P.H. in Nutrition. Later, Bell received certification as a high school biology teacher from Lincoln Memorial University. Her experiences include a student year in Japan; two years in the Peace Corps in Iran; managing and cooking in a restaurant on Sugar Loaf Key, Florida, for nine winters; traveling to three Tennessee counties as a nutritionist in the WIC program; teaching biology at the smallest K–12 school in Tennessee; and devoting years to environmental activism while staying at home on her farm with her children.

Bell's writing experience includes editing, reporting, and writing for three newsletters: *Clearwater*, monthly of the Friends of the Clinch & Powell Rivers, Sneedville, Tennessee; *Clinch Mountain Views*, quarterly, Eidson, Tennessee; and *CJE News*, quarterly, Coalition for Jobs and the Environment, Abingdon, Virginia.

Bell is a member of Lost State Writers' Guild, Abingdon, VA, and the Appalachian Studies Association, and is currently serving as Vice Chair of the Tennessee Chapter of the Sierra Club (2021–2023). She lives and gardens on her Clinch Mountain farm with her husband Gary, and dog Hildegard. You can contact Nancy Withington Bell through her website, clinchmountaingirls.com, or on Facebook.

www.ingramcontent.com/pod-product-compliance
Lightning Source LLC
Chambersburg PA
CBHW080633230426
43663CB00016B/2851